Spinoza's Book of Life

Spinoza's Book of Life

Freedom and Redemption in the *Ethics*

Steven B. Smith

Yale University Press
New Haven and London

Printed in the United States of America.
Library of Congress Cataloging-in-Publication Data
Smith, Steven B., 1951–
Spinoza's book of life : freedom and redemption in the
ethics / Steven B. Smith.
p. cm.
Includes bibliographical references and index.
ISBN 0-300-10019-1 (cloth : alk. paper)
1. Spinoza, Benedictus de, 1632-1677.   2. Free will and
determinism—History—17th century.   3. Ethics,
Modern—17th century.   I. Title.
B3999.F8S65   2003
170—dc21   2003002244
$Smith$

A catalogue record for this book is available
from the British Library.
The paper in this book meets the guidelines for
permanence and durability of the Committee on
Production Guidelines for Book Longevity of the
Council on Library Resources.

10 9 8 7 6 5 4 3 2 1

For Joseph Cropsey
Amicus Spinoza

Remember us that we may live, O King who delights in life.
Inscribe us in the Book of Life for your sake.
—*Mahzor*

God had taken a perilous risk when He created man and gave
him dominion over all the other creatures of the earth, but He
was about to promise by the rainbow in the clouds never again
to bring a flood and destroy all flesh. . . . God had granted the
sons of Adam an abundance of self-love, the precarious gift of
reason, as well as the illusions of time and space, but no sense
of purpose or justice. Man would manage somehow to crawl
upon the surface of the earth, forward and backward, until
God's covenant with him ended and man's name in the book
of life was erased forever.
—Isaac Bashevis Singer, "The Death of Methuselah"

Into Life
—Franz Rosenzweig, *The Star of Redemption*

CONTENTS

Preface

This is not the book I had initially set out to write. My aim was to complete a study of the influence of Spinoza on Jewish thought and political theory from the eighteenth to the twentieth centuries. Writing a book on Spinoza's *Ethics* was the farthest thing from my mind. And yet it became apparent as I began to think about this project that I could not let go of Spinoza, or perhaps more accurately, he would not let go of me. *Spinoza's Book of Life* is the result of that exchange.

Why a book on the *Ethics?* Despite an illustrious tradition of scholarship stretching back for over a century, there was a time up until the recent past when it was fashionable to treat Spinoza with something wavering between condescension and contempt. A reviewer of my *Spinoza, Liberalism, and the Question of Jewish Identity* tells the story of how shortly after World War II, a young American scholar sent an article on Spinoza to a leading Anglo-American journal of philosophy and was told by the editors, "We are not now and never will be interested in Spinoza."[1] For those of a positivist bent, the very idea of a system of deductive metaphysics was anathema to the empirical and skeptical spirit of modern philosophy. For others, his idea that God is the immanent cause of all things carried an odor of cloying religiosity running contrary to the secular spirit of the age. Today, fortunately, much of this has changed. Not only has there been an increased appreciation for the place of Spinoza in the history of thought, but his novel reflections on a wide range of themes, from the importance of the body, to the centrality of power, to the psychological foundations of moral beliefs, have prompted renewed interest in and respect for his ideas. New editions and translations have also made his work more accessible to contemporary readers. Even if Spinoza has never quite made the A-List, it is no longer possible to treat him, as he once was, as a "dead dog."

The present study takes the form of a selective commentary on leading themes and problems of the *Ethics*. It does not purport to be a detailed line-by-line commentary or a comprehensive analysis of Spinoza's background and influences. Both such types of work already exist. Much of the recent literature on Spinoza typically falls under the genre of what might be called analytical philosophy of history.[2] Although there is much to learn from this kind of writing, it tends to judge Spinoza as a contributor to certain contemporary philosophical problems and research programs that are not strictly his own. Not surprisingly, his arguments are often found to be faulty, unjustified, and confused. It is a premise of this work that it is precisely in those places where Spinoza's thinking is most clearly at variance with our own that we have the most to learn. I am not interested in the *Ethics* because it helps to confirm contemporary opinions and points of view, but because it challenges them. The *Ethics* can teach us something about the foundations of modernity, of which it is a cornerstone.

This book differs from other studies of the *Ethics* in a couple of respects. My earlier book focused almost exclusively on Spinoza's *Tractatus Theologico-Politicus* (*TTP*), his major work of political philosophy. The relation between the *TTP* and the *Ethics* has often baffled readers. The standard treatment of this question has been to consider Spinoza's politics as a kind of appendage, almost an afterthought, to his scientific and metaphysical interests. My own view attempted to reverse this conception by making a case for the primacy of political philosophy or the "theologico-political problem" in Spinoza around which all of his later philosophical reflections tended to gravitate. The present work more or less continues this line of thinking. While I do not argue that the *Ethics* is a piece of political philosophy in the manner of Hobbes's *Leviathan* or Locke's *Civil Government*, there is most definitely a politics in the *Ethics* that is broadly supportive of the liberal democratic framework set out in the *TTP*. The critique of supernatural teleology, the analysis of the passions, and the celebration of freedom as the highest human end all bear marked affinities with the works of Machiavelli, Descartes, and Hobbes, of whom I make opportunistic use throughout this study. It is, above all, the *Ethics* as a work of practical philosophy that I want to stress.

What this book maintains is that the *Ethics* and the *TTP* form parts of a complex whole. The *TTP* is a book mired in the world of biblical criticism, history, and contemporary politics. It was addressed to a general, if learned, audience that would play an important role in the future shape and destiny of public life. The *TTP* was a founding document of liberal democratic theory as well as the first sustained reflection on the status of Judaism within this new theologico-political regime. The *Ethics* by contrast is a work written "in geometrical manner." It appears to pay scant attention to anything that cannot be deduced or inferred from human reason alone. If the *TTP* was intended as an exercise in public philosophy, the *Ethics* is an intensely private, deeply introspective book. While the *TTP* examines the theological and political dimensions of human freedom, the *Ethics* is concerned with the moral and psychological conditions of liberty. The one examined the external, the other the internal dimensions of freedom. Together both works constitute a comprehensive account of the problem of freedom.

In the *TTP* Spinoza distinguishes between two kinds of books. There are "hieroglyphic" books, his chief example being the Bible, that require elaborate and painstaking historical reconstruction if they are to make sense. To understand such works, one requires knowledge of the language in which the text was written, information about the context and circumstances of its composition, and the character of its author. Then there are "intelligible" books, such as Euclid's geometry, for which historical information about the author and the work is extraneous and the understanding of which requires only an ability to follow a chain of reasoning from premise to conclusion. The *Ethics* was clearly intended by its author to be an intelligible work after the manner of Euclid. Yet the apparent clarity of the intention is partially undermined by the work itself. Underlying the formal propositional architecture is a highly impassioned work rich with irony, rhetoric, sarcasm, and reference to first-person experience—scarcely the model of the pure philosopher unsullied and unruffled by the emotions. We cannot read the *Ethics* as we could a mathematics textbook. It is not a work in which the author disappears into the text, but a work that bears its author's distinctive voice and cast of mind on every page. The *Ethics* is, then, neither a purely hieroglyphic nor a purely intelligible work but a hybrid of the two. To understand it, one needs to be, to varying degrees, philosopher, historian, and political theorist.

The *Ethics* is a strange book and its strangeness is not diminished even after careful study. Despite Spinoza's aspiration to a kind of mathematical certainty, the *Ethics* is not as self-contained as it first appears. It is a rambling, discursive, and discordant work. Almost nothing human is alien to it. As the title of this book suggests, the Spinoza to appear here is not the grim determinist or Stoic necessitarian made out by many of his critics and some of his friends. He is instead an exponent of the joys of life and all that it entails. Above all, the *Ethics* teaches us to embrace the world rather than flee from it, to regard freedom as a blessing rather than a curse, and to find pleasure in those things that tend to increase our sense of power and agency. The work, in short, is one of the touchstones of the modern idea of individuality. If Nietzsche was right—and I believe he was—that all philosophy is essentially autobiography, then the *Ethics* is the deepest expression of the soul of its author. It provides the fullest statement of Spinoza's views on freedom and the moral responsibility of the individual. Among other things, Spinoza's *Ethics* is the closest thing we have to an intellectual autobiography of this strange and elusive man.

The *Ethics* represents the perfection of modern rationalism, that is, the attempt to work out an account of nature, of the whole, from the sources of human reason. It is not only a classic document of modern rationalism; it belongs to that genre of books that brings to light the ancient quarrel between reason and faith, philosophy and revelation. This is the deepest and most serious problem to which the work is addressed. To understand the *Ethics* as Spinoza understood it is to regard it first and foremost as a reply to the author of Genesis. Yet this may seem to date the book, to locate it firmly at a moment in the Enlightenment's struggle against orthodoxy, its war against superstition. Indeed, the case for orthodoxy seems today to have been refuted by a combination of the methods of historical criticism and scientific method, both of which Spinoza himself helped to champion. Who today believes in the biblical account of miracles or talmudic doctrines about the resurrection of the dead? Yet the implausibility of these beliefs does not settle the case. For if the *Ethics* is an account of nature from the premises of reason alone, it is not clear to what experience or principle of logic we can appeal to verify those premises. Any appeal to reason to verify the principles of reason will be self-referential, hence question-begging. The verdict we reach on the *Ethics,* then, will be very much a verdict on modern rationalism or the Enlightenment as a whole. If Spinoza's work should unwittingly help to reveal the essential limitations of reason, this would require not an embrace of irrationalism but a reconsideration of orthodoxy.

A Note on the Texts

The *Ethics* was not published until after Spinoza's death and was originally included as part of the *Opera Posthuma* in 1677. The standard scholarly edition of the work of Spinoza is still Carl Gebhardt's *Spinoza Opera*, 4 vols. (Heidelberg: Carl Winter, 1925). Even though there is still no satisfactory edition of his collected works in English, there are at least excellent translations of individual works now available both by Edwin Curley and Samuel Shirley. Throughout this book I have used Curley's edition of the *Collected Works of Spinoza* (Princeton: Princeton University Press, 1985), which includes not only the *Ethics* but also the *Treatise on the Emendation of the Intellect* and the *Short Treatise* and Shirley's translation of the *Theologico-Political Treatise*.

References to the *Ethics*, included in the body of the text, make use of the following shorthand:

I, II, etc.	part number
p	proposition
d	demonstration
s	scholium
c	corollary
def	definition
ap	appendix
pref	preface
def.aff	definition of the affects
TTP	*Theologico-Political Treatise* (*Tractatus Theologico-Politicus*)

PT	*Political Treatise*
TIE	*Treatise on the Emendation of the Intellect*
KV	*Short Treatise on God, Man, and His Well-Being*
Ep	*The Letters* (*Epistola*)

References to the *Ethics* will take the form of IIIp9s to indicate the scholium to proposition nine of part three. I have also made occasional use of the Gebhardt pagination (included in Curley's edition) where the reference would be otherwise unclear, so IV, pref/207 refers to the preface to part four, page 207 of Gebhardt.

References to the *TTP* include chapter and Bruder section number followed by Gebhardt volume and page number—e.g., *TTP*, vii, 55; III/57, whereas references to *TIE* and *KV* include section numbers followed by Gebhardt volume and page number—e.g., *TIE*, xvi; II/9. References to *Ep* are given to the letter number only.

INTRODUCTION

Who was the author of the *Ethics?*[1] Spinoza was born Bento
Despinosa on November 24, 1632, in Amsterdam. His Hebrew
name Baruch means "blessed." His father, Michael, was a rea-
sonably well-to-do merchant who had arrived in Amsterdam
from Portugal via Nantes sometime around 1623. While there
is some dispute over the family's social standing, the fact that
Michael served two terms on the *parnas*, the governing body of
the Jewish-Portuguese community, fixes him as a member of the
upper crust of the Amsterdam Sephardim. Spinoza's mother,
Hanna, died in 1638 when he was only six years old, followed by
his father in 1654. By the time he entered early adulthood, Spinoza was entirely alone except for a younger brother, Gabriel,
with whom he later founded a fruit importing business under
the names "Bento y Gabriel Despinosa."

Little is known of Spinoza's early life. The Jewish community in which he grew up consisted largely of Marranos, that
is, Sephardic Jews of Spanish and Portuguese descent who had
been forcibly converted by the Inquisition and who later fled to
France and the Netherlands to avoid further persecution. Spinoza received a typical Jewish education at the Talmud Torah
school. His teachers included Saul Levi Morteira and Menasseh
ben Israel, the latter a man of wide learning who helped to pre-
pare for the readmission of the Jews to England. From an early
age, Spinoza's intellectual gifts were noted. He was a polymath.
In addition to Portuguese, the lingua franca of his community,
Spanish, its literary language, and Dutch, the language of trade
and commerce, he also learned Hebrew. He studied Latin at the

school of a former Jesuit priest named Frances Van den Ende, from whom he also learned the classics of ancient philosophy, literature, and drama, as well as the works of modern political theory from Machiavelli to Grotius to Hobbes.

Then on July 27, 1656, for reasons that are still unknown, an edict of excommunication or *Cherem* was visited on Spinoza by the elders of the community. According to the language of the document that still survives in the Amsterdam Municipal Archives, the twenty-four-year-old Spinoza was henceforth to be "banned, cut off, cursed, and anathematized" by the people of Israel. No official reasons for this ban—which, incidentally, has never been rescinded—are given except for some vague references to certain "evil opinions," "abominable heresies," and "awful deeds" said to be practiced and taught by him. Indeed, not only was Spinoza himself put to the ban, but the text of the *Cherem* concludes with the ominous warning that anyone who seeks to contact him either orally or in writing, who reads anything he has written, does him any favor, or even comes "within four cubits of his vicinity" will suffer the same fate.[2]

It is still a shock to read the fiery language of Spinoza's edict of excommunication. The fact that such bans were not at all uncommon in the seventeenth century makes little difference. People could be put under a *Cherem* for a whole range of offenses, from such things as arriving at synagogue with a weapon or raising a hand against a fellow Jew, to buying meat from an Ashkenazic butcher or publicly insulting the Portuguese ambassador. Further, such bans were not intended to sever entirely the individual's relation to the community. Usually a time limit was imposed and some kind of penance in the form of a fine required for readmission. What made Spinoza's excommunication unusual was not only its permanence but that he made no effort to have the ban lifted or make amends. According to an older biographical tradition, he wrote a Spanish *Apology* defending his decision not to seek readmission to the community, but this work has never been found.[3] For all of his differences with the authorities, Spinoza was not an apostate. He refused to convert to Christianity, preferring to live independent of all established religious sects and attachments.

Why was Spinoza excommunicated? There is an older hagiographical literature that regards the excommunication along the lines of the trial of Socrates or Jesus. On this account, the excommunication is seen as a struggle between the free thinker and the forces of darkness, the new science against the authority of the rabbis. More recently, scholars like I. S. Revah and Yosef Kaplan have pointed to the influence of notable Marrano free thinkers like Uriel de Costa and Isaac Orobio de Castro on the young Spinoza.[4] Marxist critics have even argued that from an early age Spinoza was a social and political radical who threatened the economic interests of the parnassim, who were all heavily invested in the Dutch East India Company.[5]

Spinoza's recent biographer, Steven Nadler, suggests, plausibly, that the excommunication was a response to both internal and external considerations.[6] Internally the *Cherem* was a tool of social control designed to enforce moral conformity on a religious community that had only recently begun to reclaim its links with tradition after being driven underground by the forces of the Inquisition. Externally, there were limits to the famed Dutch tolerance. By 1656 Spinoza had already begun to taste the philosophy of Descartes and may even have begun to contemplate a commentary. Spinoza's excommunication coincided with one of the periodic campaigns against Cartesianism in the universities. Descartes's "new science" was widely believed to have atheistic implications at odds with the established Aristotelian science and the dominant Calvinist theology. The expulsion of a leading advocate of the new science could well have been a signal to the Dutch officials that heretics of any sort were as unwelcome in the Jewish community as among their Christian hosts.

What is clear is that from a very early time, the life of Spinoza became an object of fascination. His first biography, written by the French Protestant Jean Lucas, appeared shortly after his death.[7] The question that clearly befuddled Lucas and others is what kind of person could have forsaken the minority religion in which he had been brought up yet stand apart from the majority religion, which he refused to embrace. It was the image of Spinoza as more than an ordinary philosopher—as a kind of philosophical saint—that inspired such intense curiosity. The life of Spinoza became the model for Bayle's "virtuous atheist," who was able to live a life of exemplary piety and goodness while standing alone and aloof from all established religions.[8]

Spinoza's excommunication was clearly the most significant event in what was otherwise a life of more or less uninterrupted study. By 1661 he had left Amsterdam to escape continued hostility and settled in the village of Rijnsburg. By this time he was already acquainted with members of some dissenting sects like the Remonstrants and Collegiants, so called because they met in colleges or informal meeting houses. These groups rejected the austere Calvinist theology of the Dutch Reformed Church with its doctrine of predestination. They stressed a teaching of the "inner light" rather than official creed or dogma; they were what Leszek Kolakowski has called "chrétiens sans église."[9] There is even some evidence that he came into contact with a Quaker mission in Amsterdam and helped translate a Quaker tract into Hebrew. Just as he leaned toward latitudinarianism in theology, so was Spinoza drawn toward republicanism in politics. He identified with the freedom party in Dutch politics, which meant resistance not only to the power of the Calvinist clergy but to the monarchical designs of the House of Orange. It was in order to provide a manifesto for the republican cause that he interrupted his work on the *Ethics* and wrote the *TTP*.[10]

In 1665 Spinoza left Rijnsburg and moved to Voorburg, a suburb of The Hague. It was during these years that his reputation grew beyond the Dutch Cartesians like Pieter Balling and Jarig Jellesz to include a much wider European audience. His interest in optics put him in contact with the Dutch scientist Christiaan Huygens, with whom he maintained a somewhat frosty relationship. He was also acquainted with Leibniz, who sought out his company, although Spinoza seems to have held him at arm's length ("I think it imprudent to entrust my writings to him so hastily. I should first like to know what he is doing in France" [*Ep* 72]). And he carried on a lengthy correspondence with Henry Oldenburg, the Secretary of the Royal Academy in London and a confidant of Sir Isaac Newton.

Spinoza's final years were spent in The Hague, where he witnessed the end of the golden age of Dutch politics.[11] The brutal murder of the brothers De Witt by a savage mob in 1672 led him to describe the psychology of the crowd as the "ultimi barbarorum." The next year he must have been gratified to receive an invitation to assume a professorship of philosophy at the University of Heidelberg. Of course the idea of a highly reclusive and brittle personality like Spinoza taking up the public duties of lecturing seems in retrospect almost inconceivable. He politely but firmly turned down the offer on the grounds that his own love of peace and freedom of mind would be better assured if he remained a private person (*Ep* 48). Spinoza, who had never enjoyed good health, died on February 21, 1677, at the age of forty-four; consumption had been exacerbated by the dust created by his lens grinding.

At the time of his death Spinoza had published relatively little. The only work to bear his name on its title page during his lifetime was his commentary on Descartes's *Principles of Philoso-*

phy (1663). The *TTP*, his major work of political philosophy, was published anonymously in 1670 bearing the name of a fictitious Hamburg publishing house. Several other works, including the *Political Treatise*, the *Treatise on the Emendation of the Intellect*, and the *Compendium of Hebrew Grammar*, were left unfinished at the time of his death.[12] The *Ethics* was published only posthumously, largely for reasons of prudence and safety. Despite the relative tolerance of the Dutch republic, Spinoza feared persecution and set out his reasons for the delay of publication in a letter to Oldenburg:

> At the time when I received your letter of 22 July, I was setting out for Amsterdam, intending to put into print the book [*Ethics*] of which I had written to you. While I was engaged in this business, a rumor became wide-spread that a certain book of mine about God was in the press, and in it I endeavor to show that there is no God. This rumor found credence with many. So certain theologians, who may have started this rumor, seized the opportunity to complain of me before the Prince and the Magistrates. Moreover the stupid Cartesians, in order to remove this suspicion from themselves because they are thought to be on my side, ceased not to denounce everywhere my opinions and my writings, and still continue to do so. Having gathered this from certain trustworthy men who also declared that the theologians were everywhere plotting against me, I decided to postpone the publication I had in hand until I should see how matters would turn out, intending to let you know what course I would then pursue. But the situation seems to worsen day by day, and I am not sure what to do about it. (*Ep* 68)

If this sounds like a classic case of persecution mania, it is worth remembering Henry Kissinger's dictum that sometimes even paranoids have enemies.

The influence of Spinoza's work was profound and immediate. He was routinely anathematized as a teacher of atheism and determinism in the century after his death. Leibniz, who as we have seen eagerly sought out Spinoza's opinions, led the pack. "He was truly an atheist," he wrote, "that is, he did not acknowledge any Providence which distributes good fortune and bad according to what is just."[13] Despite Bayle's appreciation for Spinoza's personal qualities (he described him as one of the *esprits forts*), he excoriated his philosophy in his entry in the *Historical and Critical Dictionary.* Bayle's opinion was echoed throughout the eighteenth century by Montesquieu, Hume, the authors of the *Encyclopédie,* and Kant for espousing a doctrine of cosmic determinism according to which whatever is, is just.

It was not until the end of the century that Spinoza was rehabilitated by the German Idealists as the bearer of a new kind of spirituality. The *Pantheismusstreit,* which we will consider in the final chapter, helped to canonize Spinoza as a kind of secular saint. The formal rehabilitation of Spinoza can be dated from 1785 with the publication of F. H. Jacobi's *Letters to Herr Moses Mendelssohn Concerning the Doctrine of Spinoza,* after which Spinoza was treated by Goethe, Schliermacher, and Novalis as the "God-intoxicated" philosopher. Throughout the nineteenth and twentieth centuries, Spinoza was turned from a philosopher into a cultural icon on whom novelists and artists could project all the aspirations of modernity. If his thought provided inspiration for the ruthless naturalism of novels like *Cousin Bette* and *Madame Bovary,* the life of Spinoza was turned by Berthold Auerbach into a tale of secular redemption through a religion of reason. It was the very loneliness of Spinoza that turned him into an existential hero for writers who could no longer be orthodox but who still felt the pull of their own Jewishness. From Bialystok to the Bronx, Spinoza came to symbolize the emancipated or secular Jew, free from tradition and authority, determined to live life on its own terms.[14]

It is more recently as a moral psychologist and a student of the passions that Spinoza has been read. This view of Spinoza was canonized by Nietzsche, who read Spinoza as his own great precursor for regarding the mind, or what Nietzsche would later call "the will to truth," as the most powerful affect. In a letter to Overbeck he wrote: "I am utterly amazed, utterly enchanted. I have a precursor, and what a precursor! I hardly knew Spinoza and that I should have turned to him just now was inspired by 'instinct.' Not only is his overall tendency like mine—making knowledge the most powerful affect—but in five main points of his doctrine I recognize myself; this most unusual and loneliest thinker is closest to me in precisely these matters: he denies the freedom of the will, teleology, the moral world order, the unegoistic, and evil. Even though the divergencies are admittedly tremendous, they are due more to the differences in time, culture, and science."[15]

It was in this "most unusual and loneliest thinker" that Nietzsche clearly felt he had discovered a kindred spirit. Further, it is not just in what he rejects but in what he affirms that makes Spinoza's "overall tendency" a profound and far-reaching precursor of Nietzsche. For in Spinoza we find a doctrine of modern individuality, creativity, and the celebration of life as freedom. Like Nietzsche, Spinoza stands opposed to everything that represents a mutilation, mortification, or repudiation of life. As with every truly great thinker, the type of freedom Spinoza valued most was the freedom of mind. The *Ethics* is not merely a testimony to that freedom; it is an expression of it.

Thinking about the *Ethics*

Spinoza's *Ethics* is by general consensus one of the most diffi-cult books ever written.[1] This is so in part because the ideas that Spinoza sought to convey are inherently difficult. The themes of substance, attribute, necessity, and eternity are not such as to allow easy access. But Spinoza's work is made doubly difficult by the method by which he attempted to communicate these ideas. As a work written *in more geometrico,* the *Ethics* consists of formal propositions, definitions, scholia, and corollaries, all of which are said to follow from one another in the manner of a formal geometrical proof. Philosophy means for Spinoza rea-soning in a deductive manner. Taking Euclid's *Elements* as its model, his work is set out as a moral geometry intended to lead the reader from a condition of moral confusion and chaos to the one true way of life. Its theme, as Leon Roth claimed years ago, is not just the True but the Good.[2]

The difficulties with the *Ethics* do not end here. Not only are there inherent difficulties with reading the book, but Spinoza's thought has proven peculiarly resistant to classification. What, exactly, has been Spinoza's achievement? Was he a medieval or a modern or, as Harry Wolfson believed, a modern with one foot still in the medieval world?[3] Was he a soulless materialist and atheist as Bayle and Hume believed or a mystical pantheist and "God intoxicated man" as Goethe, Novalis, and Emerson laid claim? Was he a ruthless determinist who believed that noth-ing, not even our innermost thoughts and beliefs, escaped the causal order of nature or an apostle of human freedom whose philosophy sought to liberate the mind from bondage to false beliefs and systems of power? A forerunner of German Idealism or Marxian materialism?[4] An individualist or a communitarian? The answer is to some degree all of the above.

Perhaps we can gain some clarity by examining Spinoza's major influences. But even here we find ourselves on no firmer ground. Like his older contemporary Thomas Hobbes, Spinoza is remarkably sparing with references to his predecessors, and when he does mention them, it is often brusquely to dismiss their various errors and fallacies. This has not stopped readers of the *Ethics* from attempting to situate the work within different intellectual contexts and traditions. According to Wolfson, Spinoza's philosophy is a kind of mélange of the works of the great Judeo-Arabic philosophers of the Middle Ages. For some, notably Edwin Curley, Spinoza belongs entirely to the world of modern philosophy, especially the Cartesian aspiration to create a "unified science" of man and nature bringing together metaphysics and morals.[5] For others, Spinoza was a product of the Marrano culture of Spain and the Iberian Peninsula who still utilized the forms of expression characteristic of a people living under the threat of persecution.[6] And for still others, Spinoza's philosophy constitutes a reworking of certain ancient Stoic moral positions.[7]

However much we can learn from historical studies of Spinoza's background, there is a sense in which he cannot be reduced to his various intellectual and cultural contexts. These may be useful for explaining this or that aspect of the *Ethics,* but all such attempts must necessarily fail in trying to make sense of the work as a whole. Spinoza was neither a renegade Maimonidean, a Cartesian, a Marrano, nor a Stoic. His work incorporates even as it transcends these various descriptions. His formal education both began and ended in the world of the Talmud Torah. This was a world deeply hostile to philosophy. The conflict between philosophy and religion, "Athens and Jerusalem," forms one of the essential motifs of his thought. Spinoza was himself a philosophical autodidact whose work drew on but was essentially independent of any particular tradition or school of thought. His readings in the philosophical literature were extensive but eclectic. He was an original who in the deepest sense of the term was a product of his own making.

To the extent that it is possible to classify the *Ethics*, it is as one of the great monuments to the modern enterprise. To be sure, modernity is an almost endlessly porous term. It can mean many things to many people. It has been defined by the rise of a scientific worldview often associated with mathematical physics, a skeptical disposition regarding religion and other traditional sources of authority, the emergence of the secular state, and the assertion of the autonomous individual as the primary locus of agency and moral responsibility. Spinoza endorses all of these features of modernity to varying degrees, although the aspect of his work to be emphasized here is his reading of human life as an adventure of self-discovery. The *Ethics* is nothing if not a testimony to the powers of human agency and the self-direction of the mind.[8]

The *Ethics* is a singular achievement written by someone who valued his own singularity. Its supreme achievement is to explore the moral and psychological postulates of freedom in a world that had been stripped, partly by Spinoza himself, of its previous theological, cosmological, and political moorings. His questions is: what place is there for human freedom in a world radically divested of divine purpose, devoid of telos, and in which human beings no longer occupy a "kingdom within a kingdom" but are rather fully articulated within a single self-contained system of nature? In this abyss of loneliness—the proverbial night in which all cows are gray—what conceivable grounds are left for the assertion of human dignity and moral responsibility? Despite its claims to geometrical certainty and mathematical truth, the *Ethics* conceals a deeply personal, even existential, work written out of an author's confrontation with his own solitude. In spite of its apparently selfless style and the author's injunction to rise above the limited human standpoint and embrace the perspective of eternity, the work is a celebration of freedom and life with all of its legitimate joys and pleasures.

Above all, Spinoza taught us to appreciate and value life — both our own and that of others. Accordingly he repudiated the classical depreciation of life as "mere" life. He also rejected the messianic emphasis on the world to come at the expense of the here and now. What is to be appreciated is not just the biological fact of existence, although this is not to be despised, but the consciousness of ourselves as rational beings who strive to increase our power and freedom even as we create obstacles that serve to frustrate those ends. The *Ethics* is a celebration of life, of joy and laughter, of sociability and friendship. Spinoza's philosophy culminates not in the grim and remorseless recognition of necessity, as is often portrayed, but in the enjoyment of the pleasures of mind and body working together as a unified whole that helps to secure the conditions for human autonomy. He is a tireless advocate of individual liberty in its moral, psychological, and metaphysical dimensions, and these taken together form a pendant to his liberal politics.

What Kind of Book Is the *Ethics*?

The kinds of questions raised above are made even more problematical when we ask what kind of book this is and who is its intended audience. Spinoza himself gives little by way of introduction. The title page announces only that it is a work in five parts which treats of the following subjects:

Spinoza's relative taciturnity on the purpose of the *Ethics* and its readership stands in marked contrast to the *TTP*, his major work of political philosophy. In the preface to the *TTP* he is remarkably candid about the larger aims of the work. It was written to separate the claims of philosophy from theology and to put them on entirely different footings (*TTP*, pref, 27; III/10). Philosophy is concerned with the realm of truth, theology with moral practice and obedience to God. Spinoza presents himself as protecting philosophy from those who would make reason bow to the claims of Scripture, and also protecting the sanctity of religion from the philosophical systematizers and rationalizers. Furthermore, this distinction is said to serve a political end. The goal of the *TTP* is not merely to protect theology from false systems of philosophy but to demonstrate that freedom to philosophize can be granted without any injury either to piety or to the peace and security of the state.

In addition Spinoza tells us a great deal about the intended audience for the *TTP*. In a letter written to Henry Oldenburg five years before the book was published he spoke frankly about whom he was trying to reach:

> I am now writing a Treatise about my interpretation of Scripture. This I am driven to do by the following reasons: 1. The prejudice of the theologians; for I know that these are among the chief obstacles which prevent men from directing their minds to philosophy; and to remove them from the minds of the more prudent. 2. The opinion which the com-

mon people have of me, who do not cease to accuse me falsely of atheism; I am also obliged to avert this accusation as far as it is possible to do so. 3. The freedom of philosophizing, and of saying what we think; this I desire to vindicate in every way, for here it is always suppressed through the excessive authority and impudence of the preachers. (*Ep* 30)

The distinction Spinoza draws here between the "prudent" reader (*prudentiorum*) and the "common people" (*vulgus*) is repeated in the preface to the *TTP*, where he refers to the "philosophical reader" (*philosophe lector*) and the "multitude" (*multitudo*) (*TTP*, pref, 33; III/12). Yet, while claiming to address the philosophical reader, in the very next breath Spinoza notes that everything to appear in the work will be "more than adequately known to philosophers." He seems to be positioning his audience between the "vulgar" or the "multitude" who live under the sway of superstition and prejudice and the true philosophers who already know what he is saying and for whom the book will be redundant. The audience seems to comprise not philosophers in the strict sense but potential philosophers, philosophers in the making, who still remain under the partial sway of theological prejudice but who can be induced by reason to reflect critically on the source of prejudice. It is a book written by a philosopher for potential philosophers out of a love for them and indeed out of a love for philosophy itself. The *TTP* is a book addressed to those who, in the words of Leo Strauss, "love to think."[9]

If the *TTP* is a work addressed to potential philosophers in order to cure them of their prejudices, the *Ethics* is a work that takes no prisoners. "I do not assume that I have discovered the best philosophy," he confidently asserts, "but I know that I understand the true one" (*Ep* 76). This sense of confidence pervades the work as a whole. The *Ethics* is addressed to philosophers pure and simple. What Spinoza means by a philosopher is addressed in a letter to William van Blyenbergh in which he alludes to his correspondent as "a pure philosopher who . . . has no other touchstone of truth than the natural intellect and not theology" (*Ep* 23). To be a philosopher means to accept the authority of reason pure and simple. A work of philosophy, as Spinoza understands it, is a work that can be understood by reason or the "natural intellect" alone. It makes no concession to time, place, and circumstance. It requires only a reader who can follow a chain of reasoning and accept unflinchingly what is found there. It will accept no argument that is not acceptable to reason. Spinoza's silence about his audience expresses the anonymity of reason itself. The *Ethics* is in the literal sense not Spinoza's philosophy at all; it is the philosophical biography of the idea of reason. In this respect the *Ethics* can truly be called a book for everyone and for no one.

Yet the impersonality of the book and its audience can be overstated. Even if the intended audience for the *Ethics* is smaller, perhaps infinitesimally smaller, than for the *TTP,* Spinoza still wrote the book with a practical intent in mind. The perfect philosopher, like the ancient sage, is at best an ideal, a heuristic, against which any actual reader should be judged. In the preface to part four of the *Ethics* he speaks of "a model of human nature to which we may look" (IVpref/208). Although he never uses this expression again, it is clearly the idea of the philosopher or the philosophic life that he is thinking of. Presumably for such an exemplar of human nature a book like the *Ethics* would be unnecessary, but for the less-than-perfect readers who actually exist, it might actually prove useful.

Spinoza's purpose was to liberate the mind from bondage to the passions and to encourage certain traits of character that he believes will increase the stock of human happiness. Among the virtues he recommends are the qualities of *animositas* and *gene-*

rositas—tenacity and nobility—both of which are described as aspects of the comprehensive virtue of *fortitudo* or strength of character (IIIp59). This is the highest of the moral virtues to which the book aspires. The point or purpose of the *Ethics* as a whole is clearly a pedagogic one, that is, to foster an ideal state of human character. Its goal is precisely to lessen emotional distress, or what Spinoza calls *fluctuatio animi*, vacillation of mind, which is the principal cause of so much misery and human conflict. The *Ethics* is intended as a work of moral therapy in which the reader is simultaneously analyst and patient.

In More Geometrico

Perhaps the single greatest obstacle to entering the world of the *Ethics* is cracking the style of the book. The work is presented in the form of a moral geometry. This has led many readers to wonder what is the purpose of the geometrical form and what is its relation to the content of the work as a whole.[10] Is the axiomatic method in some sense required by Spinoza's philosophy or is it a matter of choice or convenience, much like a poet's decision to write in iambic pentameter? There were certainly many styles of philosophical communication open to him—the dialogue (Plato), the treatise (Aristotle), the autobiography (Augustine), the disputed question (Aquinas), or the essay (Montaigne). Why, then, present oneself in the manner of a geometer? There has been a variety of answers to this question.

The standard view of Spinoza, the textbook image of him passed down in countless introductory courses of philosophy, is that of a relentless rationalist who sought to prescribe how the human mind could achieve clear and distinct ideas by means of the unaided intellect. The mathematical method of reasoning seemed best suited to this pursuit of truth unencumbered by reference to revelation, history, or imaginative experience. Spinoza was among the first to present his philosophy as a "system" in which all problems—moral, metaphysical, political—could be deduced from the axioms and premises of pure reason alone. The *Ethics* gives classic expression to the view of philosophy as an activity carried out *sub specie aeternitatis,* from the aspect of eternity. It consists of taking a God's-eye view of the human condition, a position sometimes diminished by its detractors as the "view from nowhere."

This standard view of Spinoza is also bound up with the image of the philosopher as a kind of self-effacing rationalist for whom all traces of individuality or subjectivity must be expunged from his thought. Long before the advent of poststructuralism Spinoza seemed bent on eliminating the author or the subject from his own discourse. "He thus eliminated from the presentation of his philosophy the concealed means of persuasion and of engaging the imagination of the reader which are part of ordinary prose writing," Stuart Hampshire claims. "He wished the true philosophy to be presented in a form which was, as nearly as possible, as objective and as free from appeals to the imagination as is Euclid's *Elements.* He wished to be entirely effaced as individual and author, being no more than the mouthpiece of pure Reason." [11] The "majestic impersonality" of this system, Hampshire continues, is even more apparent in Spinoza's correspondence, where "the philosophical argument is deployed straitly and rigorously, and only occasionally, when intolerably provoked by the obscurantism of some moralizing or devout critic, does he allow a note of irony or of indignation to appear." [12] As we shall see shortly, there are others who believe that these outbursts of irony and indignation are more than simply occasional grace notes to the system, but reveal what lies hidden just behind the geometrical method.

This view of the *Ethics* as a piece of rationalistic metaphysics constitutes what could be called the standard view of Spinoza.

On this reading of the *Ethics,* the geometrical method is not just a matter of convenience but is taken to express the actual structure of physical reality. In fact the geometry is not a method strictly so called, but is logically entailed by the subject matter of philosophy. There is, on this account, the strongest possible connection between Spinoza's use of the geometrical order of exposition and his views about the ontological structure of reality. That there is a necessary connection between the order of nature and the clear and distinct ideas of a geometrical proof is suggested by Spinoza himself: "The order and connection of ideas is the same as the order and connection of things" (IIp7). According to this statement, the laws of nature act according to the same necessary and immutable principles as do the laws of thought. Nature and thought, the realm of extension and the realm of ideas, are not two causally connected substances but part of the same world seen from two points of view. There is, then, a necessary, not a contingent, relationship between the form and matter, the method and content, of the *Ethics.*

There are, of course, objections to this standard view of Spinoza. In the first place, it is not clear that Spinoza believed the geometrical method has some kind of unique relation with the truth. It seems to play the role of a pedagogical device for exposing the sources of error and false belief. For example, Spinoza employs the geometrical method in his *Principles of Descartes's Philosophy* to demonstrate propositions he believed to be manifestly untrue. More importantly, the idea that the geometrical method represents a kind of mirror of nature is widely believed to be false. The world may be susceptible to mathematization, but this does not make reality mathematical any more than a picture of water is wet. The view that philosophy is the self-articulation of nature and the philosopher merely the voice through which nature speaks fails to address a variety of post-Kantian concerns regarding subjectivity and personal expressions of the self.[13]

Nevertheless, Spinoza's commitment to the geometrical method is often taken to be part of his residual Cartesianism.[14] Descartes certainly had a special fondness for mathematics. Like him, Spinoza is convinced that all genuine knowledge is demonstrative or deductive in form. The geometrical method is intended to provide the *Ethics* with the form of a deductive system that reasons from self-evident propositions to substantive conclusions about the nature of things. This same procedure was advocated by Descartes in the *Discourse on Method:*

> Those long chains composed of very simple and easy reasoning, which geometers customarily use to arrive at their most difficult demonstrations, had given me occasion to suppose that all the things which can fall under human knowledge are interconnected in the same way. And I thought that, provided we refrain from accepting anything as true which is not, and always keep to the order required for deducing one thing from another, there can be nothing too remote to be reached in the end or too well hidden to be discovered. (AT, vi, 19)[15]

Descartes's infatuation with geometry was part of the new science and its attempt to achieve the complete mathematization of nature. For the apostles of this science—Galileo, Gassendi, Kepler, Hobbes, and a host of others—geometry seemed the ideal language of explanation whereby the ordinary world of perceptual phenomena revealed a whole new world of particles in motion. The sense of philosophical paranoia evinced in Descartes's dreams of evil geniuses is but the expression of the growing realization that the world of sensible forms, teleological explanations of natural happenings, and geocentric universes were all a kind of immense fiction from which mankind was only gradually awakening.[16] The answer to this kind of problem was provided by the language of geometry, which alone could establish grounds for certainty when everything else seemed liable to systematic doubt.

Descartes's use of mathematics was itself derived from Galileo's claim that "nature is written in the language of mathematics" (*grandissimo libro scritto in lingua mathematica*). The metaphor of the "two great books," nature and Scripture, were both taken to be mirrors of the divine. For Galileo, mathematics was henceforth conceived as the language of God: "Philosophy is written in that great book, the universe, which stands continually open to our gaze. But the book cannot be understood unless one first learns to comprehend the language and read the letters in which it is composed. It is written in the language of mathematics, and its characters are triangles, circles, and other geometric figures, without which it is humanly impossible to understand a single word of it; without these, one wanders about in a dark labyrinth."[17]

The model of scientific proof was accepted as authoritative not only by Galileo and Descartes but by many of their most important contemporaries. Consider the well-known story from John Aubrey's life of Hobbes: "Being in a gentleman's library, Euclid's *Elements* lay open, and 'twas the 47th Proposition of the first Book. He read the Proposition. By God, said he . . . this is impossible! So he reads the demonstration of it, which referred back to such a Proposition; which proposition he read. That referred him back to another, which he also read. And so on, until at last he was demonstratively convinced of that truth. This made him in love with Geometry."[18]

Hobbes's passion for geometry underwrites his attempt to establish a political science founded only on mathematical exposition. In *Leviathan*, geometry, which is called "the only science that it hath pleased God hitherto to bestow on mankind," is but the science of names (*Lev*, iv, 12).[19] It consists in settling on definitions and drawing out the necessary consequences therefrom. The problem with all previously existing philosophies has been the failure to agree on certain definitions and axioms at the outset of reasoning. Consequently the result has been to doom their efforts to "cant" and other forms of useless speech. Unlike prudence or "knowledge gotten from experience," reason consists "first in apt imposing of names, and secondly by getting a good and orderly method in proceeding from the elements, which are names, to assertions made by connexions of one of them to another . . . till we come to a knowledge of all the consequences of names appertaining to the subject in hand; and this is it men call SCIENCE" (*Lev,* v, 17).

Like Hobbes, Spinoza was an amateur mathematician in comparison to Descartes. Neither left any permanent contributions to mathematical knowledge. Perhaps due to his autodidacticism, Spinoza carried the geometrical project even further than Descartes had thought possible. The Cartesian method always presupposed a dualism between a materialist theory of nature and an immaterialist theory of the mind. There is evidence, however, that Spinoza regarded the geometrical method as more than an exposition of the nuclear structure of physical reality. He saw it as a universal method that in principle encompasses not just physics but psychology, ethics, and politics. While Descartes refrained, apparently from prudential grounds, from extending his geometrical approach to controversial subjects like theology and ethics, Spinoza tells us in the autobiographical preface to the *Treatise on the Emendation of the Intellect* *(TIE)* that all the sciences serve a single end and that politics, too, can be treated as a branch of the science of substance (*TIE,* xvi; II/9).

This view seems to fit with another of Spinoza's major tenets, namely, that there can be no kingdom within a kingdom, no quarter of reality that is not subject to the same causal laws and processes as everything else (IVpref/137). The uniformity of method is based on the belief that there is in the final analysis only one science capturing within its scope a diverse class of entities and activities that might otherwise appear to be irreducibly diverse. It is part of the reductive strategy of the *Ethics* to peer behind the phenomenological diversity of appearances in order to discover their foundations in the common order of nature. There is nothing in the *Ethics* to approximate Aristotle's threefold classification of the sciences into the theoretical, practical, and productive branches of knowledge. In place of this older tradition, Spinoza offers a new conception of philosophy in which the human and nonhuman alike are treated by same method. As he puts it in the preface to part three: "I shall consider human actions and appetites just as if it were a question of lines, planes, and bodies" (IIIpref/138).

How Many Spinozas?

The conception of the *Ethics* as a work of deductive metaphysics is obviously not false. One can easily say of Spinoza what Aubrey reported of Hobbes, that he was "in love with geometry." It is under this guise that Spinoza has seemed to many a kind of protopositivist trying to reduce or replace our everyday commonsense language and beliefs with a cryptoscientific vocabulary of substance, modes, and attributes. However, the image of Spinoza as a committed positivist devoted only to what can be demonstrated by means of clear and distinct ideas is profoundly misleading. Indeed, the first person to provide this misreading of Spinoza's work was Spinoza himself. A careful reading of the *Ethics* is enough to show that it is not a purely axiomatic work, as he sometimes makes it appear. It is a work that draws on a wide range of human experiences—historical, moral, imaginative, even autobiographical—to make its case. The geometrical method, far from a logically impregnable form, is in fact a kind of rhetoric that, like all rhetoric, often conceals more than it reveals. The standard conception of Spinoza has itself come under suspicion from those who have advised that we look, in Harry Wolfson's fine phrase, "behind the geometrical method."[20] What is it that we can expect to find there?

According to Wolfson's argument, Spinoza's geometrical method is not intended as an exact representation of the structure of the universe, but as a pedagogical device for presenting philosophical arguments. Wolfson even speaks of this method as a "literary form," that is, "a peculiar piece of writing" that Spinoza adopted for expository purposes.[21] He regards this method not as expressing Spinoza's ontological commitments but as a matter of convenience for expressing complicated trains of thought in a relatively shorthand manner. As such, the geometrical form is merely the external casement in which Spinoza chose to cast his major ideas.

The choice of this method was not, however, altogether arbitrary. Wolfson accounts for this choice as a product of the peculiar circumstances in which the work was written. Because of the conditions of his exile, Spinoza lacked challenging students and friends who were prepared to ask tough questions and hold his feet to the fire. His correspondents and associates were genial laymen who lacked the ability to serve as an effective sounding board for his ideas during the developmental stages of his thinking. Spinoza's use of the geometrical method was intended as an exoteric cover in which to conceal some of his more polemical and controversial conclusions.[22]

Wolfson adds an important moral element to Spinoza's use of the geometrical method. It is not simply a matter of convenience but an important instrument of moral self-control. It grew out of a sense of caution and decorum: "In this strange environment, to which externally he seems to have fully adjusted himself, Spinoza never felt himself quite free to speak his mind; and he who among his own people never hesitated to speak out with boldness became cautious, hesitant, and reserved. It was a caution which sprang not from fear but from an inner sense of decorum which inevitably enforces itself on one in the presence of strangers, especially strangers who are kind."[23] The geometrical method had the effect of boiling Spinoza's complicated thought down to its "concentrated essence," and this essence conceals more than it reveals. "The *Ethics*," Wolfson avers, "is not a communication to the world; it is Spinoza's communication with himself."[24]

That the geometrical method is directly related to Spinoza's habitual caution and need for restraint has been even further developed in an important article by Efraim Shmueli entitled "The Geometrical Method, Personal Caution, and the Idea of Tolerance."[25] Shmueli distinguishes the strictly geometrical and propositional parts of the *Ethics* from the "non-geometrical" portions, in which he includes the prefaces, appendices, extended notes, and corollaries that help to fill out and provide some flesh to the bare geometrical skeleton of the work. The geometrical method was developed as "a form of caution, and indeed, as a pedagogical device of self-restraint" in contrast to "the non-geometrical assertions loaded with harsh rebukes, refutations, ridicule, and scorn."[26]

Shmueli rejects the view that the *Ethics* forms a single, unified whole, but argues that the nongeometrical portions of the work have a distinctive character that do not follow deductively from the metaphysical premises. These are the parts of the work in which Spinoza lets down his guard and allows his true views to shine through. The result of Shmueli's reading is to turn the *Ethics* into two books that often seem to be "highly antagonistic" to one another. Spinoza was a man of strong passions who was torn by deep apprehensions and intellectual doubts. The *ordus geometricus* thus served as a form of moral self-discipline through which Spinoza sought to restrain his "aggressive impulses," which might have otherwise brought his ideas into even further disrepute. The geometrical method thus served "consciously or semiconsciously as a device for restraining his strong temper when dealing with views whose treatment by him might have annoyed the public. Such discussion indeed called for increased caution and for self-conquest."[27]

A further radicalization of the two-Spinoza thesis has been argued by the French Spinozist Gilles Deleuze.[28] The *Ethics*, he argues, is not one book or even two but three. The elements of the three *Ethics* consist of affects, concepts, and essences. These correspond to the three forms of knowledge or three very different languages discussed in part two of the work. In place of a rigorous, deductive metaphysical system, Deleuze deconstructs the work into several discontinuous treatises held together by only the loosest of connections. Like Wolfson and Shmueli, Deleuze argues that underneath the apparent calmness and serenity of its propositional structure, the *Ethics* contains another polemical and rhetorical discourse within the various scholia and corollaries. While the language of the propositions is likened to an "ageless ship that follows the eternal river," the scholia are compared to "a broken chain, discontinuous, subterranean, volcanic, which at irregular intervals comes to interrupt the chain of demonstrative elements, the great and continuous fluvial chain." "Each scholium is like a lighthouse that exchanges its signals with the others, at a distance and across the flow of the demonstrations. It is like a language of fire that is distinguishable from the language of the waters. It is undoubtedly the same Latin in appearance, but one could almost believe that the Latin of the scholia is translated from the Hebrew. On their own the scholia form a book of Anger and Laughter, as if it were Spinoza's anti-Bible."[29] The difference between the propositions and the scholia, he concludes, are like "two versions of the language of God."[30]

The idea that the scholia form an independent Hebrew work, if taken literally, is absurd. But Deleuze is at least half right to say that Spinoza wrote his book as an "anti-Bible," although he overlooks the way in which he modeled it on the original. Like the Torah, the *Ethics* is a book written in five parts, a Pentateuch of sorts. But the *Ethics* is much more than an anti-Bible. It takes to heart and with the utmost seriousness the Shemah, the biblical injunction known to every Jew: "Hear O Israel, the Lord is God, the Lord is One." The book as a whole can be seen as a sustained midrash on this biblical passage. What is it to think of God as One? If God truly is One—the locus of all power and perfection—how is it possible for him (or it) to create something outside of and independent of himself that would seem to limit his power and perfection? Further, if God is truly One, this would seem to make not just human beings, but rocks and birds and all of the things under the earth and in the heavens a part of this One, no longer objects with an independent existence but, literally, parts of God. He seems committed to denying the ontological status of individuals. These are the questions that inform virtually every page of the *Ethics* and from which the logic of the work unfolds.

The theme of Oneness, which in the philosophical tradition goes back to Parmenides and the pre-Socratics, for Spinoza grows out of the biblical tradition of the single God. To be sure, the God of Spinoza is set up in direct opposition to the God of Genesis. The God of the *Ethics* is not the creator of heaven and earth but is an extended substance composed of an infinity of attributes that is purely immanent throughout nature. Spinoza wrote the *Ethics* in part to free men from the historical practices of religion and from the revealed script upon which those practices were based. His theology, such as it is, is based on a new kind of piety with a new form of worship, the worship of nature. His formula *Deus sive natura,* God or nature, denies the transcendent status of the divine in part because he seeks to divinize the natural world. He invests nature and natural processes with an element of sublimity that makes the *Ethics* a worthy companion to Kant's *Critique of Judgment.*[31]

THE STYLE IS THE MAN

The efforts to read Spinoza's choice of the geometrical method as a literary form or a pedagogical device have considerable merit. In particular they cast doubt on the element of necessity that is often attributed to this form. The idea that there is a relation of logical entailment between Spinoza's view of the world and his geometrical method is false. There are many ways of communicating truth that do not require axiomatic form. But even if there is no logical necessity in Spinoza's manner of presentation, this is not to say that his choice of this method was purely fortuitous. Even if there is no logical necessity, there is still a moral necessity to Spinoza's choice of method.

The geometrical method was for Spinoza, Hobbes, and Descartes strongly related not just to a model of knowledge but to their very ideas of the individual. It has a definite moral purpose, but it is not one of self-abnegation or self-denial, as both Hampshire and Wolfson believe, but rather of individual self-creation. The mathematical method was not for these early moderns a means of purging their philosophies of all personal touches or expressions of individuality, but was closely bound up with a vision of human beings as the products of their own making. Mathematics as a system of symbolization became the paradigm for the individual as, literally, something self-constructed.[32]

Spinoza's views on the moral and constructivist uses of geometry were suggested a generation before him by Descartes. Descartes had set out to turn mathematics, especially geometry, into the veritable model for all human knowledge. The model for Descartes's geometry was, of course, Euclid, who had set out the basic form and structure of geometrical reasoning that held sway for centuries. While Renaissance humanists and philologists turned to Euclid as part of the project of the rehabilitation of ancient arts and letters, Descartes wanted to move beyond the humanistic reception of his work in one crucial respect. While mathematics represented for Descartes's Renaissance predecessors one possible mode of knowledge, for him it took on a privileged character, due in part to the purity of its concepts and their expression in symbolic language. It was, above all, this independence from ordinary language and traditional means of expression that was connected to Descartes's essentially productivist conception of knowledge as a science of human mastery. The term *mathesis universalis,* used for the first time in his *Rules for the Direction of the Mind,* was intended to demonstrate that there was just one royal road to science and this was the path of geometry (AT, ix, 378).

The method of analytical geometry was valid for Descartes not because it represented the "mirror of nature," but because it was a form of self-making. Much of the prestige of modern mathematics derived from the fact that it was a purely self-created system. Its virtue was that it was a heuristic that could be transported from one discipline to another. "The artificial nature of mathematical concepts," Amos Funkenstein has written, "guarantees their absolute unequivocation. Mathematics is the paradigm for all other sciences because we created it ourselves out of nothingness: its veracity is entirely convertible into its construction."[33] Funkenstein's association of mathematics with creation out of nothingness suggests a theological dimension to the image of man as self-creator. In fashioning mathematical entities we are imitating God's original *creatio ex nihilo*. Hobbes applied this analogy to the study of politics when he wrote in the introduction to *Leviathan* that political society is an artificial construction made by imitating God's absolute and arbitrary sovereignty over nature (*Lev*, intro, 1).[34]

Descartes's mathematization of knowledge was more than an epistemological or scientific strategy. It formed an essential move in the late-sixteenth and seventeenth-century creation of the quarrel between the ancients and the moderns. The place of mathematics in this struggle has been brilliantly analyzed by David Lachterman in his aptly titled *The Ethics of Geometry*.[35] "The 'quarrel of the ancients and the moderns,'" he writes, "was much more than a literary parlor game, a bookish battle of shadow-contestants. Indeed, the literary versions of the quarrel often recapitulate in illuminating ways prior engagements on the field of philosophy and science; thus, Perrault, spokesman for modern writers toward the end of the seventeenth century, invokes the superiority of Copernicus and Descartes as proof of modern superiority."[36]

The novelty of the moderns turned on their alleged insight into the constructed character of all knowledge. Today we are inured to hearing about the "social construction" of reality and that terms like *race* and *gender*, previously thought to be biological "givens," are in fact social constructions. Much of the authority of this language comes from adopting, consciously or unconsciously, a Cartesian mind-set. Terms like *doing, producing, constructing,* and *generating* were all used to convey the idea that, however it may appear, all knowledge is a form of human making, an active and self-conscious projection of the mind. Geometry provides a litmus test for this view of knowledge as making. Mathematics is the clearest illustration of the principle that *verum et factum convertuntur*, or that the mind can know only what it makes.[37] It is a feature of all genuine knowledge that it is radically constructed by the knowing subject. To cite Lachterman again:

> Under the sign of making or construction, modernity is an empty form, indeed, the form of endlessly iterable projection, but it is so because it is receptive to all those possible contents which carry the seal of human "fabrication" in its most literal sense. Projection, then, belongs to the idea of modernity, as the programmatic anticipation of an endless sequence of human feats, while productive virtuosity is the touchstone of discriminating genuine from bogus feats, determining when a content did or did not result from a deliberately crafted project. Similarly, the polar antithesis between ancient and modern no longer simply marks off chronologically distinct periods, but turns on an ontological axis; the genuine and the bogus are distinct styles of being. The ancient, necessarily retained in memory as what modernity had to negate in order to secure its own identity, now names the inauthentic itself, that is, the recollected absence of the projected infinitude of human making.[38]

As Lachterman's terms like "genuine" and "bogus" suggest, the Cartesian conception of a universal mathematics is more than an epistemological enterprise; it is part of a larger project of self-transformation that entails notions of personal integrity and authenticity. Philosophers have generally focused on Descartes's two-substance doctrine, his mind-body dualism, to describe this self. Others have in mind Descartes's famous skepticism regarding all knowledge that does not stand up to the rigorous test of clarity and distinctness. Only what is self-evidently true or certain counts as knowledge for him. While Cartesian dualism and skepticism capture important moments of the modern self, they fail to grasp Descartes's truly novel emphasis on the self as the product of its own making. It is the experience of subjectivity or the "I" that marks the real originality of Descartes. The very idea of the individual is itself a product of Descartes's constructive image of knowledge. The features of this new self include liberation from tradition and authority, especially the authority of opinion as congealed in certain ancient books; the mastery of method by which we can arrive at certain truths that can be validated by a well-regulated mind; and finally the control of the passions in order to achieve an ideal of autarchy or individual autonomy that Descartes described by the term *un vrai homme* (AT, vi, 59).

Descartes uses the term *un vrai homme*—a true man, a real man—only once in the *Discourse,* but it is his highest term of praise. To be a real man is to have the qualities of courage, resoluteness, and authenticity necessary for a free life. Central to his idea of freedom is the notion that life is an adventure in self-making. To be free is to be authentic, to be oneself. The real man is one who is true to himself. The Cartesian emphasis on authenticity puts him in a line of Renaissance moralists going back to Montaigne's *Essays* and Charron's *De la sagesse.* It is the emphasis on authentic individuality, as opposed to various forms of role playing and dissimulation, that finds its expression in Spinoza's praise of the *vir fortis,* the noble or, literally, the manly man.

The role of Descartes in the creation of our modern ideas of individualism and individuality is acknowledged by no less authority than Tocqueville. In the opening sentences of volume two of *Democracy in America,* Descartes is presented as more than the founder of a new school of philosophy, but as the discoverer of a whole new world. While the people in the United States pay less attention to philosophy "than in any other country in the civilized world," Tocqueville asserts, their democratic social state leads them "naturally" to adopt something like the principles of Cartesian methodology. Tocqueville defines the main outlines of this method as follows: "To escape from imposed systems, the yoke of habit, family maxims, class prejudices, and to a certain extent national prejudices as well; to treat tradition as valuable for information only and to accept existing facts as no more than a useful sketch to show how things could be done differently and better; to seek by themselves and in themselves for the only reason for things, looking to results without getting entangled in the means toward them and looking through forms to the basis of things."[39] The Cartesian method is not just a philosophical method; it is a democratic method. "So of all the countries in the world," Tocqueville says, "America is the one in which the precepts of Descartes are least studied and best followed. No one," he adds, "should be surprised at that."[40]

AN ETHIC OF RESPONSIBILITY

The *Ethics* is a book that begins with God and ends with human freedom. What on first sight appears to be a chain of bloodless propositions is on closer examination an exodus of the mind from a state of bondage to false beliefs and systems of power to the promised land of clarity and self-knowledge. It is a work of moral therapy that seeks to liberate the reader from the power of the passions and give us control over our lives. Although the *Ethics* is structured in the formal manner of a geometrical proof, it is a work infused with biblical images of bondage, freedom, love, and redemption. It is not just a demonstrative but a dialectical work, leading the reader from the most general definitions and axioms to the more concrete specifications of what is entailed in those initial generalizations. It leads us from lesser to greater degrees of adequation. Like the Torah, the *Ethics* begins with a general account of God's provenance in the world, his power and attributes, and moves quickly to an exploration of the human condition within the causal order of nature. It concludes with a soul-swelling conception of freedom as "the intellectual love of God."

It is not an exaggeration to say that Spinoza makes freedom into the core of the *Ethics*. His treatment of God, body, mind, and the passions are all written with an eye to how they illuminate the great problem of human freedom. Indeed, what distinguishes Spinoza from prior theological and philosophical thinkers is the value and shape that he accords to the idea of freedom. In contrasting the philosophies of Aristotle and Spinoza in his book *Morality and Conflict,* Stuart Hampshire had it more or less correct when he wrote: "There have been changes both in knowledge and in ways of life, which have the effect of making Aristotle's construction of moral and particularly political thought seem incorrigibly incomplete. The succinct phrase for the barrier, and for the missing element, is the concept of freedom, which is applied in individual psychology and politics."[41]

Spinoza's status as a prophet of modern freedom entailed a profound transformation and rupture not just with Aristotle and the classical tradition but with the prevailing orthodoxies, both theological and philosophical, of his own time. Unlike his greatest philosophical contemporaries, Spinoza does not equate freedom with the mastery and control of nature. There is not the kind of "prometheanism" associated with the Baconian or Cartesian quest to turn us into the masters and possessors of nature.[42] Nowhere do we find the dream of a science of universal human mastery of the kind associated with Descartes's *Discourse of Method* (AT, vi, 62). Spinoza seems less impressed with our capacity to transform nature than with our embeddedness within it. Our attainment of autonomy is predicated on our understanding of the various natural and causal contexts in which our lives—both our ideas and choices as well as our behavior and bodily states—are governed. Freedom is not achieved by liberation from nature but through our capacity to understand it. The idea that we cannot escape the causal order of nature often gives the misleading impression that Spinoza equates freedom with the understanding of and reconciliation with necessity, that freedom means understanding why things have to be the way they are, or that it culminates in a kind of Stoic acquiescence to fate.

There is a stern and unyielding necessitarianism in the *Ethics* that has a neo-Stoic dimension to it. However, understanding nature, including the various causal contexts of our lives, does not amount in the end to an ethic of resignation. To increase our powers of understanding is but the first step toward increasing our powers of moral agency. Once we understand the external and internal factors governing our lives, we cease to be passively dependent upon them but can learn to take control of ourselves and responsibility for our actions. The *Ethics* is very much an ethic of responsibility. It teaches that while we cannot escape nature and that much that goes on within it will forever elude human control, we can take responsibility for our lives and how we choose to live them. Accepting responsibility is a necessary component of human freedom. Spinoza teaches us not only to take responsibility for our lives but to find joy and happiness in doing so. He is a thoroughgoing eudaimonist. He makes the joy of life itself his greatest good.

There is an even further difficulty in coming to terms with the *Ethics* arising from the very title of the work. The *Ethics* is not a conventional treatise of moral philosophy. Its subject matter seems both more and less than we would expect from a work called the *Ethics*. It is an ambitious and multifaceted work, bold to the point of audacity. While the work contains materials directly relevant to the content of ethics, such as the source of our judgments of good and bad and discussions of the principal motivations or causes of human action, there is a great deal that points beyond the sphere of ethics conventionally understood. "Ethics," Spinoza writes to a correspondent, "as everyone knows, ought to be based on metaphysics and physics" (*Ep* 27). But ought it? This is by no means obvious, and surely "everyone" does not know this. In particular how are the metaphysics and psychology of parts one and two related to the ethical and political discussions of parts three and four, and how are both related to the treatment of divine love in part five of the work? These kinds of questions have led some readers to wonder why Spinoza called his book the *Ethics* at all.

To be sure, most readers have accepted that the title of Spinoza's work is appropriate without reflecting much on what makes it so. This is strange, because a reading of the book reveals that there is no Spinozistic equivalent of the Aristotelian golden mean, the Kantian Categorical Imperative, or the Benthamite principle of utility. Anyone looking to the book in search of that kind of moral rule is bound to be disappointed. The author of the *Ethics* is not an ethicist in the sense of a person of high moral standards. He is a *moraliste*, that is, someone who sees through layers of convention, custom, and social appearance in order to discover what makes people tick.[43] The *Ethics* offers no answer to the question "what ought I to do?" because it sets out to answer the prior and more fundamental question "how ought I to live?" Spinoza is less interested in the rules governing social life than in questions involving the good life and the supreme happiness for a human being. It is a work of moral pedagogy similar to the other great philosophical and literary romances of education—Plato's *Republic*, Rousseau's *Emile*, Hegel's *Phenomenology of Mind*, and Thomas Mann's *The Magic Mountain*.

Its aim is emancipatory and redemptive. The *Ethics* is not a book of moral dos and don'ts; it is nothing less than a book of life.[44]

One important difference that distinguishes Spinoza from other early modern thinkers is worth noting at the outset. It is a standard conceit of early modern thought to deny the viability of final causes of all sorts and to regard human desires as produced by efficient causes. The result of both claims was to see all human behavior purely in terms of power and power relations. Machiavelli and Hobbes both saw politics as a science of power. So did Spinoza. But unlike his predecessors, he did not attempt to divest power from some notion of telos or human perfectibility. Spinoza was a critic of the doctrine of divine or supernatural teleology, which he took to task in the appendix to part one and the preface to part four of the *Ethics*. But he still regarded human beings as teleological creatures whose actions only make sense as expressions of certain goals or purposes. This does not rule out the proposition that our ends have antecedent causal conditions, but to know the background causes of an action is only to know a part. It is a central theme of the *Ethics* that we are essentially goal-directed animals and that life is, at bottom, the expression of an ideal or goal. We are beings who are constituted by a desire or endeavor (*conatus*) not just to live but to live freely, and freedom, properly understood, constitutes the perfection of the individual. There is a single word that unites Spinoza's psychology, politics, and ethics. That word is *freedom*.

The *TTP* sought to liberate its readers from the authority of Scripture and its ecclesiastical interpreters. Its aim was the creation of a tolerant republic in which each person would be free to think what he likes and say what he thinks (*TTP* xx; III/239). The *Ethics* is concerned more with the ethics and psychology of freedom. Its concern, in contemporary usage, is not "freedom from" but "freedom to." The free individual requires more than the absence of external impediments in order to realize his liberty, but the exercise of certain powers of mind and understanding that make it possible. For Spinoza, freedom is not a natural condition into which we are born. The natural condition is rather one of bondage to the passions and the imagination. Freedom is an achievement of reason that comes about through the harnessing of power and the proper understanding of the passions. The originality of Spinoza consists in his attempt to combine a politics of negative freedom with an ethics of positive freedom. The *TTP* and the *Ethics* constitute the two sides of the problem of freedom.

The *Ethics* is not only a piece of practical philosophy; it is also a profoundly Jewish book, as I have already suggested. Spinoza's indebtedness to and critique of the Jewish tradition has already been developed in a number of previous biographical and interpretive studies.[45] For now I would like to express my agreement with Leon Roth, who may have exaggerated the point but was in my opinion substantially correct when he wrote:

> Now Spinoza was not only, nor even primarily, interested in external nature and the physical sciences. His interest in nature and science was indeed . . . in some sort, incidental. His primary concern was with man and human conduct, and it was in search of a way of life that he set out on the path of science . . . Spinoza's interest in morals came to him by inheritance. He is a descendant of a people which, from the earliest times, had cared little for abstract theories, everything for practical conduct; he is the product of a literature dominated by the ideal of righteousness, of a history which is one long appeal for justice. In spite of himself, and in spite of the Amsterdam community, he remained in his innermost being a son of the People of the Book.[46]

It is hard to say with a straight face that Spinoza "cared little for abstract theories." The *Ethics* is full of such theories—his theory of the oneness or unity of nature, mind-body parallelism, the physiological theory of the passions, and so on. Nevertheless, the insight that all of these theories are subordinate to the practical aim of the *Ethics* is important and a point that needs making. The point of the present study is to return Spinoza to his place among the great moralists of modernity and as a guide of the perplexed to people in all times.

2

Thinking about God

Starting points are always difficult in philosophy, and Spinoza is no exception. He makes it appear that if we do not understand the opening definitions and axioms of the *Ethics* we cannot possibly hope to understand the demonstrations that follow from them. This reading would have some plausibility if the work unfolded in a rigorously deductive manner from self-evident first principles. But it doesn't. The *Ethics* is continually punctuated by digressions, repetitions, polemics, and rebuttals. The geometry forms a kind of surface rhetoric below which we can better determine Spinoza's purpose. Nowhere is this more apparent than in the opening part of the *Ethics*, entitled simply "Of God."

The striking feature of the *Ethics* is Spinoza's decision to put God at the very beginning. Knowledge of God is, apparently, a precondition for knowledge of anything else. The opening eight definitions, followed by seven axioms, are intended to establish the framework for the system as a whole. These provide in a highly compressed and elusive manner the elements, the fundamental categories, of substance, attribute, infinity, causality, freedom, and eternity. The God that emerges in the opening pages of the *Ethics* is not the God of Scripture, of Abraham, Isaac, and Jacob who created man in his image, but of an infinitely extended substance with neither beginning nor end and who is not distant from the world but immanent within it. Spinoza retains the biblical conception of the one God, but denies that it is a just and loving God accessible through prayer and supplication. Spinoza's God is so abstract and impersonal as to be virtually indifferent to human well-being.

The *Ethics* begins with an account of substance. "By substance," Spinoza writes, "I understand what is in itself and is conceived through itself, i.e., that whose concept does not require the concept of another thing, from which it must be formed" (Idef3). Upon this definition, it could be said, the whole of the *Ethics* rests.

With this single sentence Spinoza announces his break with the ancient and medieval philosophical traditions. For Aristotle, with whom the debate about substance essentially begins, the concept of substance indicated the rational form or shape of any species. It identified the characteristic or characteristics that marked off each species from every other species. Accordingly, there were as many substances as there were species in Aristotle's polyglot universe.[1] By the time of Descartes, the plurality of substances had been effectively reduced to two—thinking substance and extended substance. How these two substances were related gave rise to the famous mind-body problem on which so much has been written. For Spinoza, however, there is only a single substance possessed of an infinity of attributes that radiates throughout the whole of nature. Spinoza is the first thinker to consider the substance underlying all things not as a form but as a power. Substance is not a static, timeless form, but a dynamic unfolding power from which all things in nature emanate.

The idea of substance grew out of a discourse about the nature of change, of coming-into-being and passing away. To understand how things come to be is to inquire into their causes or origins. All explanation is, for Spinoza, causal explanation; it is the investigation into the causes or principles of things. The search for causes is, however, potentially endless. Since each effect will have a cause that will in turn be the effect of some prior cause, causal explanation seems to open up the possibility of an infinite regress. If thinking is not to be involved in a potentially endless regression, there must be a point at which the chain of causality comes to an end, that is, there must be something which is not itself caused by some other thing but which is the ground of all causation. That something which brings all further explanation to an end Spinoza calls substance.

There are two features of substance that Spinoza especially wants to emphasize. Substance is unique, that is, it is not the result of some other cause, as is everything else in nature. Substance is rather sui generis or self-contained, not caused by anything outside itself, but its own cause. Further, substance is One. There cannot be multiple substances as in the Aristotelian universe because this would only raise the question of how these substances were related to one another, which would drive the need for explanation further back. Neither does substance stand apart from the various things throughout nature that are said to be its modes and attributes. Spinoza does not posit substance as a separate and distinct first cause like the God of creation. Substance is fully articulated within the causal order of nature, with which it is identical.

From what has just been said, it is clear that there is only one thing that, strictly speaking, qualifies as substance and this is God. In part one of the *Ethics* Spinoza develops his idea of what it is to think of God as a single substance. "By God," he writes, "I understand a being absolutely infinite, i.e., a substance consisting of an infinity of attributes, of which each one expresses an eternal and infinite essence" (Idef6). In the opening propositions of the book this conception of God as substance is awarded a dazzling array of attributes. By "attribute" is understood "what the intellect perceives of a substance, as constituting its essence" (Idef4). Among the attributes possessed by God are existence, eternity, indivisibility, and necessity. God is, in short, coterminous with nature, with the entire system of things that we associate with the created world. This is the basis of the *Ethics*'s famous formula *Deus sive Nature,* God or nature. What does this doctrine entail?

The *Ethics* takes for granted that God exists and that to deny his existence involves us in fatal self-contradiction (Ip11d). But while Spinoza affirms the existence of God, he sets out to prove that God truly conceived cannot be anything like the biblical God portrayed in the opening chapters of the book of Genesis. The God of Genesis is first and foremost a creator who stands apart from and independent of his creation. It is the biblical God who sets in motion a series of separations, first between light and darkness; heaven and earth; the earth and the sea; the sun, moon, and stars; water animals and birds; and finally land animals and man. It is only man who is created in God's image, a fact that accounts for God's giving him dominion over all the rest of creation.[2]

Part one of the *Ethics* represents Spinoza's answer to the author of Genesis and the account of creation given there. The question is What does the Bible mean by the God of creation? It must be admitted that the text itself is not clear. The idea of creation is often taken as analogous to that of artistic production. To create means to give form or shape to a preexisting raw material, as when a sculptor forms a torso out of a lump of clay. This is, for example, the way Plato considered the art of divine craftsmanship in the *Timaeus.* The god of the *Timaeus* was conceived as a heavenly craftsman working from a pattern. The idea of God is understood here as a demiurge or artisan who imposes form on a previously inchoate matter. The image of a divine craftsman may seem to have a certain plausibility—Socrates refers to it as a "likely tale"—but it does not do justice to the account of Genesis.

It is fundamental to the biblical account of creation not only that God created the world, but that he stands utterly alone and apart from the object of his creation. There can be no analogy or correspondence between the laws of causality by which a sculptor makes a vase and that by which the universe is brought into being. To think of divine creation along the lines of the arts is to conceive God in terms of purely human concepts and categories. It is a kind of anthropomorphism, something that the Bible expressly forbids. It follows, then, that if God is the creator of all that is, his act of creation must be completely different from the ordinary human processes of production and generation. God's creation of the world ex nihilo is a unique act for which there is no precedent or analogue on earth. God's creation of the world is and remains a mystery for which nothing in experience offers an explanation.[3]

The aim of the *Ethics* is to remove the mystery of creation ex nihilo not by interpreting it but by replacing it with a causal explanation of the universe and its operations. By placing God outside the causal operations of nature, the Bible maintains the majesty and mystery of the creator but empties the term of all explanatory power. If we think of God as a creator we must think of him as limited by what it is that he creates. But if God is truly self-sufficient and self-contained then it follows that he can suffer no limitation. Further, to regard God as the creator of the world implies an absence of perfection, but by definition God contains all necessary perfection within himself; therefore to see him as creating something outside himself is not to celebrate God's perfection but to doubt it. In short, it is the very idea of God as a creator that Spinoza finds philosophically incoherent.

In answer to the God of creation, the *Ethics* offers a conception of nature as a vast causal network without will or purpose, the understanding of which can be attained from principles and premises internal to nature itself. Reason alone without recourse to revelation can provide both the necessary and sufficient conditions for understanding nature. This is the principle of sufficient reason, according to which the interpretation of nature must be drawn from the resources of reason alone. According to this principle, the world is governed by a necessity of the kind that were "X" to happen then "Y" would have to happen. Note that this is not merely an empirical statement about one thing or class of things following another. It is rather a statement of the necessary conditions for why things happen the way they do and not otherwise. The result is a purely immanent conception of causality such that for every possible state of affairs there is some explanation of it (Ip18). To refer the workings of nature to the actions of a creator being is already to inscribe a measure of arbitrariness or willfulness into nature. By expelling such an idea of God, Spinoza attributes an absolute, logical necessity for everything that is. Reason is the understanding of causes, and nothing can happen in nature that is not the result of some prior cause. The unity of nature and reason is thus made complete.

To be sure, the discontent with the biblical account of creation has long been a staple of the philosophical tradition. The famous quarrel between Athens and Jerusalem has long turned on the issue of whether the universe is eternal and necessary or created in time by an act of divine will.[4] At issue is not only a theological or cosmological, but a moral and political difference. For if the law of sufficient reason proves true, then it would be fatal not only to a conception of God as a transcendent divine being but to the idea of persons as free agents endowed with the attributes of will and choice. All efforts to bridge the gap between these two fundamental alternatives seem to have resulted in failure. It suffices to recall the story about the great Jewish philosopher Hermann Cohen, who had given a lecture on his philosophical concept of God at a Marburg synagogue. After presenting his ideas, he was asked by a pious member of the congregation, "Professor, your philosophical concept of God is very interesting. But where in it is the *boray olam* [Creator of the world]?"

At this point, it is said, the philosopher had tears in his eyes.[5] Suffice it to say that Spinoza would not have wept.

PANTHEISM OR ATHEISM?

The first fifteen propositions of the *Ethics* propose Spinoza's countertheology. His conception of God not as an intending agent but as a system of laws of which all things are but the expression is given radical formulation in Ip15: "Whatever is, is in God, and nothing can be or be conceived without God." This insight is explicated with the help of the following demonstration: "Except for God, there neither is, nor can be conceived, any substance, i.e., thing that is in itself and is conceived through itself. But modes can neither be nor be conceived without substance. So they can be in the divine nature alone, and can be conceived through it alone. But except for substances and modes there is nothing. Therefore, nothing can be or be conceived without God, q.e.d." (Ip15d).

That God is a unique substance in which all things partake is the source of Spinoza's famous (or infamous) pantheism. Pantheism is not only associated with the principle of sufficient reason, that is, the belief that nothing can happen without a cause and there are no causes that cannot be known by reason; it is identified with a determinism such that everything that happens occurs from a necessity such that it could not have happened otherwise. Pantheism, so understood, is thought to be a denial not only of moral agency but of an autonomous moral point of view. The idea that God is a cause immanent in all things is believed to underwrite the liquidation of all moral values. Pierre Bayle was but the first to satirize Spinoza's view that all things, good and bad alike, are but modifications of God: "Several great philosophers, not being able to comprehend how it is consistent with the nature of the supremely perfect being to allow man to be so wicked and miserable, have supposed two principles, one good, and the other bad; and here is a philosopher [Spinoza] who finds it good that God be both the agent and the victim of all the crimes and miseries of man . . . Thus in Spinoza's system all those who say 'The Germans have killed ten thousand Turks' speak incorrectly and falsely unless they mean 'God modified into Germans has killed God modified into ten thousand Turks.'"[6]

But what does it mean to say that all things are in God and God in all things? If God is identical with nature, it would seem that he is inseparable from the creaturely and created things we see around us. Is a bird or a house a property of God? Can we not think of them without thinking that they are somehow in God? If all things are in God, that is, parts of some infinitely complex whole, this would appear to deny the ontological status of individuals. Are persons as a complex of mind and body to be understood as modes of a singular substance without either individuality or self-identity? This would seem to be implied by Spinoza's belief that literally everything that is follows from the nature of the divine substance.

Even more troubling is the idea that Spinoza's monism denies our status as moral agents with the capacity for will and choice. Roger Scruton captures this point nicely when he writes: "Spinoza's monism generates a highly paradoxical idea of the human person. The individual person is not, it seems, an individual at all. Nor is anything else. The identity, separateness, and self-sufficiency of the person all seem to be denied by Spinoza, and man, as part of nature, seems to be no more important a feature in the scheme of things than are rocks and stones and trees."[7] This is a "paradoxical idea," given that Spinoza will wish to show later on precisely that we are beings capable of forming plans, acting on purposes, and accepting moral responsibility for our actions.

These are difficult charges to answer. Let it be noted that the phrase "God or Nature," a virtual catch-phrase identified with Spinoza, is actually used sparingly throughout the *Ethics*. One place where it occurs is used to show that God is a system of causal laws that knows neither beginning nor end but is infinite in its scope and contains all possible perfection. God is not an agent, as conceived by the biblical tradition, but a system or, more properly, a concatenated set of causal laws that make up the system of nature. God is equivalent not so much with nature but with the causal order, the underlying set of laws and relationships, that constitutes the system of nature: "Nature does nothing on account of an end. That eternal and infinite being we call God or Nature acts from the same necessity from which he exists. The reason, therefore, or cause why God, or Nature, acts, and the reason why he exists, are one and the same. As he exists for the sake of no end, he also acts for the sake of no end. Rather, as he has no principle or end of existing, so he also has none of acting" (IVpref/206-7).

It is easy to see how Spinoza's pantheism can easily slide over into atheism or at least the charge of atheism. For if God is in all things, there is no way of effectively separating off God from what he is not. There is little practical difference between the views that all things are in God and no things are in God. Furthermore, if God is in the strong sense of the term "in" the world, this would seem to make God a corporeal being since, after all, extension is an attribute of God's activity. This corporealization of God makes the atheistic interpretation of Spinoza even more plausible since in the Jewish tradition all such corporeal representations of God are absolutely forbidden. On this account the term *God* is a holdover or perhaps even a ruse that Spinoza uses to describe an inexorable system of nature. If *God* is simply a synonym for everything that is, then nothing is added by referring to this causal system in God-terms.

Clearly aware of these implications, Spinoza backs away from the strong view that God is literally identical with nature. To say that God is in all things is not the same as saying that he is all things. The God of the *Ethics* is more like the general ordering principles of nature by which the various created and creaturely things we encounter are constituted. God is to nature as a cause, not a divine or transcendent cause but an internal or immanent cause (Ip18). In describing God as the immanent, not the transient, cause of all things, Spinoza means that God is the intelligible core of nature. God is like the laws of physics, eternal, because these laws are always what they are (Ip19). There is no development or evolution of this system. It is at any single moment what it is and always will be. Further, these laws are said to exist necessarily (Ip29). There are no contingencies or accidents in nature. Everything exists because it has to exist and could not be otherwise. "A thing is called contingent," Spinoza writes, "because of a defect of our knowledge" (Ip33s1). Knowledge of God is equivalent to understanding the necessity for why a thing exists.

There is much evidence throughout part one to support the reading that God is not coterminous with everything that is, but only with the general laws or ordering principles of nature. There is first the statement that God acts only by "the laws of his nature alone" (Ip17). To say that God acts freely is only to say that he is compelled by nothing outside himself. God's actions are the result of an entirely self-generated system of causal laws. Most importantly, Spinoza repeatedly warns against thinking of God in human terms, as an agent or subject possessed of such human qualities as body and mind. To speak of God as "he" (much less "she") is to fall prey to a form of primitive anthropomorphism that consists of thinking of God as a human being, like ourselves, although of infinitely greater power: "There are those who feign a God, like man, consisting of a body and a mind, and subject to passions. But how far they wander from the true knowledge of God, is sufficiently established by what has already been demonstrated. Them I dismiss. For everyone who has to any extent contemplated the divine nature denies that God is corporeal . . . Nothing more absurd than this can be said of God, viz. of a being absolutely infinite" (Ip15s1).

The same is true for those who attribute the capacities of will and intellect to God. Will and intellect are human qualities and as such cannot be attributed to the divine substance: "Further— to say something here also about the intellect and will which we commonly attribute to God—if will and intellect do pertain to the eternal essence of God, we must of course understand by each of these attributes something different from what men commonly understand. For the intellect and will which would constitute God's essence would have to differ entirely from our intellect and will, and could not agree with them in anything except the name. They would not agree with one another any more than do the dog that is a heavenly constellation and the dog that is a barking animal" (Ip17s2).

The two passages just quoted show Spinoza attempting to divest his understanding of God of all human characteristics. God must be completely deanthropomorphized if he is to be made acceptable to reason. In his recent study *The God of Spinoza* Richard Mason has argued that Spinoza's deity is very much like what Pascal disparaged when he spoke of the God of the philosophers, that is, a philosophical construction utterly disconnected from the historical reality of religion and the actual practice of ordinary believers.[8] This understates the difference. Spinoza's God differs from that of Pascal's rationalists and systematizers in one crucial respect. The aim of the *Ethics* was not to provide a philosophical rationalization for the God of creation, but to replace it. Spinoza's purpose was not to provide better reasons for believing in the God of Scripture, but sufficient reasons for not believing in him at all.

Deus sive nature is a formula for the atheism that Spinoza either could not or would not admit to. All of his philosophical contemporaries—Leibniz, Locke, Bayle—believed his views to be deeply atheistical. Of course, since the nineteenth century it has become common to regard Spinoza as misunderstood by those contemporaries and a victim of the narrowness and parochialism of the Jewish community that expelled him. It is alleged that he may not have been an orthodox theist, but that his "God or Nature" bespeaks a sense of genuine religious reverence and even awe. Even otherwise tough-minded analytical critics have come to hold this view, arguing that "Spinoza did accept pantheism as a kind of religion, and apparently did not think of himself as an atheist."[9]

I regard this as utterly naïve. No person of religious sensibility could believe that the famous Roman adage *vox populi vox dei* was a statement of genuine religious belief. It is rather a way of saying that the will of the people is the highest court of authority from which there is no further appeal. The appeal to God is merely a manner of expressing what counts as the ultimate source of authority. The same is true of Spinoza's *Deus sive nature*. God or nature is Spinoza's way of saying that nature is the ground of all things beyond which we need make no further inquiries. It is the place where the buck stops.

Regarding the statement that Spinoza "did not think of himself as an atheist," it is impossible to say what Spinoza thought of himself apart from what he wrote. No one in his time and in fact no one well into the twentieth century could admit publicly to atheism without severe repercussions. Spinoza had already been expelled from one community and remained only tenuously connected to another. The idea that he could have boldly proclaimed what might have been a death warrant is historically disingenuous. A close look at what he means by nature in the expression "God or Nature" should be sufficient to dispel the view that he was a theist of any kind. His view of nature, as we shall see, is utterly void of any kind of purpose for humankind or concern for our well-being. It is hard to imagine what kind of religion could be inspired by the view of God as absolutely indifferent to the distinction between good or evil or that "He who loves God cannot strive that God should love him in return" (Vp19). Spinoza does not deny that there is a difference between good and evil, only that we are the cause of the distinction and it exists purely for the sake of human utility.

Morale par Provision

The issue of whether Spinoza regarded himself as discovering things about God or denying his (its) existence is central to how we understand the *Ethics*. After the statement cited above affirming his belief that Spinoza was a theist, Jonathan Bennett goes on to add that from the point of view of "philosophical truth, it would make no difference if he saw himself as an atheist."[10] I disagree with this point completely. It is surely a matter of great philosophical interest whether the *Ethics* is intended to undermine or support religious belief and practice. The idea that philosophical problems can be treated as a class apart from a writer's theological commitments can be true only of the narrowest conception of philosophy. Ordinarily, whether a writer sets out to prove or disprove the existence of God would be considered a crucial aspect of determining what kind of philosopher he or she is.

The opening propositions of the *Ethics* are among the most difficult in the work and intentionally so. Spinoza follows what appears to be a traditional procedure of defining the nature and attributes of God. The geometrical method seems at first as if it is intended to come to the aid of religion, to place our ideas about God and nature on a sounder basis secure from the corrosive blasts of skepticism and doubt. He goes out of his way to assure the reader that "God necessarily exists" (Ip11d). Yet the God that Spinoza affirms is so radically different from anything that his readers may have understood by that term as to render his intentions questionable. He may not deny the existence of God, but he transforms it into something so strange and unfamiliar as to amount to virtually the same thing. Whether one chooses to call this atheism or not is bound to excite debate. The point is that Spinoza himself was aware that he was skating on thin ice and took pains to protect himself from a plunge. In this respect he had an important predecessor whose work he could take as a model: René Descartes.

Descartes and Spinoza were engaged in a common research program, but each began by grasping a different end of the nettle. Spinoza began by trying to elucidate the general structure of nature, while Descartes began from the thinking ego or self. Each was deeply concerned with how the new science would affect morality and ultimately how a deterministic account of nature could be rendered compatible with the qualities of freedom and responsibility necessary to uphold a moral point of view. Accordingly, each felt compelled to answer critics who saw this science as subverting not just traditional philosophy but morality and religion. Each engaged in complicated strategies of evasion and denial in order to prove the broadly "conservative" nature of their moral teachings against the charges of heresy and unbelief.[11]

Descartes was a master of the double teaching. In the letter-preface to the French edition of the *Principles of Philosophy* he invokes the metaphor of a tree of knowledge to indicate the place of morality within his completed system of philosophy: "The roots are metaphysics, the trunk is physics, and the branches emerging from the trunk are all the other sciences, which may be reduced to three principal ones, namely medicine, mechanics, and morals." Of these three branches, only morality, apparently, requires further elucidation. "By 'morality,'" Descartes writes, "I understand the highest and most perfect moral system which presupposes complete knowledge of the other sciences and is the ultimate level of perfection" (AT, ixb, 14). Descartes speaks here of the "perfect moral system" that only comes to light within a complete knowledge of the other sciences. Recognizing that this completed moral science is the capstone of a system which includes physics, metaphysics, and medicine, Descartes had to provide an answer to the question of what kind of morality should be followed until this system is achieved.

This question is addressed explicitly in the *Discourse on Method,* where he sets out a number of rules, which he calls *une morale par provision,* intended to protect the inquirer from the destabilizing effects of systematic doubt. Descartes imagines himself in the situation of an architect building a new home who must arrange for some temporary lodgings while he is waiting for the new dwelling to be constructed. In order to "live as happily as I could" while the new work is in progress, Descartes enumerates a provisional morality consisting of "three or four maxims" that he knows to be "imperfect" but which must be followed until the better one comes along. The maxims of the *morale par provision* are listed as follows:

> The first was to obey the laws and customs of my country, holding constantly to the religion in which by God's grace I had been instructed from my childhood, and governing myself in all other matters according to the most moderate and least extreme opinions—the opinions commonly accepted in

practice by the most sensible of those with whom I should have to live . . . My second maxim was to be as firm and decisive in my actions as I could, and to follow even the most doubtful opinions, once I had adopted them, with no less constancy than if they had been quite certain . . . My third maxim was to try always to master myself rather than fortune, and change my desires rather than the order of the world . . . Finally, to conclude this moral code, I decided to review the various occupations which men have in this life, in order to try to choose the best. Without wishing to say anything about the occupations of others, I thought I could do no better than to continue with the very one I was engaged in, and devote my whole life to cultivating my reason and advancing as far as I could in the knowledge of the truth, following the method I had prescribed for myself. (AT, vi, 23–27)

The issue perplexing every student of Descartes is the relation between the provisional morality of the *Discourse* and the "perfect moral system" alluded to in the *Principles*. The first thing to note about the *morale par provision* is that it is precisely that, provisional. It is not Descartes's last word on the subject. It consists of a set of rules or precepts for ordinary use that allows the moral agent to persevere even in the face of sustained or systemic doubt. Descartes does not make clear when he thinks the perfected moral science will be ready for adoption or if it will ever replace the provisional moral code. The term *par provision* carries the double meaning of both a stopgap policy to be adopted until something better comes along and the suggestion of equipping oneself with provisions in order to endure a long siege. As is the case with Spinoza, it will take a particular kind of individual who can adopt the morality of self-sufficiency developed in Descartes's later *Passions of the Soul*. The key virtue of this morality, we will see later, is generosity redefined not as conferring benefactions on others but as a specific form of admiration or self-esteem.

In the *TIE* Spinoza follows almost verbatim the maxims of Descartes's *morale par provision*. Here he sets out a largely defensive strategy for accommodating himself to the opinions and beliefs of those around him. While the new philosophy is still in the incubation stage, it is necessary to develop a modus vivendi for negotiating the transitional period. It is therefore "necessary" to assume certain "rules of living" as good. These are the following:

1. To speak according to the power of understanding of ordinary people, and do whatever does not interfere with our attaining our purpose. For we can gain a considerable advantage, if we yield as much to their understanding as we can. In this way, they will give a favorable hearing to the truth.

2. To enjoy pleasures just so far as suffices for safeguarding our health.

3. Finally, to seek money, or anything else, just so far as suffices for sustaining life and health, and conforming to those customs of the community that do not conflict with our aim. (*TIE,* xiii; II/9)

Spinoza's rules for living have received much less attention than Descartes's *morale par provision,* but the similarities between them are striking. Both appear in relatively early works that are set out as propaedeutics to a completed system. They both form parts of intellectual autobiographies in which the authors express concern for maintaining their moral equilibrium during times of crisis, but also for the sake of prudence and personal safety. Spinoza's strategy of accommodation to the understanding of the multitude testifies to the existence of a double teaching between publicly and privately stated ethical doctrines. Unlike Descartes, however, Spinoza did not describe his rules of conduct as provisional. Perhaps this is because he believed such rules would always be necessary. If so, they form an important background feature of the *Ethics*. They express Spinoza's habitual reticence and caution even in the midst of his proposals for the overthrow of religious orthodoxy.[12]

THE CONSTITUTION OF THE IMAGINATION

The most important aspect of part one is not only Spinoza's formal account of the nature and properties of God, but his explanation of what stands in the way of accepting his account. To be sure, there are the inherent difficulties in following the exposition, difficulties he is as at pains to clarify in his various notes and demonstrations. But more importantly, there are the mental and psychological obstacles that we must be taught to overcome. This is what I meant in calling the *Ethics* a work of moral pedagogy. Its aim is to free the reader from the false beliefs that stand in the way of accepting the teachings of the *Ethics!* The core lesson here is a negative or polemical one. It is to remove the "prejudice" that God is a transcendent creator who takes an active interest in our lives and who can be persuaded through ritual practice, prayer, or right conduct to ensure that things come out all right in the end. Remove this prejudice and everything else will fall into place. How will this happen?

In the appendix to part one of the *Ethics* Spinoza provides a powerful psychological explanation for this kind of anthropomorphic mentality. The belief that God is a person or agent who acts with purposes is the product of a particular mental faculty that Spinoza calls the imagination. The imagination is the power on which all the errors, superstitions, and prejudices of revealed religion rest. It is a term that has none of the later positive connotations we associate with human sympathy and creativity. The world of the imaginary, drawn from our lived experiences, is always fragmentary and confused, the source of error and false belief. In particular, the imagination is projective: it projects human ends and purposes onto the artifacts of nature. Because we are purposive beings, we imagine purposiveness is built into the world around us, assuming that what we find there is made for the sake of serving human life. There is a deep-seated human need to attribute to God the basic qualities and attributes of human beings. "The basic prejudice, on which all the errors of revealed religion depend," Leo Strauss writes, "is the assumption that all things, even God Himself, act as men do, according to purposes."[13]

The causes of prejudice grow out of a threefold foundation rooted in human nature: "that all men are born ignorant of the causes of things; that they all want to seek their own advantage; and are conscious of this appetite" (Iap/78). The crucial assumption here is that nature sets no end or telos for all that we do, but rather provides a range of materials and opportunities that we are free to use for our own advantage or disadvantage. The ends we pursue are created, not discovered. "Nature," he writes, "has no end set before it . . . all final causes are nothing but human fictions" (Iap/80). Because nature is nothing other than a universal means to our survival, the human mind comes to believe that the various objects we encounter in nature are put here for the sake of our well-being. The idea that nature does nothing in vain or that nature intends certain purposes for us is simply a fiction of the imagination. It is based on the false belief that, because we act for the sake of certain ends, nature itself has an end. Because we conceive plans and act on purposes, the imagination is led to believe that God is a being like us who also makes plans and has purposes. This is the source of the false understanding of God as a prince, judge, or law-giver who exercises some intending influence over human affairs.

The anthropomorphic fallacy is at the root cause of prejudice or revealed forms of religious belief. By prejudice Spinoza means organized forms of superstition of the type found in the major religions, as understood and practiced by ordinary believers as opposed to the way these religions are understood by philosophical rationalizers and systematizers. According to this conception, God is a being like us, although of infinitely greater power, endowed with the human attributes of willing, judging, and acting as well as the qualities of mercy, anger, justice, and love. This projection of human qualities onto God is the cause from which all the errors of organized religion are shown to follow. The emancipation of the mind from these organized bodies of belief is not an easy task for the reason that the causes of superstition are built into human nature itself. Spinoza was keenly aware of the power of the imagination in causing and maintaining superstitious beliefs. We are, above all, the superstitious animal or the animal prone to believe the figments of our own imaginations.

Superstitions persist because the power of the imagination is strong: "Among so many conveniences in nature they had to find many inconveniences; storms, earthquakes, diseases, etc. These, they maintain, happen because the Gods are angry on account of wrongs done to them by men, or on account of sins committed in their worship. And though their daily experience contradicted this, and though infinitely many examples showed that conveniences and inconveniences happen indiscriminately to the pious and impious alike, they did not on that account give up their long-standing prejudice" (Iap/79).

Spinoza attacks this anthropomorphic conception of God in a way that is both ironical and reverential. He views the belief that God is a purposive agent as a denigration of his power and self-sufficiency. If God acts for the sake of some end, this must imply a lack or deficiency for the sake of which he is acting. The attribution of human qualities to God is merely a symptom of our ignorance of natural causes. It explains further why, when misfortunes and disasters occur, so many are quick to attribute it to the will of God, who must then be placated through prayers, sacrifices, and supplications (*TTP*, pref, 1; III/5). Men end up living in a condition of fear of a vengeful or wrathful deity rather than seeking out the natural causes by which their circumstances are determined and which they might then begin to alter. The idea that everything that happens is due to the will of God is said to be the last refuge of ignorance:

> For example, if a stone has fallen from a roof onto someone's head and killed him, they will show, in the following way, that the stone fell in order to kill the man. For if it did not fall to that end, God willing it, how could so many circumstances have concurred by chance (for often many circumstances do concur at once)? Perhaps you will answer that it happened because the wind was blowing hard and the man was walking that way. But they will persist: why was the wind blowing hard at that same time? If you answer again that the wind arose then because on the preceding day, while the weather was still calm, the sea began to toss, and that the man had been invited by a friend, they will press on—for there is no end to the questions which can be asked: but why was the sea tossing? why was the man invited at just that time? And so they will not stop

asking for the causes of causes until you take refuge
in the will of God, i.e., the sanctuary of ignorance.
(Iap/80–81)

The denial of any sort of natural teleology or divine providence has an ethical corollary. The *Ethics* deflates the idea that
our moral judgments of approval and disapproval have any coun-
terpart in nature. Moral and aesthetic categories like good and
evil, beautiful and ugly, are simply human creations made for
our own convenience and utility. Like Hobbes, Spinoza emphasizes the way that judgments of value vary enormously from one
person to another and that these differences express our diverse
perceptual and physiological responses. It is pointless to believe
that nature or the world provides any guide to morality or the
ends of life: "For example, if the motion the nerves receive from
objects presented through the eyes is conducive to health, the
objects by which it is caused are called beautiful; those which
cause a contrary motion are called ugly. Those which move the
sense through the nose, they call pleasant-smelling or stinking;
through the tongue, sweet or bitter, tasty or tasteless; through
touch, hard or soft, rough or smooth etc. and finally, those which
move the ears are said to produce noise, sound, or harmony. Men
have been so mad as to believe that God is pleased by harmony"
(Iap/82).

Spinoza's attack on teleology and his reduction of our moral
categories and concepts to our diverse physical states is all part of
an effort to liberate the mind from the power of the imagination.
People governed by the imagination are continually swayed by
the passions of hope and fear. This in turn makes them susceptible to a belief in a supernatural being who rewards and pun-
ishes us for our sins. "All the notions by which ordinary people
are accustomed to explain nature," Spinoza writes, "do not indicate the nature of anything, only the constitution of the imagi-

nation" (Iap/83). It is the constitution of the imagination that keeps us in a state of mental slavery not only to our passions and systems of false belief but to the various ecclesiastical and political authorities who profit from this condition.

ON TELEOLOGY

Spinoza's attack on the doctrine of final causes in the appendix to part one has been one of the most widely debated aspects of the entire work. Readers have been puzzled about how far he intends to take the repudiation of teleology. For some readers, the *Ethics* seems to be an attack on the very idea of purpose and the idea that even human ends and ideals can be translated into the nonteleological language of impulses and appetites.[14] For others, it is an attack only on the idea of divine purpose, leaving open whether or to what extent human activity can be characterized as purposive or goal-directed. At times Spinoza writes as if he were rejecting only divine teleology, that is, the ascription of purposes to God or nature. This is the minimal sense in which Spinoza's denial of purpose can be read. It is certainly the case that the rejection of divine teleology was a highly controversial position to take in the seventeenth century. The Aristotelian tradition of teleological explanation was still very much alive, as the repeated attacks on it by the likes of Descartes and Hobbes make clear.[15]

The *Ethics* not only denies the idea of divine purpose but offers an explanation of it. The belief in divine teleology, we have seen, is a prejudice that is itself explained by the tendency to attribute to nature or God the same kinds of purposes that we have as human beings. We are, Spinoza appears to say, teleological beings and we cannot help fancifully ascribing similar ends to other objects in nature and history. "Men commonly suppose that all natural things act, *as men do*, on account of an end," he writes (Iap/78; emphasis added). Not only is this tendency a function of the imagination—a projection of human wants and desires onto the world around us—but it is also inconsistent with other more rational beliefs we hold about God. Typically, human purposes take the form of desires of some sort. I have a desire for a cup of coffee and this desire in turn explains why I begin to fill up the coffee pot. The desire is for something I want but now lack. To attribute desires to God implies a deficiency. How could God be deficient in anything? If God is the locus of all power and perfection, the attribution of purpose to him is a non sequitur. God or nature is always perfect exactly as it is and can never be in want of anything.

Elsewhere in the *Ethics* Spinoza appears to go further and to repudiate not just divine teleology but the very concept of purpose. In a passage from the appendix to part one, cited earlier, he writes that "nature has no set end before it and . . . all final causes are nothing but human fictions." The statement that "all final causes" are "human fictions" applies not just to divine but to human teleology. Human purposes are likewise *figmenta* of the imagination, which are in turn reducible to antecedent causes or conditions. Spinoza shows how all allegedly final causes are themselves just efficient causes in disguise. In a passage from the preface to part four he writes: "What is called a final cause is nothing but a human appetite insofar as it is considered as a principal, or primary cause, of some thing. For example, when we say that habitation was the final cause of this or that house, surely we understand nothing but that a man, because he imagined the conveniences of domestic life, had an appetite to build a house. So habitation, insofar as it is considered as a final cause, is nothing more than this singular appetite. It is really an efficient cause, which is considered as a first cause, because men are commonly ignorant of the causes of their appetites" (IVpref/207).

This passage is generally taken as evidence of Spinoza's belief that talk of final causes is simply a mistaken way of speaking about efficient causes. We have seen that he is wary of attributing final causes to natural objects, in that this implies consciousness or a conscious designer. To say that "the eyes are for seeing" or "the heart is for pumping blood" implies that these organs were created with that end in mind. But not only does he deny purpose to natural bodies, he seems also to deny that human activities can be understood as expressing purposes. The argument against teleology in the explanation of human behavior is that final causes refer to some future state yet to be achieved, which is then used to explain an antecedent condition. To explain the present by reference to the future is something that Spinoza says "turns nature completely upside down. For what is really a cause it considers an effect, and conversely" (Iap/80).

The repudiation of human purpose is carried to an even further degree in Spinoza's letter to Schuller in which the two debate the nature of freedom and necessity (*Ep* 58). Here Spinoza reiterates his definition of freedom, according to which a "thing is free which exists and acts solely from the necessity of its own nature" (Idef7). From this he believes it follows that all created things are determined by external causes. "For every single thing," he writes, "is necessarily determined by an external cause to exist and to act in a fixed and determinate way."

Consider the case of a stone rolling downhill. What might such a stone think, Spinoza wonders, if it possessed the powers of consciousness and will? "Now this stone, since it is conscious only of its endeavour and is not at all indifferent, will surely think it is completely free, and that it continues in motion for no other reason than that it so wishes. This, then, is that human freedom which all men boast of possessing, and which consists solely in this, that men are conscious of their desire and unaware of the causes by which they are determined" (*Ep* 58). This passage confirms the view that human beliefs and desires—first-person states—are not freely chosen but the result of antecedent conditions. If efficient causes for action are exhaustive, then appeals to states of consciousness like intentions and reasons can only be a form of superstition.

The denial of all teleology, including human rational teleology, is often seen as part of, even necessary for, Spinoza's wider scientific metaphysics. All teleological concepts on this account are taken to be relics of an older Aristotelian or theological universe in which the model of explanation is purposive striving rather than inertial motion. Those who hold this view think of Spinoza as maintaining a thoroughly homogeneous conception of nature, including human nature, so that everything— our thoughts, desires, deliberations, and imaginings—are subject to the same laws of motion and rest. Richard Mason has provided a particularly striking reformulation of this reading: "Spinoza tells us plainly that 'Nature has no fixed goal' and that 'all final causes are but figments of the human imagination'; and this should give us the clearest pointer towards his position. Of course we use teleological explanations all the time, both for our own actions, the actions of others and, most strikingly, but not always with care, in biology. But such explanations are not correct; we *imagine* them and, in this way at least, our imagination leads us astray . . . The distinction between human and nonhuman final explanations is just a matter of being less or more obviously wrong."[16]

Mason is here defending the strongly antiteleological reading of Spinoza developed earlier by Bennett, for whom all explanation in terms of purposes is reducible to efficient causes based on the concepts of appetite and aversion. Spinoza's concept of appetite, Bennett avers, is "free of the supposedly noxious elements in teleological concepts," although he admits that this is easy to overlook in the appendix to part one, where Spinoza is clearly more concerned with repudiating divine rather than human teleology. Spinoza's "seeming concessions" to human rational teleology, Bennett speculates, may be due to the fact that he wrote his attack against divine teleology before his case against all teleology had occurred to him and then neglected to go back and revise the earlier part in the light of the later discoveries. "Anyway," Bennett continues, "the radical attack on teleology should be taken seriously. For one thing, it is needed for the attack on divine teleology: if human beings were allowed to act purposively, Spinoza would have as much reason to say that God has purposes as he does to say that God thinks. Furthermore, brief as it is, the radical attack on teleology is there, and many aspects of Part 3 cannot be understood unless one grasps that Spinoza is trying to develop a nonteleological theory of human motivation. Miss that and you miss most of what is interesting in Part 3."[17]

Bennett is correct to see that the attack on teleology in the appendix to part one is connected to Spinoza's doctrine of the *conatus* in part three. The issue of teleology is only raised, hardly settled, by his initial remarks. However, Spinoza's conative theory of human motivation is shot through with teleological content that the attempt to reduce it to purely physiological or biological impulses cannot deny. A large part of what it means to be a human being, we shall see in the next chapter, means to have the power of reflective thought and choice, which can in turn be used to revise and correct our moral beliefs and desires in an indefinite process of self-perfection.

In any case, I read the passage from the appendix to part one somewhat differently and in a way that is more consistent with what Spinoza says later in the *Ethics*. Spinoza is not denying all final causes, and the statement about turning nature upside down is preceded by the remark that "Nature has no end set before it." He is denying only natural teleology, the attribution of purpose to nonhuman parts or wholes. Human activities are by contrast thoughtful and purposive. They are deliberate responses to human situations. To return to the example cited about the house: the desire for habitation is an efficient cause of having a house built, but the desire also contains an end or purpose to be accomplished. The desire for a house alone cannot devise a house. We cannot understand the desire without grasping the end that the desire contains. This is not to explain the present in terms of the future, but to recognize that human activities have a rational and conscious component that cannot be explained simply in terms of antecedent conditions. Human beings do not build houses in the way that spiders spin webs, but rather as the self-conscious expenditure of energy and intelligence. To be sure, work, like all events in nature and history, forms part of a causal process, but it also exhibits an internal structure that is goal-directed.

Marx, who may have had Spinoza's example in mind, brilliantly captures the purposive nature of work in a passage from *Capital*, volume one: "We presuppose labor in a form that stamps it as exclusively human. A spider conducts operations that resemble those of a weaver, and a bee puts to shame many an architect in the construction of her cells. But what distinguishes the worst architect from the best of bees is this, that the architect raises his structure in imagination before he erects it in reality. At the end of every labor-process, we get a result that already existed in the imagination of the laborer at its commencement. He not only effects a change of form in the material on which he works, but he also realizes a purpose of his own that gives the law to his modus operandi, and to which he must subordinate his will."[18]

What is at stake in this rather scholastic dispute about the limits of teleology? First, there is the issue of the consistency or coherence of Spinoza's teaching. For some readers, if substance is One and all things are modes of this singular substance, it follows that there must be a single mode of explanation for all aspects of substance. It is a leading idea of the *Ethics* that there is no kingdom within a kingdom, no sphere that escapes the causal order of nature. As Spinoza's example of the stone falling on a man's head indicates, every action or event in nature is a link in a chain of causes that can be traced back to infinity. Similarly, the stone hitting someone's head will initiate a new chain of events that will extend infinitely into the future. The view that there is a final cause at which the explanation of an event stops is an illusion. Of course, we may simply run out of answers or give up searching for new causes, but this has more to do with the limitations of the human intellect than with the causal chain under consideration. Every human wish, hope, want, or desire is simply part of a causal chain without beginning or end, that is, infinite in duration.

The same readers who insist on the denial of all teleology in the *Ethics* are often perplexed by Spinoza's explicit use of teleological language throughout much of the work and his other writings. In the *TIE* he speaks unequivocally about directing all the sciences toward the attainment of "one end and goal," that being "the highest human perfection" (*TIE*, xvi; II/9). The *Ethics* itself is predicated on the belief that there is an ultimate human good, love and knowledge of God, that results in salvation or beatitude, Spinoza's terms for human happiness. Running throughout the work is a conception of action as both cause and effect, active and being acted upon (IIIdef2). That is to say, human beings are not only folded within the causal order of nature; we are both natural objects existing within time and space and rational agents with beliefs and desires. We can be viewed both under the aspects of extension and thought. The unity of nature does not rule out the possibility, even the necessity, of internal complexity. Explanation in terms of causes does not deprive us of acting for the sake of reasons. It does not deprive us of our rational agency.

The core of this debate over the scope of teleology concerns the place of freedom in the *Ethics*. If all human behavior, including our thoughts and beliefs, is part of the causal order of nature, then the scope of human freedom must be severely curtailed. A consistent naturalism would rule out of bounds moral concepts like freedom, choice, guilt, and responsibility. Freedom would consist of little more than an ability to understand our place in nature and learn how to adapt to it. It would mean successful adaptation rather than acting on freely chosen ends and purposes. Indeed, Spinoza often delights in deflating our moral vocabularies, showing them to be little more than an expression of bodily states and emotional desires. Yet it would be a strange reading of the *Ethics* that would deprive the work of all ethical substance.

It is tempting to view Spinoza in this light, in part because he often writes as if he were doing precisely this. Throughout the *Ethics* he constantly engages in a kind of reductionism that seems to make moral choices little more than appetites we happen to have (IIIp9s). But as we shall see in more detail in the next chapter, we are not just natural objects but rational agents with the powers of reflection and choice. The *Ethics* is constructed around a conception of human agency, and the idea of agency without related notions of purpose and meaning is unintelligible. In Spinoza's language we are conative beings who not only have a built-in desire to preserve ourselves but also desire to enhance our powers and take control over our lives. This is not to say that our lives are undetermined. Thoughts and desires have their antecedent conditions in other thoughts and desires. This is all a part of Spinoza's singular vision. We are beings who act and are acted upon, simultaneously both subject and object. Far from a denial that we are purposive beings, it is central to the scheme of the *Ethics* that we are. The plan of the work is not to deny that we have purposes but to help us realize them more effectively.

3

Thinking about Thinking

The transition from part one to part two marks an important change in the overall direction of the *Ethics*. In part one Spinoza dealt with the biblical theme of the unity and oneness of God. To take seriously the proposition that God is one meant thinking about God not as the transcendent creator of nature, but as fully articulated within the natural world and its causal processes. In part two, however, Spinoza turns away from the unitary structure of nature as a whole to consider the issues of personal identity, the relation of mind to body, and the basic composition of the human personality. It marks the point of transition from theology or onto-theology to psychology as the focus of the work.

Part two is called "Of the Nature and Origin of the Mind." Its terms are set mainly by the psychology of Descartes and especially the way in which human beings as a complex of mind and body can be said to have an identity or form an "I." The framework of Cartesian psychology can be summarized in terms of Descartes's famous two-substance doctrine. Human beings are in the first instance bodies whose motions and interactions with other bodies form part of a general science of mechanics. As physical organisms we are subject to the same laws of attraction and repulsion as is the rest of nature. But humans are possessed not just of bodies but of an entire internal world of will, consciousness, and reason, which Descartes called by the classical designation of the soul. In the science of the soul, its strivings and desires are not reducible to physical states but belong to an autonomous sphere of mind. Minds or souls are as much constituent parts of reality as are bodies or material substances. The question is how to account for the relation between the motions of the body and the stirrings of the soul. How are these two related? Or do they simply form two entirely different substances? Descartes struggled to solve this problem in a quasiphysicalist manner by suggesting that these two substances were mediated through the pineal gland located at the base of the skull—a theory at which Spinoza takes aim later in the book (Vpref/278). It was this answer that Spinoza found unsatisfactory and to which the second part of the *Ethics* is a response.

PARALLELISM

On the basis of part one of the *Ethics* it might appear that Spinoza is a thoroughgoing materialist. He conceives God in terms of the extended order of nature; he regards everything within nature, ourselves included, as subject to an all-embracing causal necessity; and he reduces our moral judgments of good and evil to the shifting physical states of the body. There is nothing that escapes the world of physical causation and nothing that cannot be explained in terms of its antecedent conditions. Spinoza often writes as if the idea of freedom is itself a kind of illusion from which we must be disabused. Mental terms such as *volition* and *will* are rejected as so many "fictions" to which nothing in reality corresponds: "In the Mind there is no absolute, or free, will," he writes, "but the Mind is determined to will this or that by a cause which is also determined by another, and this again by another, and so to infinity" (IIp48). Spinoza explains the above proposition by means of the following demonstration: "The Mind is a certain and determinate mode of thinking and so cannot be a free cause of its own actions, or cannot have an absolute faculty of willing and not willing. Rather, it must be determined to willing this or that by a cause which is also determined by another, and this cause again by another, etc." (IIp48d).

Part two of the *Ethics* begins by adding another dimension to its account of God. God is characterized not only by the attribute of extension, but also of thought: "Thought is an attribute of God, or God is a thinking thing" (IIp1). While earlier he had maintained that God is constituted by an infinity of attributes (Ip16), Spinoza now singles out the properties of thought and extension as primary. It is here that he articulates his famous idea that thought and extension are not two different substances but rather two modes of the same substance.

The idea that thought and extension are two modes of a single substance forms the basis of what is known as Spinoza's doctrine of parallelism. This doctrine means that extension and thought, body and mind, run on two separate but parallel tracks, each obeying its own sphere of causality. Physical events cause other physical events; mental events cause other mental events, but there is no causal flow between body events and mind events. Instead of a causal relation there is an overall correlation between body events and mind events. A change in the state of my body will not cause a change in the state of mind; it *is* a change in my mind. The world of bodies and the world of minds are not two different worlds but the same world, albeit described from two different points of view.

Spinoza denies that there is any causal flow between mind and body, a proposition expressed most vividly at IIp7: "The order and connection of ideas is the same as the order and connection of things." This proposition, he avers, follows from what was said in the first part of the *Ethics*, according to which there is but one substance, which can be comprehended under the mode of extension and under the mode of thought. In the scholium to this proposition Spinoza adds that "some of the Hebrews"—he does not say which ones—"seem to have seen this, as if through a cloud, when they maintained that God, God's intellect, and the things understood by him are one and the same."[1]

The term almost universally applied to Spinoza's mind-body doctrine is *parallelism*. Spinoza, it should be said, nowhere used this term, and it seems to have been coined by Leibniz, who used it to designate a correspondence between autonomous or independent series.[2] Spinoza seems to be aware of how odd this doctrine must sound, because at one point he beseeches his readers "to continue on with me slowly, step by step, and to make no judgment on these matters until they have read through them all" (IIp11s). The proposition that thing and idea, body and mind, are "the same" means that the mind is an embodied thing and the body is an ensouled one. Each forms part of a complex functioning organism that we call a person. In the propositions following IIp7 Spinoza comes closest to giving a purely materialist or corporealist theory of mind. The mind, he maintains, cannot be conceived apart from the body and the ideas that constitute the human mind are nothing but the ideas of the body to which that mind is attached (IIp11).

Accordingly, our ideas will be as simple or complex, as weak or strong, as the body they are ideas of. No one, Spinoza affirms, will ever understand the mind unless they first understand the body:

> We also cannot deny that ideas differ among themselves, as the objects themselves do, and that one is more excellent than the other, and contains more reality, just as the object of the one is more excellent than the object of the other and contains more reality. And so to determine what is the difference between the human Mind and the others, and how it surpasses them, it is necessary for us, as we have said, to know the nature of its object, i.e., of the

human Body. I cannot explain this here, nor is that necessary for things I wish to demonstrate. Nevertheless, I say this in general, that in proportion as a Body is more capable than others of doing many things at once or being acted on in many ways at once, so its Mind is more capable than others of perceiving many things at once. And in proportion as the actions of a body depend more on itself alone, and as other bodies concur with it less in acting, so its mind is more capable of understanding distinctly. And from these [truths] we can know the excellence of one mind over the others. (IIp13s)

Spinoza's doctrine of parallelism is intended to replace two competing theories of the mind-body relation. The first is the Cartesian doctrine of dual substances in which the mind is viewed as inhabiting the body in much the way that a person inhabits a house. What goes on in the mind will push outward and cause the body to act. It is our reasons, intentions, and interior mental states that explain actions the mind causes to happen. The Cartesian distinction between the body and the mind maps onto a related distinction between the public and the private. To be sure, this argument has a certain prima facie plausibility. On this view, what goes on in the inner theater of the mind is private and known only to the subject, while the external actions of the body are public and belong to the world of observable behavior. It is a distinction that derives in part from the theological belief about the immortality of the soul. It also provides the basis for the modern liberal separation of the private and public spheres of life. The Cartesian problem turned on its attempt to explain the relation between the content of the mind that is knowable only by the agent and the causal mechanisms to which the body is subject. This use of mental concepts to explain bodily states was later ridiculed mercilessly in Gilbert Ryle's *The Concept of Mind* as a legacy of the Cartesian doctrine of the "ghost in the machine."[3]

The second doctrine that Spinoza sought to dispel might be called the theory of mind-body interactionism. The interactionist thesis maintains that mind events can cause body events and body events can cause mind events. At IIIp2 he makes a special point of denying that body and mind can codetermine each other's functions: "The Body cannot determine the Mind to thinking, and the Mind cannot determine the Body to motion, to rest or to anything else" but rather "Mind and Body are one and the same thing, which is conceived now under the attribute of Thought, now under the attribute of Extension."

Once again Spinoza expects to encounter resistance to his views. So deeply entrenched is the opinion that the body moves or rests by the mind's command that readers cannot be induced to consider his views fairly unless they can be confirmed by experience. He proposes a new kind of experimental science that may yet demonstrate that many of the things we now attribute to the powers of the mind are in fact due to the motions of the body. The study of the body is still in its infancy, he argues, and may one day explain a great many things we commonly attribute to intentional human activity: "And of course, no one has yet determined what the Body can do, i.e., experience has not yet taught anyone what the Body can do from the laws of its own nature . . . For no one has yet come to know the structure of the Body so accurately that he could explain all its functions—not to mention that many things are observed in the lower Animals that far surpass human ingenuity, and that sleepwalkers do a great many things in their sleep that they would not dare to do awake. This shows well enough that the Body itself, simply from the laws of its own nature, can do many things which its Mind wonders at" (IIIp2s).

Spinoza is clearly aware of how much his view jars with ordinary experience. We are commonly accustomed to believing that our bodily and physical activities are dependent upon prior mental states. My decision to speak (a mental event) causes my tongue to move (a body event). But does it? He takes an evident delight in reducing in scope those areas where we mistakenly believe that our actions are self-determining: "Human affairs, of course, would be conducted far more happily if it were equally in man's power to be silent and to speak. But experience teaches all too plainly that men have nothing less in their power than their tongue, and can do nothing less than moderate their appetites. . . . So the infant believes he freely wants the milk; the angry child that he wants vengeance; and the timid, flight. So the drunk believes it is from a free decision of the Mind that he speaks the things he later, when sober, wishes he had not said. So the madman, the chatterbox, the child, and a great many people of this kind believe they speak from a free decision of the Mind, when really they cannot contain their impulse to speak" (IIIp2s2).

The *Ethics* rejects both the two-substance and the interactionist theses on the ground that they assume we are composite beings made up of body and mind. The fact is we are not two things but one or, more precisely, one being that can be looked on from two points of view. Mind and body are one and the same thing seen under the aspects of extension and thought. Conceived as an aspect of the attribute of extension, we are embodied creatures whose behavior is entirely of a piece with the system of physical causation. For every action or event there is some set of antecedent causal conditions sufficient to explain it. We are links in a universal chain of causality that can be studied purely naturalistically. Conceived, however, as an aspect of the attribute of thought, we are rational agents who have the power of reflection and choice and are capable of taking responsibility for our own actions. As rational and reflective beings we have the capacity to control and reform those aspects of our mind that had been previously dominated by unconscious or ill-considered appetites, feelings, and passions. This is not to say that our actions are undetermined, but that the explanation derives from our own context of understanding, including our own first-person perspective.

The Identity of Mind and Body

The question faced by any reader of the *Ethics* is the relation between the two attributes of thought and extension. In what does the correlation of mental to physical modes consist? It must be admitted that the near-universal description of Spinoza's doctrine as parallelism is somewhat misleading. R. G. Collingwood observed that parallelism is a geometrical term that presupposes two lines running equidistant from each other but never meeting. But the idea that there is some two-dimensional space separating body events from mind events cannot be literally true.[4] So what kind of relation is it between the causal and rational explanations of human behavior?

Deleuze usefully distinguishes three different aspects of the doctrine of parallelism. It implies, first, a formal symmetry or correspondence between two modes. Two things can be said to correspond with one another if they fulfill a similar or related function, as when we say runs in baseball correspond to points in soccer. They are functional equivalents. Second, parallelism implies equality or isonomy between the things being considered, suggesting that neither part is superior to the other. Mind is not superior to body, nor body to mind, but each is required for and presupposes the other. Deleuze gives this a strongly democratic interpretation: "By his strict parallelism Spinoza refuses any analogy, any eminence, any kind of superiority of one series over another, and any ideal action that presupposes pre-eminence; there is no more any superiority of soul over body, than of the attribute of Thought over that of Extension."[5]

Finally, the term implies not just a formal symmetry but a literal identity of thought and extension. *Parallelism* implies that mind and body are not two things but one considered only from different points of view. Changes in one do not effect changes in the other; they are changes in the other. Mental states and physical states do not describe two independent substances but the same substance from two different angles. A person may be described as a complex of physical and chemical processes as well as a complex of feelings, beliefs, and self-interpretations. Each describes what a person is from one limited point of view. We can describe a person running as a set of physical processes in motion or as expressing the beliefs and purposes of the runner, say, the desire to win the New York City marathon. Like Wittgenstein's duck-rabbit experiment from the *Philosophical Investigations*, where we can see a picture one way as a duck and another way as a rabbit, human nature has these dual aspects. We can be viewed as bodies existing in space and time or as minds expressing purposes and desires, but both are aspects of the same human identity. Both of these are equally valid descriptions and may even be necessary for a complete picture, although they are incommensurable and irreducible to one another. They form parts, albeit radically heterogeneous parts, of a comprehensive science of human nature.

Readers of the *Ethics* have long pondered how Spinoza's doctrine of mind and body is supposed to work. Unfortunately, Spinoza rarely illustrates his views by means of an example, so the reader is left largely to ponder his own. Consider the following example suggested in a *New York Times* Op-ed article by paleontologist Stephen Jay Gould.[6] Gould raises the old question of the role of mind in athletic ability. In particular, how do we explain why a gifted second baseman like former New York Yankee Chuck Knobloch suddenly makes repeated throwing errors in otherwise routine operations that he has performed literally thousands of times before? When an athlete fields a difficult ground ball, we are apt to say he did it "effortlessly" or "instinctively" or that he "made it look easy." But when the same person becomes plagued by errors of an inexplicable kind, we are apt to say he is suddenly "thinking too much," as if a mental event, thinking about what to do, has somehow interfered and caused an error in the physical process of doing it. That is, we think of mind and body as two different activities that have an external, causal relation to one another. Is it thinking about what to do, then doing it that has caused Knobloch's throwing errors? From Spinoza's viewpoint this is a false inference.

Consider the enormously complex activity involved in hitting a baseball. Of course before getting up to the plate the batter may well deliberate where he believes the pitch will be thrown, what kind of pitch (a curve, a changeup) to expect, and even where would be the ideal location to hit it. But in the split second it takes a ninety-mile-an-hour fastball to leave the pitcher's hand and cross the plate, there is simply no time for the batter to process information about what to do and then do it. But just because the swing of the bat is not preceded by overt mental reflection, it does not follow that it is done unthinkingly or instinctively. Rather, the relation between thinking and doing, mind and body, is different from a causal, sequential one. A skill that has been honed over many years and countless hours of practice is not the result of mind; it is an expression of mind. We can use metaphors like "physical intelligence" or "muscle memory" to indicate that body and mind are more closely intertwined with one another than might appear. Hitting requires both physical skills of strength and hand-eye coordination and mental skills of dedication and commitment. It is not the case that the body acts independently of intelligence or that the mind causes the body to act, but both form parts of the same activity.

What is true of sports is equally true of a whole range of other activities. Playing a musical instrument is an activity that takes great patience, practice, and concentration, but the activity itself is not regulated by overt mental calculations over what to do. Countless books have been written on the art of playing the piano, but none can explain just how the movements of the fingers are connected to the operations of the brain. In his recent work *Notes from the Pianist's Bench*, Boris Berman explains that the dexterity of the fingers must be matched by the performer's emotional technique, which he calls the "technique of the soul."[7] It is the unity of physical and emotional maturity that constitutes the performer's art. The musician's craft is neither simply a mental activity nor a physical one, but one that expresses body and mind together in a single performance. Perhaps the best way of putting it is that the mind-body relation does not work in sequence but in tandem. The relation between them is one of identity.

FREEDOM AND DETERMINISM

Spinoza's solution to the mind-body problem, namely that the relation between them is one of identity, has hardly proved conclusive for many readers. His denial that mental concepts like will and volition can determine behavior and his belief that states of mind are dependent on states of the body appear to allow little or no room for freedom, at least as that word is ordinarily understood. Like many modern-day behavioralists, Spinoza seems here to believe that the more knowledge we possess about our bodies and their physical processes, the fewer will be those areas of human behavior usually thought to be free or under our own control. If our minds are indeed part of the same singular substance as our bodies, subject to the same laws of physical causality, then the freedom of choice, the freedom to do or not to do, is made redundant, at least for explanatory purposes. Knowledge and freedom appear to be on a direct collision course. Further, Spinoza's embrace of mind-body identity seems to allow the mind no independence, none of the reflective distance necessary for critical judgments of evaluation and appraisal. The use of moral terms of praise and blame, guilt and responsibility, also seems correspondingly to diminish as knowledge of causal processes increases.

The issue of freedom and determinism cuts to the core of the *Ethics*. For many readers, Spinoza's embrace of determinism is incompatible with any affirmation of human freedom. We can call this position the incompatibility thesis.[8] On this view, freedom requires some significant area of choice or volition whereby it is possible to say that a person chose to do one thing rather than another, this rather than that. Freedom thus always involves some degree of indeterminacy. If one's choices could always be known or predicted in advance due to certain background features of one's situation or due to identifiable traits of personality, our freedom would be correspondingly diminished. Freedom requires that an action is mine in the sense that it is something I initiate, not something that merely happens to me. The view that I am the source of my own activity rather than a link in a chain of causal transactions is closely bound up with our ideas about autonomy and moral agency, without which a person could hardly be considered free.

The case against Spinoza, or at least the argument that his conception of mind-body leads to a radical diminution of freedom, has been stated powerfully by Isaiah Berlin. Characterizing what he takes to be Spinoza's doctrine in the *Ethics*, Berlin writes: "Given Spinoza's premises—that the universe is a rational order, and that to understand the rationality of a proposition or an act or an order is, for a rational being, equivalent to accepting or identifying oneself with it (as in the old Stoic notion)—the notion of choice turns out to depend upon the deficiencies of knowledge, the degree of ignorance. There is only one correct answer to any problem of conduct, as to any problem of theory. The correct answer having been discovered, the rational man logically cannot but act in accordance with it: the notion of free choice between alternatives no longer has application."[9]

Berlin's idea is not that Spinoza's embrace of determinism is false. If determinism were simply false, it would not be incompatible with freedom; it would be irrelevant to it. Berlin, like other incompatibilists, sometimes even concedes that, with advances in empirical science, a predictive science of human behavior is not out of the question. His main concern is that if such a science were to come about, it would not only deny us the power of self-initiation but would rob us of the moral vocabulary of praise and blame, guilt and responsibility, tied to that power. That is to say, if determinism were true, it would make no sense to blame or praise individuals for actions they commit because in an ethically important sense these would not be their actions at all. Our moral vocabulary presupposes that we are agents who can make choices and can be held accountable for those choices. How could we be praised or blamed for doing something over which we had no choice, that merely happened to us, or for which we were but the conduit? My decision to offer a seat to an elderly person on a crowded subway would not be so much a free choice as a response drummed into me through certain antecedent forces of socialization and habituation. It would not be me who committed the act, but the act that committed me.

To be sure, knowledge of causes or antecedent conditions can help us make certain decisions more effectively, can increase our sense of power and control over the future, but cannot make us free. Berlin writes of this dilemma as follows: "I see no reason to suppose that a deterministic doctrine, whether about one's own behaviour or that of others, is in principle incoherent, or incompatible with making choices, provided that these choices are regarded as being themselves no less determined than other phenomena. Such knowledge, or well-founded belief, seems to me to increase the degree of rationality, efficiency, power; the only freedom to which it necessarily contributes is freedom from illusions. But this is not the basic sense of the term about which controversy has been boiling for twenty-two centuries."[10]

Berlin and other incompatibilists deny that causal understanding can do anything more than free us from comforting illusions about the role of the unconstrained free will. And yet Spinoza regards causal knowledge as contributing to the common stock of freedom in a more substantive way. To understand the causes of why something is the way it is allows us the freedom to react or respond to it intelligently. To act rationally or deliberately and not emotionally is a positive enhancement of our power not only over events but just as decisively over ourselves. Thus, when I understand the causes of a traffic tie up (rush hour, an accident, a holiday weekend), I can respond intelligently to it and not allow my emotions to govern my behavior. My understanding of the causes will not, of course, make the traffic move any faster, but it will alter my response to it. Rather than succumbing to road rage, I can accept the situation for what it is and in this sense free myself from purely negative feelings of anger and frustration.[11]

At issue, then, between Spinoza and his critics is the question whether determinism is compatible or incompatible with freedom. The crux of the incompatibilist thesis turns on what it regards as two rival and incompatible forms of explanation. These forms of explanation have been given different names in the philosophical literature, objectivist and subjectivist, naturalist and antinaturalist, external and internal. They will be referred to here as agent-centered and event-centered accounts respectively.

Agent-centered accounts of human action typically rest on two assumptions about the relation between the individual and the world. First, it assumes that we are intelligent, purposeful beings capable of framing reasons for our actions and acting on those reasons. And second, agent-centered accounts require privileging a person's own first-order desires, reasons, and beliefs in the explanation of an action. Because each person is said to have a privileged insight into the contents of his or her own mind, it follows that the agent's conscious desires and first-person descriptions form the platform for any possible understanding of action. To understand why a person committed an act, it is enough to find out the reasons that informed the action at the time of the performance. Acting for reasons, it is further believed, is necessary if our moral notions of freedom, guilt, and responsibility are to make any sense at all. Agent-centered explanations, then, require recovering the motives and reasons we have for acting, beyond which no further explanation is either necessary or possible.

These two assumptions about human agency are in turn connected to the belief that agent-centered explanations are not only different from but incompatible with causal theories of behavior. To provide a causal explanation of human behavior is to seek out a set of antecedent conditions prior to the action being explained. However, to explain an action in terms of the agent's first-order reasons and beliefs is not to point to a set of prior conditions, because these reasons are, strictly speaking, a part of the action itself. My intention to take a vacation to San Juan is not the cause of my vacation; it is my reason for it. Motives and reasons do not function as the springs and levers of behavior but something like the informing principles. It may make sense to ask whether these reasons were good or bad, based on complete or faulty information. But the reasons for an action can never serve as causal conditions. They are rather the point or purpose of the act in question.

Agent-centered explanations of the kind just described are widely believed to be incompatible with event-centered explanations favored by a range of behavioral psychologists, sociologists, and philosophical naturalists. Event-centered explanations are based on two assumptions that are the mirror image of the ones described above. In the first place, event-centered explanations do not so much deny that we are rational beings who have motives and purposes as they insist on putting our motives and purposes within a causal framework in which our mental states are said to be but the last link in a chain of causation. This is not to deny such things as will and choice, but to regard them as merely the proximate causes of our actions. And second, event-centered explanations force us to look outside ourselves and our self-interpretations to the world and events surrounding us if we are to understand why we have the beliefs and desires that we have. On this account, human beings are part of the causal order of nature. Our choices and reasons are not things that arise sui generis. They have their causal conditions, and the more we learn about these conditions the less autonomy and influence in the world do we seem to exercise. From this point of view, it is a piece of vanity to see ourselves as self-legislating or self-determining agents when in fact our actions are simply part of the course of events that not only carries us along, but carries all persons and things in its wake.

Despite the vast differences between these two modes of explanation, there is one point on which agent-centered and event-centered theories agree, namely, that the degree to which one of them is true, the other will be false. Freedom and determinism are engaged in a zero sum game such that the more there is of one, the less there will be of the other. Classic examples of such causal explanations are Marxism and Freudianism, which treat our mental states and beliefs either as "ideologies" to be explained by external material conditions or as the result of repressed memories that must be exhumed from the vast well of the unconscious. In each case the notions of individual moral will and agency are explained by the operation of causes of which the individual may be partly or even wholly unaware. If determinism of this kind is true, critics like Berlin believe that we are correspondingly deprived of the qualities of reflection and choice so necessary for agent-centered morality. If we regard ourselves as links in a chain of causal determination, then the concepts of freedom, guilt, responsibility, and blame have at best a radically diminished application to our moral lives. Antisocial or criminal behavior will be explained not as the result of choice and character but as the product of social conditioning and a range of other external determinants.

Rationality and Human Agency

The incompatibilist thesis, according to which freedom and determinism are rival and incompatible models of explanation, remains in crucial respects the standard position in the philosophical literature. On whatever side of the divide one falls, the view remains that these represent polar and antagonistic alternatives. These two alternatives set the stage for the debate between materialists and idealists, naturalists and antinaturalists, from the eighteenth to the twentieth centuries. It is in part as an anticipation of those debates but in part as a response to them that Spinoza's answer to the free-will versus determinism controversy remains of interest.

The *Ethics* is not the first, but it is the most powerful statement of the position that the free-will versus determinism debate rests on a mistake. He articulates what could be called the compatibilist thesis, according to which explanations in terms of rational agency and explanations in terms of causes need not be and are not in conflict with one another. Compatibilism denies the claims of agent-centered idealists that rational explanations must necessarily be at the expense of causal explanations; and against event-centered materialists, compatibilism asserts that causal explanations are not necessarily at the expense of our powers of free agency. Let us see how Spinoza makes good on this claim.

The *Ethics* sets out to dispute the claim that free agency is incompatible with causality. The alleged incompatibility between freedom and determinism is based in the first instance on a false idea of freedom. Spinoza takes up this point specifically when rejecting the idea of the "will" as the locus of freedom. Attributing freedom to some occult quality called the will, he affirms polemically, is a "privation of knowledge," that is, "a mutilated and confused" idea (IIp35). He goes on to "explain the matter more fully": "Men are deceived in that they think themselves free, an opinion which consists only in this, that they are conscious of their actions and ignorant of the causes by which they are determined. This, then, is their idea of freedom—that they do not know any cause of their action. They say, of course, that human actions depend on the will, but these are only words for which they have no idea. For all are ignorant of what the will is, and how it moves the body; those who boast of something else, who feign seats and dwelling places of the soul, usually provoke either ridicule or disgust" (IIp35s).

This passage, and others like it, can be treated as a denial of human agency, but this would be mistaken. Spinoza is not denying our capacity to act as free agents, but only one understanding of freedom. Freedom is not the result of an unconstrained will or the freedom to act in such a way that one's behavior is arbitrary, indeterminate, or otherwise underivable from known facts about one's personality or situation. It is hard to see why such behavior would be called free. Freedom is not guaranteed by unpredictability but by the ability to form reasons and to act upon them. Our actions are not the product of will but of understanding. We live in a world of *intelligibilia*. It is not because we have a will but because we possess intelligence, the ability to understand a given situation and respond intelligently to it, that we are free agents. It is by virtue of our possession of a reflective consciousness capable of conceiving, imagining, wishing, and doing that we are free. To say, as Spinoza does, that freedom and determinism are compatible is not to assert that human beings follow the same causal patterns as nonhuman objects. He is not committed, as Berlin implies, to a form of reductionism in which all explanation must conform to the same causal pattern as a physical, biochemical, genetic, or any other kind of process. Rather, Spinoza maintains that there are at least two different and irreducible conceptual vocabularies, a language of bodies in motion and a language of minds with reasons and purposes.

Spinoza's point is different from that of many contemporary critics of causality. For some, as we have seen, causal explanation is incompatible with rational explanation. To explain an action or event in terms of its causes requires us to specify a set of antecedent conditions independent of the event to be explained. But an agent's reasons or desires for doing something do not qualify as antecedent conditions. Our reasons are not independent of our actions but are conceptually related to them. They specify not so much the cause of the action as its point. Thus, it is believed, we cannot predict an action on the basis of an agent's reasons because these reasons are simply first-person descriptions of the action to be performed. In fact our reasons for acting are not predictors of what we are going to do; just as often they serve as rationalizations, excuses, deliberate or even unconscious eva-sions of what we will do. Reasons are not causes but are part of the puzzle that needs explanation.

These points are well taken but they are not Spinoza's. *Causa* and *ratio* are not so distinct for him as they have been taken to be in the post-Kantian world. First, he regards reason as a form of causal power in the soul, a *conatus*, which impels a person to act. The recognition that reasons can serve as a causal power is not intended by him to diminish but to enhance the role of human agency (IIIdef2). To show that an action is caused is not to say that it could not have been otherwise. For Spinoza it is to specify an event or state of affairs that it is in our power to produce or prevent from happening. Second, it is not his aim, as Berlin suggests above, to deny the role of evaluation or moral judgment in the explanation of action. To understand all is not to forgive all. Spinoza's Latin term *causa* carries with it strong moral implications of guilt, blame, accusation, and responsibility. To ask who or what is the cause of something is to ask who is responsible for it.

The fundamental insight of the *Ethics* is that freedom and determinism are not incompatible, but form two ends of a chain that must be held together. Freedom does not amount to some form of indeterminacy. To act freely means to act for reasons. But to act for reasons is not to set oneself outside the chain of causality; it is to be determined by one's own desires and beliefs.[12] A person's thoughts and desires do not arise ex nihilo; they are part of the individual's broader life history. To recognize that desires and beliefs have a causal context is not to say that we do not choose them, but that our choices form part of a set of background circumstances that make them intelligible. It follows, then, that causal explanations do not undermine our status as agents nor do rational explanations deny the causal contexts, including the mental context of ideas and beliefs, of actions.

Rather, causes and reasons are equally explanatory and equally necessary. The truth of determinism, a truth to which Spinoza is passionately committed, does not dispute the truth of rational agency. The point is not whether causal explanation or rational explanation is true, but how the *Ethics* is able to combine conceptual dualism within the framework of an ontological or theological monism.[13]

Just as the *Ethics* tries to prove that reasons can serve as causes, so too does it attempt to show that causal explanations in terms of material processes and events need not impugn our capacities as free and rational actors. To be sure, Spinoza sometimes writes as if his purpose is to replace altogether the idea of ourselves as agents capable of initiating actions. His polemic at IIp48, quoted above, that "there is no absolute or free will" and that the mind "cannot be a free cause of its own actions" seems bent on replacing explanation of action in terms of reasons, intentions, and purposes with a purely materialistic account of the mind in terms of its causal conditions. The extreme limit of this reductive materialism occurs in IIp13, where we read: "The object of the idea constituting the human Mind is the Body or a certain mode of Extension which actually exists, and nothing else." Spinoza understands by this "not only that the human Mind is united to the Body" but that "no one will be able to understand [this union] adequately, or distinctly, unless he first knows adequately the nature of our Body" (IIp13s).

The priority given to the knowledge of the body leaves the impression that the *Ethics* is committed to eliminating all traces of mental causation from the explanation of human behavior. The fact that we believe ourselves to be free, that such beliefs may be deeply imbedded in our ways of thinking, does nothing to vouchsafe the truth of those beliefs. "So experience itself," Spinoza writes, "no less clearly than reason, teaches that men believe themselves free because they are conscious of their own actions, and ignorant of the causes by which they are determined, that the decisions of the Mind are nothing but the appetites themselves, which therefore vary as the disposition of the Body varies. For each one governs everything from his affect; those who are torn by contrary affects do not know what they want, and those who are not moved by any affect are very easily driven here and there" (IIIp2s2).

That Spinoza sometimes seems committed to a sort of eliminative materialism undermines his conviction that body events and mind events each have their own integrity and that neither can be reduced to or explained by the other. Causal explanation and rational explanation are neither incompatible nor mutually exclusive, but aspects or modes of the same moral universe. Consider the following example. It was once widely believed that alcoholism was the result of sin, vice, or simply the bad choices people have made about their lives. The elimination of alcohol was seen as a legitimate object of moral reformers and temperance advocates. It was the subject of sermons, pamphlets, and lectures. Today, however, medical science understands that what previously appeared to be the result of free agency has a biological or genetic component. There is in some cases a "predisposition" toward certain kinds of self-destructive behavior, like alcoholism, that can be accounted for in terms of chemical and physical properties of the body. Does recognition of this fact deprive us of choice and moral responsibility for our actions? Is scientific investigation at odds with the claims of morality?

It is widely feared that the more we know about the causal antecedents, including the genetic and chemical conditions, of our behavior the less free we will be. The dangers ascribed to determinism are less epistemological than moral. To view ourselves and our actions as part of a natural causal order will produce a sense of passivity and weakness. In fact it will lead to the belief that we are not agents at all, but merely the products and manifestations of our environment. Spinoza regards this fear as mistaken. Knowledge of mechanism is not itself mechanism. Far from rendering us passive, knowledge makes it possible for us to intervene in and alter the causal network of events in which we are embodied. Knowledge of causes is not just a passive transcription of reality, but an active power that renders the world different from what it was before. Knowledge is a form of power that not only interprets the world but changes it.

Let us return to the example cited above. To identify the genetic causes for alcoholism or any destructive behavioral tendency does not absolve us of responsibility for our actions. To the contrary: it enhances this responsibility. Once we are made aware of our causal makeup, we are in a better condition to understand the consequences of taking that first drink. Spinoza believes that once we understand the causes of our behavior, we are in a better position to control and even resist them. Knowledge of causes can help us produce effects that would not have previously been available to us. Further, to understand that our actions have a causal component of which we may have been previously unaware is to relieve us of the feelings of shame, guilt, and loathing that will inevitably accompany self-destructive behavior. To understand is to be able to correct and, one would hope, gain control over our lives. But this reform of understanding is always an operation of the mind and cannot be produced by genetic causes alone. Once again, causal knowledge does not impugn our freedom but enhances it.

The consequence of Spinoza's solution to the mind-body problem is to see that it is not really a problem at all. Spinoza's theory of mind-body is better described by the term *compatibilism* than *parallelism*. Stuart Hampshire's account of this mind-body compatibilism is the best statement of the position known to me: "The essential and often neglected insight which follows from Spinoza's metaphysical doctrine of the two attributes, is that there is no incompatibility, and no competition, between the two systems of explanation, the immaterialist and the materialist systems of explanation. They are both valid and indispensable, and each is independent of the other and complete in itself. Therefore there is no need, and no proper place, for the kind of arguments which have divided both psychiatrists and the lay public when materialist conceptions of personality are proposed."[14]

It is wrong, I believe, to regard the *Ethics* as a defense of a "materialist monism" as some have done. "It is hard to see how any philosopher," Edwin Curley writes, "could give greater priority to knowledge of the body than Spinoza has."[15] It would be hard to disagree. Spinoza frequently writes that the mind is dependent on the body, that there are no changes in our mental states that are not caused by prior changes in the body, and that our ideas are always determined by the order of nature. Ideas are always ideas of a body, and the differences between ideas express only the differences between the bodies the ideas represent. "Ideas differ among themselves," Spinoza writes, "as the objects themselves do, and that one is more excellent than the other, and contains more reality, just as the object of the one is more excellent than the object of the other and contains more reality" (IIp13s). The *Ethics* is in many respects a celebration of the body and its powers and has clear anticipations of the materialism of Feuerbach, Marx, and Nietzsche.[16]

Yet for all this, Spinoza attributes a power of spontaneity and self-direction to the mind that is irreducible to bodily states. There is, above all, a desire for freedom, an inner-*conatus*, that aspires to a condition of autonomous agency and cannot be explained by naturalistic means alone. To act freely here does not mean to act arbitrarily or to be undetermined. Acting for reasons means that the cause of our actions is in our minds, that we are self-determining beings whose actions are the product of forethought and deliberation. Far from regarding rationality, as does Hobbes or Hume, as an instrument for mediating between the passions, Spinoza attributes a causal power to reason that is genuinely transformative. It is hard to imagine a thinker, with the possible exception of Plato, who attributes greater power to the mind to liberate itself from the obstacles and impediments that stand in the way of its own freedom.

The Odyssey of the Mind

The active power of the mind is the explicit subject of IIp40–43, where Spinoza treats the ascent of knowledge from the confused and conflicted world of the imagination to the intelligible world of reason and adequate ideas. The famous "three kinds of knowledge"—*imaginatio, ratio,* and *scientia*—constitute the ascent of the mind from lesser to greater modes of adequacy. Like Plato's image of the Divided Line in the *Republic,* Spinoza's three kinds of knowledge depict the mind's efforts to free itself from error, illusion, and the sources of false belief. It is a kind of odyssey which the mind undertakes in its struggle for freedom.

The *Ethics* presents the imagination and the ideas of common reason as stages through which the mind travels on the road to truth. And yet these are not merely steps on a ladder to be kicked aside when we have reached the top. They are both necessary components of knowledge and as such indispensable to an interconnected grasp of all levels of human experience. While it is easy to read the appendix to book one of the *Ethics* as attempting to banish the imagination as the principal cause of superstition and prejudice, book two has as its aim the limitation, not the elimination, of the power of the imagination.

Knowledge of the first kind is grounded in the imagination. It consists of random experience (*experientia vaga*) acquired through the senses but in ways that are described as "mutilated, confused, and without order" (IIp40s2). This type of knowledge consists of signs derived either from hearsay or reading or ideas based on memory and recollection. In either case, knowledge of this type is said to pertain to ideas derived from "the common order of nature," which as such remain confused and contradictory (IIp29c). What Spinoza means by the common order of nature is a random association of ideas rather than an investigation into their causes. Imaginative thinking is not an oxymoron, but it tends to rely on established conventions and dogmas, not critical or investigative thinking. There is a strict correlation between the imagination and the passions or inadequate ideas. Thus the imagination is the source of mental passivity, of our enslavement to the affective-passionate life.

Marxist readers of the *Ethics* have typically associated the world of the imagination with "ideology" or the discourse of everyday life.[17] In the *German Ideology* Marx made the statement that the ideological consciousness turns everything upside down as in a camera obscura. Under the reign of the imagination, Spinoza contends, there is a reversal of the order of causality, whereby the causes appear as effects and vice versa. Thus the imagination makes it appear as if our desires, wishes, and beliefs are the causes of our actions rather than the effects of previous causes. In particular the imagination is responsible for the belief that we are an "empire within an empire," an island within the natural world, rather than beings subject to the same natural laws as all other beings. The imaginative faculty constitutes the social world and its fictions.

Certainly Spinoza calls knowledge of the first kind "the only cause of falsity" and denigrates the imagination as the source of confused thinking and conflicting emotions (IIp41). Yet the world of the "social imaginary," as it has been called, is not simply a piece of false consciousness. Spinoza stresses that we are all creatures of sense and imagination and cannot be otherwise. So long as we live, we will not cease to imagine, and the products of the imagination are many and various. "The imaginations of the Mind," Spinoza states, "considered in themselves contain no error" and "the Mind does not err from the fact that it imagines" (IIp17s). That the mind does not err because it imagines is a truly remarkable statement, given Spinoza's attack on the power of the *imaginatio* in the appendix to part one as the root cause of prejudice and superstition. What has happened? Did Spinoza forget what he had just written just a few propositions earlier?

It is not that Spinoza has forgotten what he had said earlier about the imagination or changed his mind. It is that now he is trying to locate the imagination within the entire phenomenology of human knowledge, as it were. Knowledge acquired through the imagination is one aspect of a comprehensive system of human knowledge. The imagination is the source of human diversity, and its expressions are as various as are the life experiences of individuals and society. This explains why a soldier who sees a picture of a horse thinks of battle and war, while a farmer thinks of fields and plows (IIp18s). There is no logical connection between these mental acts; it is a loose, psychological association based on memory and experience. The imagination is not only the cause of confusion and error, but of the differences between how we live, what we think, and what we aspire to. It is the source not only of differentiation but of individuation and even moral diversity.

The second kind of knowledge pertains to certain universal or general ideas "common to all men." Spinoza explains the cause of these universal ideas as follows: "These notions they call Universal, like Man, Horse, Dog, etc. have arisen from similar causes, viz. because so many images (e.g., of men) are formed at one time in the human Body that they surpass the power of imagining—not entirely, of course, but still to the point where the Man can imagine neither slight differences of the singular (such as the color and size of each one, etc.) nor their determinate numbers, and imagines distinctly only what they all agree in, insofar as they affect the body" (IIp40s1).

The ideas of common reason form the basis for our ordinary conceptual discourse (*ratio*) because they derive from certain universal human experiences. As such, common notions do not constitute the essence of any particular thing; rather they provide the conceptual armory that allows us to order and classify particular things into relevant genera and species. This does not mean, however, that such ideas do not vary from person to person. These common notions of reason merely express the general characteristics of each thing or class of thing rather than their individual essences. Spinoza uses this opportunity to poke fun at the reasons for our very differing accounts of human nature. "Those who have more often regarded men's stature with wonder will understand by the word 'man' an animal of erect stature," he writes. "But those who have been accustomed to consider something else, will form another common image of men—e.g., that man is an animal capable of laughter, or a featherless biped, or a rational animal" (IIp40s1).

The ideas of common reason are among the most fundamental in all of the *Ethics*. They make possible certain common standards of deliberation and judgment that enable us to distinguish right from wrong, justice from injustice, in particular cases. These general ideas form common patterns that serve as models for deliberation in areas like science, law, and history. Legal or scientific reasoning, just like historical reasoning, relies on common standards of evidence, the balancing of competing claims, and listening impartially to authorities in order to arrive at a decision. All of these activities require common standards without which they would be impossible. Yet at the same time, the very use of such standards testifies to a weakness in our powers of rationality. If we could see things from a God's-eye point of view, we would have no use for general ideas, but rather judge each case on its merits alone. We could see each individual as it is in itself rather than as an instance of a general rule or law. Unable to grasp things in their radical particularity, we are forced to fall back on generalizations to do the work for us.

In a remarkable passage that sheds light on this issue, Tocqueville noted that the use of general ideas does not bear witness to the powers of human intelligence but rather its inadequacy: "If a human intelligence tried to examine and judge all the particular cases that came his way individually he would soon be lost in a wilderness of detail and not be able to see anything at all. In this pass he has recourse to an imperfect though necessary procedure which aids the weakness that makes it necessary. After a superficial inspection of a certain number of objects he notes that they resemble each other and gives them all the same name. After that he puts them on one side and continues on his way."[18] However, he adds to the above: "General ideas have the excellent quality, that they permit human minds to pass judgment quickly on a great number of things; but the conceptions they convey are always incomplete, and what is gained in extent is always lost in exactitude."[19]

In the above passage Tocqueville emphasizes the limitations of general notions of the intellect. He does not acknowledge quite so clearly their necessity for the existence of shared moral practices and a common way life. Neither does Spinoza. His emphasis is on the failure of *notions communes* to arrive at the truth. All knowledge may be mediated through these ideas, but they do not constitute the whole of knowledge. In addition to the second kind of knowledge, there is a third that Spinoza calls by the name *scientia intuitiva*. Whereas knowledge of the first kind is false or at least a "cause of falsity," knowledge of the second and third kinds is true or adequate knowledge. The difference between them is that while the former arrives at its conclusion from general principles or axioms, the latter is based on an immediate apprehension of the truth. Typically, Spinoza describes the difference in terms of an example taken from Euclid:

> Suppose there are three numbers, and the problem is to find a fourth which is to the third as the second is to the first. Merchants do not hesitate to multiply the second by the third, and divide the product by the first, because they have not yet forgotten what they heard from their teacher without any demonstration or because they have often found this in the simplest numbers, or from the force of Demonstration P7 in Bk. VII of Euclid, viz. from the common property of proportionals. But in the simplest numbers none of this is necessary. Given the numbers 1, 2, and 3, no one fails to see that the fourth proportional number is 6 — and we see this much more clearly because we infer the fourth number from the ratio which, in one glance, we see the first number to have the second. (IIp40s2)

In describing knowledge of the third kind as intuitive, Spinoza does not mean that it is irrational or mystical, inaccessible to the ordinary forms of knowledge acquired through sense and reason. Rather, he emphasizes that the notions of common reason are a precondition for knowledge of the third kind. The difference is that while *ratio* provides an adequate idea of the properties common to bodies, *scientia* grasps the essence of individual things in their particularity. All genuine knowledge is for Spinoza ultimately knowledge of particulars. "The more we understand individual things, the more we understand God," he says at Vp24. It is ultimately knowledge of nature in all of its details that matters and that is strongly connected later in the *Ethics* to Spinoza's idea of freedom and the intellectual love of God.

The transition from imagination to intuition represents an ascent from inadequate to adequate ideas. The question is what makes an adequate idea adequate? This has been the subject of controversy. However, an adequate idea, knowledge of essences, is likened to a self-evident truth of reason. A statement or proposition can be said to be self-evidently true if it is verified by the very terms used to define it. For example, to say that a triangle is a three-sided figure the sum of whose angles equals 180 degrees is self-evident to anyone who knows the terms *line, angle,* and *equal.* A self-evident truth is logically self-contained, that is, it cannot be doubted without falling into self-contradiction. Such truths exist necessarily rather than contingently; they are independent of any matter of fact or experience for their verification (IIp44). Thus when Descartes sought to establish his system on the clear and distinct proposition *cogito ergo sum,* he meant to show that we cannot doubt the fact that we think without simultaneously proving the truth of the proposition that we are thinking beings. This is what Spinoza means when he says that an adequate idea, knowledge of the highest sort, contains its own criteria of truth—or that "truth is its own standard" (IIp43s).

What finally distinguishes *scientia* is not that it is mystical or nondiscursive, but that it contains the crucial aspect of re-flexivity not present in the lower forms of knowledge. It is not just truth about the world but about the mind; it is a form of self-knowledge similar to the Delphic injunction "know thy-self." The question of the self or the thinking "I" is central to Spinoza's conception of knowledge. As we shall see in the next chapter, the mind contains a *conatus* or desire for self-under-standing. The mind may desire to know everything, but if it does not know itself, the thinking vessel, it cannot be said to really or truly know anything. This kind of self-knowledge is not in the strict sense caused by anything outside the mind, but is the product of the thinking mind itself. It is innate to the mind. This process of self-reflection not only has an intellectual, but a moral component. There is a teleological or perfectionist com-ponent to this kind of knowledge. Knowledge of the third kind, he reports later, is the highest good (IVp28).

4

Thinking about Desire

The *Ethics* is generally regarded as a work of scientific psychology akin to Descartes's *Meditations* and the opening chapters of Hobbes's *Leviathan*. Following the examples of these two predecessors, Spinoza took mathematics, and especially geometry, as providing the model for all reasoning. All the sciences are to proceed from the same clear and distinct premises as constitute a mathematical formula. Mathematics provides a kind of universal language that cuts across the study of nature and the so-called human sciences, like politics, history, and morality. In one of his most decisive utterances on this approach, Spinoza tries to justify his use of the geometrical method in the study of the passions: "Most of those who have written about the Affects, and men's way of living, seem to treat, not of natural things, which follow the common laws of nature, but of things which are outside nature. Indeed, they seem to conceive man in nature as a dominion within a dominion. For they believe that man disturbs, rather than follows, the order of nature, that he has absolute power over his actions, and that he is determined only by himself" (IIIpref/137).

The task of the moralist, he seems to say, is not to indulge in judgments of praise and blame, but to understand the virtues, like all other things, as the result of anterior causes. He adopts what appears to be a purely scientific, value-free treatment of the passions. Since nothing happens or can happen contrary to nature, it follows that our judgments of good and bad, better and worse, are always expressions of our knowledge of "the laws and rules of nature." The virtues are but forms of the affects or passions, and these he promises to treat "by the same Method by which, in the preceding parts, I treated God and the Mind, and I shall consider human actions and appetites just as if it were a Question of lines, planes, and bodies" (IIIpref/138).

It is often believed that Spinoza's commitment to the mathematical method deprived his philosophy of any serious interest in or appreciation of the stuff of politics and history. At times he writes as if the human and political world can simply be deduced from premises embedded in the common structure of nature. Human beings are presented as simply elementary units of power that strive to preserve their motion and independence vis-à-vis other elements in nature. Humans may be distinguished by a certain level of internal complexity, but there is essentially no difference in kind between human and nonhuman nature. Each is subject to the same laws and causal processes. Both are ostensibly explicable in terms of efficient, not final, causes. We are simply modes or attributes of a single substance within which our individual characteristics and distinctive qualities have been bleached away. On this reading Spinoza's formula that there is no *imperium in imperio,* no kingdom within a kingdom, is his way of denying such traditional human qualities as will, agency, and responsibility.

The attempt to read the *Ethics* as a piece of purely behavioristic psychology aimed at eliminating the role of freedom, will, and choice has always had its defenders. Spinoza himself advises us to read human nature as entirely continuous with nature as a whole. But while Spinoza gives a thoroughly naturalistic and deterministic account of the causes of human behavior, this reading does not take into consideration the central role accorded in part three to the ideas of action, human agency, and self-reflection. The central concept of Spinoza's psychology is the idea of the *conatus,* roughly translated as the desire or endeavor to persevere in one's being, although it might be equally rendered by the contemporary term *empowerment*. To speak of desire is always a form of power. Desire is always a desire "for" something, to do this or to be that. The desire to persevere is not just to be determined by antecedent causal conditions, but to be governed by some idea of rationality and purpose. Spinoza's conception of human activity and rationality is teleological through and through.

It is often pointed out that Spinoza borrowed his *conatus* concept from the Stoics or perhaps from Hobbes, but as always he gives it a distinctive twist of his own. The *conatus*, or desire to persevere, is the chief affect or passion by which we are governed. But Spinoza distinguishes between two sets of affects, the passive and the active. The passive affects are interior causes by which we are determined; the active affects are those by which we determine ourselves. The psychological program of the *Ethics* is to encourage all of those passions of the soul that cause us to be active, energetic, powerful—the cause of our own actions. The conative power, we will see, is more than a desire to maintain life, but a desire that leads us to enhance our existence, to live in a state of continuous and never ending joy. Not a grim asceticism but a sense of *hilaritas,* the kind of reflective pleasure a human being takes at the sheer enjoyment of life, is the ethical purpose of the work. Its aim is the enhancement of human power.

The *Conatus* as Power

Part three of the *Ethics* begins with a recognition of the power of the passions over human life. "No one to my knowledge," he boldly asserts, "has determined the nature and power of the Affects, nor what, on the other hand, the Mind can do to moderate them" (IIIpref/137). He takes issue here with "the celebrated Descartes" for his belief that the mind can exercise control over the affects. Descartes is said to share the same fallacy as the ancient Stoics, who likewise believed that the passions depend on the will and that we command them absolutely (Vpref/277). The issue separating Spinoza from both Descartes and the Stoics concerns the mind's power over the passions, which Spinoza seems to believe is far more limited. The strategy he pursues for gaining control over our emotional and affective life consists in playing the passions off against one another.[1] Only one passion can limit the power of another passion. Reason cannot control the passions directly. Rather it can align itself with one passion or set of passions to gain power over others. The *Ethics* here seems to anticipate James Madison's claim in the *Federalist Papers* that only ambition is sufficient to counteract ambition and that human interest must be enlisted to protect constitutional rights.[2] We can call this Spinoza's indirect strategy of using reason as an intermediary to control and offset the passions.

The power of the affects over life is given expression in Spinoza's doctrine of the *conatus*, or the power exercised by each and every being to persevere in its own existence and to resist invasion and domination by the other beings that exist around it. "The striving by which each being strives to persevere in its being is nothing but the actual essence of the thing," Spinoza writes at IIIp7. His identification of "the actual essence of the thing" with the conative desire for self-preservation has been the basis for tremendous moral controversy. There is, first, the formal issue of what entitles Spinoza to this opinion. What in the previous sections of the *Ethics* has prepared for it, and how legitimate is the derivation of the doctrine? To what extent does Spinoza's theory of the *conatus* commit him to a form of moral egoism? Are these claims true?

Consider first the derivation of the *conatus*. Spinoza believes it follows from the affective or passionate nature of the mind.

Human nature is such that it is dominated by the affects. It is typical to think of the affects as something that happen to us, that maintain us in a state of passivity, even slavery, until we can be liberated. This is not Spinoza's view. The affects have a dual nature that can be either active or passive: "By affect I understand the affections of the Body by which the Body's power of acting is increased or diminished, aided or restrained, and at the same time, the ideas of these affections. Therefore, if we can be the adequate cause of any of these affections, I understand by the Affect an action; otherwise a passion" (IIIdef3). At the end of part three, under the heading "General Definition of the Affects," Spinoza defines the term again: "An Affect that is called a Passion of the mind is a confused idea, by which the Mind affirms of its Body, or of some part of it, a greater or lesser force of existing than before, which, when it is given, determines the Mind to think of this rather than that" (IIIdef.aff/203).

Spinoza's definition of the affects as a "passion of the mind" indicates that reason and passion are far more interconnected than the Cartesian model suggests. An affect is said to be a "confused idea," that is, one which we do not fully understand. But a confused idea is still an idea, albeit a partial and fragmentary one. Passions always contain shards of moral reasoning. They are called inadequate or confused ideas to indicate not that reason and passion are antithetical but that the affects are susceptible to rationality. Insofar as we are governed by affects of which we are unaware or have only incomplete knowledge, these are called passions; those affects that we understand are actions. We call something an action when we are the cause, a passion when something happens to us. The hope of the *Ethics* is to convert passions into actions, not by repressing human affectivity but by bringing it to a higher level of self-consciousness.

Spinoza's *conatus* doctrine is almost universally regarded as a form of psychological egoism, although it should be noted that the doctrine is initially introduced not as a psychological but as a physical theory. It is a general consequence of the inertial physics of bodies and motion developed in the so-called Physical Digression at IIp13–14.[3] According to this physics, any body will tend to remain in a given state of activity or passivity unless affected by an external cause. Spinoza formulates this hypothesis at IIIp6 as follows: "Each thing, as far as it can by its own power, strives to persevere in its being." Spinoza goes out of his way to detach the *conatus* from the human perspective. It is not a theory about human behavior but about the motion of things in general and their tendency to seek a state of equilibrium.

He elucidates this idea with the following demonstration: "For singular things are modes by which God's attributes are expressed in a certain and determinate way, i.e., things that express, in a certain and determinate way, God's power, by which God is and acts. And no thing has anything in itself by which it can be destroyed, or which takes its existence away. On the contrary, it is opposed to everything which can take its existence away. Therefore, as far as it can, and it lies in itself, it strives to persevere in its being, q.e.d." (IIIp6d).

It is not until three propositions later that Spinoza associates the *conatus* with a specifically human power, namely, the power of the mind to become conscious or aware of this striving to persevere in its being: "Both insofar as the Mind has clear and distinct ideas, and insofar as it has confused ideas, it strives for an indefinite duration, to persevere in its being and it is conscious of this striving it has" (IIIp9). The mind's desire to preserve itself is defined as the will, but the mind and body together is appetite. "This Appetite," he writes, "is nothing but the very essence of man, from whose nature there necessarily follows those things that promote his preservation. And so man is determined to do those things" (IIIp9s).

Spinoza's theory of the *conatus* reveals itself in the first instance as a theory of power. All of our psychological and emotional states, even the mind itself, represent a striving for power. Each being strives to preserve and expand itself. Power is the universal medium through which our preservation is achieved. Each being is an individual quantum of power that will expand until confronted with a larger mass. The idea that each of us is a unit of power is often identified, as mentioned above, with a theory of moral egoism. This is at best half true. The virtues of love, friendship, and sociability are all power enhancing. Power is not simply a zero-sum game. Rather, we often increase our capacities by learning to join and cooperate with others for shared ends. Each of us is by nature not so much an egoist as an individual locked up in the private world of our wants, beliefs, and desires. This is not a moral defect, a failure on the part of human nature. Spinoza makes clear in the preface to part three that there are no defects in nature (IIIpref/138). The striving after power that is characteristic of every individual is not a failure or sin, but a part of nature that becomes a defect only in society. It is not the failure of nature, but the condition of nature, as we shall see in the next chapter, that is responsible for society.

The *Conatus* as Rationality

The idea that all human striving is a form of power implies a far-reaching doctrine of realism or naturalism that bears the fingerprints of Hobbes and Machiavelli.[4] All the passions are interpreted as forms of power; philosophy itself is but the science of power. Much of Spinoza's bravado consists of his attempt to reduce all human activities to expressions of power. But is this true? Are all the virtues really reducible to the desire for power? The attempt to derive a doctrine of the virtues, what we ought to do, from a purely conative theory of what we are caused to do, seems to commit Spinoza to a naturalism that deprives the virtues of their inherent dignity and grandeur. His seems to be a classic, perhaps *the* classic, version of the naturalistic fallacy, so-called for its effort to extract an "ought" from an "is."

Many readers take Spinoza's naturalism to be in the service of a purely mechanistic, nonteleological theory of human behavior. The language of appetites and desires sounds like the same kind of causal mechanics supposedly developed in the appendix to the first part of the *Ethics* that aims to eliminate all talk of ends and purposes. Leon Roth provides an especially vivid description of what he regards as Spinoza's position: "Human beings . . . like everything else and in spite of the fact of self-consciousness, work out from conditions which are already set, not towards ideals which are to be realised . . . What is appetite? Blind impulse. We follow ends and ideals, but these ends and ideals are projected from behind us."[5]

In his gloss on this passage Jonathan Bennett alleges that this "feels right," although he regards the statement that our impulses are "projected from behind us" to be unhelpful "even by the standards of metaphor."[6] For Bennett, the *conatus* refers only to some intrinsic condition of a person completely apart from any future or anticipated state of affairs. For example, a person moves toward the fire not in order to get warm but because he is cold. It is never legitimate to explain a piece of behavior by reference to the end that the behavior seeks to bring about: "In this account, a desire or appetite is identified with some aspects of the essence or nature of the person, something which could be fully described without mentioning any subsequent state of affairs . . . The plain man thinks that an action can be caused or explained by a desire which essentially involves the future — meaning by 'the future' 'something causally subsequent to the action.' Spinoza replaces that concept of desire by one which he thinks covers roughly the same territory without implying that anything involving the future helps to explain the present."[7]

Neither of these views does justice to Spinoza's *conatus* doctrine in my view. *Conatus* is a Latin word that can be translated as "trying," "attempting," "striving," or "endeavoring." These are verbs with a clearly teleological meaning. To strive is always to strive for something; it points to a future condition that is yet to be realized. The *conatus* is not just an efficient cause of action; it forms the basis for a theory of rational agency. As rational beings we not only desire to live, but to live in ways that give meaning and purpose to our lives. We are self-interpreting beings who strive to make our lives an object of rational self-reflection. An element of critical reflexivity is built into the very idea of the *conatus*.

Human behavior is goal directed, the expression of our thoughts and purposes. Even our impulses and appetites are shot through with rationality. Mental predicates like will, appetite, and desire are shown to be the psychological reflexes of this rationality. "Between appetite and desire," Spinoza writes, "there is no difference, except that desire is generally related to men insofar as they are conscious of their appetites. So desire can be defined as appetite together with consciousness of the appetite" (IIIp9s). A desire is, then, a self-conscious appetite, an appetite brought up to the level of critical reflection.

It is not at all clear in what sense the understanding of an appetite transforms it from something passive to something active. How does this transition occur? How is an appetite turned into a desire by virtue of our awareness of it? An affect or appetite, we recall, is defined as a "confused idea." The more we understand our affects and their causes the more actively and imaginatively can we pursue them. Consider smoking, a standard philosopher's example. My desire for a cigarette is often said to be caused in me by my body's craving for nicotine. This is not something I choose, but something that happens to me. My desires are caused in me by physical and chemical processes of which I am not the author. But for Spinoza this is not the end of the story. Once I become aware of this desire, I can choose to pursue it self-consciously. My desire for a cigarette, rather than a passive affect, becomes an active source of empowerment and creativity. The pleasure I feel at lighting up gives me a renewed feeling of power and control over my life. It provides a source of pleasure and aesthetic satisfaction, one that increases sociability as I find others with whom I can share my passion. I can, of course, use my increased awareness to try to give up smoking. But this does not necessarily follow from Spinoza's perspective. Unlike the Stoics who recommend an austere discipline for controlling the affects, the *Ethics* wants us to pursue our affects vigorously and joyously. In fact the more affects we have, the more truly alive we are. The point is neither to give in to our affects, nor to repress them, but to pursue them with vigor and imagination.

As evidence for the above, Spinoza argues that once we understand the source of our affects, they cease to be mere physical promptings and acquire a kind of moral force. Consciousness and understanding endow our strivings with a sense of moral purpose. It is here for the first time that Spinoza alludes to the relation between moral considerations of good and bad and the conative tendency toward self-preservation. Moral judgments of good and evil are the expressions of our desire for what contributes to or detracts from our sense of well-being. It is here for the first time that the *Ethics* advances its famous conception of psychological egoism. "We neither strive for, nor will, neither want, nor desire anything because we judge it to be good," he claims. "On the contrary, we judge something to be good because we strive for it, will it, want it, and desire it" (IIIp9s).

An Ethic of Joy

Spinoza regards all the virtues as forms of power and the desire to preserve and enhance our being. But our *conatus,* as he understands it, is not identical to the desire for self-preservation alone; it is not a bare biological urge. Rather it is a rational desire (*conatus intelligendi*) to increase our sense of empowerment and wellbeing. Power is good if and only if it is accompanied by certain positive affects like joy (*laetitia*) and cheerfulness (*hilaritas*). What enhances these emotions is good; what diminishes them is bad. The virtues, then, are those affects that enable us to live joyously with a sense of purpose. Nature itself knows of no distinction between good and bad except what the mind puts there. As Antonio put it in Shakespeare's *Twelfth Night:* "In nature there's no blemish but the mind / None can be called deformed but the unkind."[8]

Spinoza's *conatus* is often and with justice compared to Hobbes's moral psychology. Spinoza's remark at IIIp9 that good and evil are merely predicates of our desires strongly echoes the subjectivism of Hobbes's statement that "whatever is the object of any man's appetite or desire that is it which he for his part calleth Good . . . for these words [*good* and *evil*] are ever used with relation to the person that useth them" (*Lev.*, vi, 24). Hobbes infers this moral theory from a broader psychological portrait of human motivation. Human life consists of motion, of two kinds: vital motions like respiration and the circulation of the blood and voluntary motions like speaking, moving, and endeavoring. Of voluntary motions there are in turn two kinds. When it is movement toward something we want, the motion in question is an appetite, and when it is away from something we dislike it is an aversion. Life is nothing but a kind of nonstop motion "forward" and "fromward" that terminates only with life itself.

Human beings are not such that we only have desires. Our desires are magnified by the memory of desires fulfilled or frustrated and the imagination of new desires yet to be attained. The multiplication of our desires is what leads to conflict. In part this conflict is due to a struggle over scarce resources, but more importantly human competition is intensified by the influence of pride. A part of the enjoyment of any good is the sense of pride we feel at having outdone others in the pursuit of it. Above all, we desire to be convinced of our own superiority. As Gore Vidal once said, it is not enough that I succeed; others around me must be seen to fail. This feeling of superiority, of having bested others in the race of life, brings with it a sense of glory or joy that is the crown of our desires: "*Joy,* arising from imagination of a man's own power and ability, is that exultation of the mind which is called *GLORYING:* which if grounded upon the experience of his own former actions, is the same with *confidence;* but if grounded on the flattery of others, or only supposed by himself, for delight in the consequences of it, is called VAIN-GLORY" (*Lev,* vi, 39).

Hobbes does not let the matter rest here. If pride and glory were truly our strongest passions, life would represent an interminable free for all, a war of all against all. So great is the power of pride that not even reason is sufficient to restrain it. Only one passion can check another passions. Thus the pride we feel in besting others is coupled with the fear of dishonor and even death that comes with being bested ourselves. Hobbes sometimes writes as if it were fear of death or violent death that is the strongest human motivation, but just as often it is the fear of humiliation that is the strongest constraint. The moral life is, then, a ceaseless tension between pride and fear, the one passion urging us ever onward, the other counseling prudence and restraint. It is from the passion of fear that we learn about the importance of self-preservation, for without life the enjoyment of any good would be impossible. Good and evil may be simply names for desires and aversions, but for Hobbes there is one desire that trumps (or should trump) all others and that is the desire for life itself. This the moral foundation on which the entire edifice of *Leviathan* rests.

The preservation of life is, then, the highest imperative in Hobbesian psychology. Note, however, what Hobbes is not saying. He is not saying that human beings prefer their self-preservation in all situations. He does not believe that self-preservation is a cause of behavior in the same way that stones roll down hill. It is not a natural inevitability but a moral law that we ought to obey (*Lev*, xv, 40–41). Nor is he saying that we characteristically avoid dangerous courses of action or ways of life for risk-averse ones. There are many human beings—proud aristocrats who prefer death before dishonor, religious zealots prepared to sacrifice themselves and others for the sake of salvation in the hereafter—who do not properly value life.

Hobbes is not out to convince them so much as the rest of us that life is an end in itself with no higher end or purpose: "The Felicity of this life, consisteth not in the repose of a mind satisfied. For there is no such *finis ultimus* (utmost aim), nor *Summum Bonum* (greatest good), as is spoken of in the books of the old morall philosophers. Nor can a man live, whose desires are at an end, than he, whose senses and imaginations are at a stand. Felicity is a continual progress of the desire, from one object to another; the attaining of the former, being still but the way to the latter" (*Lev*, xi, 1).

Spinoza's account of the affective life, from his moral subjectivism to his psychological egoism, bears important affinities with Hobbes. Certainly he could never be accused of downplaying the role of self-interest in human behavior. He returns to this theme in the fourth part of the *Ethics*. Here he virtually identifies virtue with the ability to seek our own advantage. Consider the following string of propositions:

> The more each one strives, and is able, to seek his own advantage, i.e., to preserve his being, the more he is endowed with virtue. (IVp20)

> Acting absolutely from virtue is nothing else in us but acting, living, and preserving our being (these three signify the same thing) by the guidance of reason, from the foundation of seeking one's own advantage. (IVp24)

> No one strives to preserve his being for the sake of anything else. (IVp25)

The comparison between Hobbes's and Spinoza's theories of egoism and self-preservation is correct up to a point. However, the differences are almost equal to the similarities. Spinoza and Hobbes agree in making the selfish desire for self-preservation the foundation of justice and duty. Without a strongly self-interested motive, they reasoned, human beings would have little incentive to obey the rules of social morality, much less restrain their desires to do whatever is in their power. But the Spinozistic *conatus* is not simply the desire for safe, secure, and comfortable living, as it often appears in Hobbes (*Lev*, xv, 40). It is tied to an idea of human perfection that involves more than prolonging the duration and ease of life. It is true that all the virtues have their foundation in the desire for self-preservation, but the issue is not simply one of preservation but of the self that is being preserved. Despite the moral subjectivism implied in the statement that we call something good because we desire it, the *Ethics* attempts to provide an objective foundation for our moral values and beliefs. The doctrine of the *conatus* is Spinoza's attempt to identify human perfection with an increase in our power of acting and the sense of joy that comes with our awareness of the increase of those powers (IIIp53).

The point is what entitles Spinoza to attribute to the *conatus* a telos not just of survival and duration but of the enhancement and fulfillment of life. The striving to persevere in our being may grow out of a desire for survival, but it develops into a richer conception of life understood in terms of rationality and agency. The striving to exist entails the striving to exist as something, as this rather than that. This is the moral equivalent of the logical maxim that every affirmation is at the same time a negation. Yirmiyahu Yovel nicely captures Spinoza's transition from the *conatus* understood in the Hobbesian sense as the desire for self-preservation to more expansive conception of individual self-enhancement. "Self-preservation," he writes, "maintains its primary position even as it is transcended, while its meaning becomes more complex. It is no longer the ultimate goal but a restriction, a limiting condition on self-enhancement; and it does not bar all exposure to danger. On the contrary, self-preservation itself demands taking the risks of initiative and action, and balancing them against the risks of passivity and inaction."[9]

Yovel's point is that the *conatus* entails an idea of activity. Far from endorsing a crabbed, ascetic life, something like Max Weber's joyless Puritans, Spinoza embraces an almost Nietzschean sense of joy at the sheer overflow of life itself. There is an erotic element in the *conatus* that does not lock us up within our solitary selves, but leads us to seek out the company and friendship of others as ways of exploring and enhancing our selves. To exist as a conative being is not just to seek survival, but is a way of life that increases our powers of judgment and reflexivity, to exist as a *conatus intelligendi* (IVp26).

The chief point of difference between Hobbes and Spinoza turns on the greater perfectionism of the *Ethics*. For Hobbes, as we have seen, there is no greatest good, only a greatest evil, fear of violent death. Spinoza's *conatus*, by contrast, has a more expansive meaning encompassing more than the desire to avoid pain. The *conatus* is closer to our sense of the word *empowerment* with its implications of self-reliance, self-enhancement, and autonomy. Thus the fulfillment of one's *conatus* is measured by an increase in joy (*laetitia*) and a decrease in sadness (*tristia*) (IIIp11). That which increases our powers of activity necessarily increases our perfection and is therefore good. The distinction between joy and sadness is the difference between that which enhances and that which diminishes our sense of life: "We see, then, that the Mind can undergo great changes, and pass now to a greater, now to a lesser perfection. These passions, indeed, explain to us the affects of Joy and Sadness. By Joy, therefore, I shall understand in what follows that passion by which the Mind passes to a greater perfection. And by Sadness, that passion by which it passes to a lesser perfection" (IIIp11s). And later in the *Ethics* he returns to this point: "Cheerfulness is a Joy which, insofar as it is related to the Body, consists in this, that all parts of the Body are equally affected. I.e. the Body's power of acting is increased or aided, so that all of its parts maintain the same proportion of motion and rest to one another. And so Cheerfulness is always good, and cannot be excessive" (IVp42d).

The *Ethics* is, then, an ethic of joy. Yet this ethic is strongly attuned to the enormous psychological diversity among human beings. What causes joy in one person brings pain to another. There are as many causes of joy and sadness as there are kinds of human beings (IIIp39s). These differences are correlated in turn to our desires and imaginative capacities. Spinoza treats the affects as to some degree "primitive" or fundamental, that is, determinative of the types of beings we are. He is overall impressed less by the equality than the diversity of our desires. The affects, he believes, explain not only the diversity between the species but between individual members of the same species. "Each affect of each individual differs from the affect of another as much as the essence of the one from the essence of the other," he writes at IIIp57.

This diversity between human beings is built into the very constitution of human nature, as he explains with the following scholium: "Both the horse and the man are driven by a lust to procreate; but the one is driven by an equine lust, the other by a human lust. So also the lusts and appetites of insects, fish, and birds must vary. Therefore, though each individual lives content with his own nature, by which he is constituted, and is glad of it, nevertheless that life with which each one is content, and that gladness, are nothing but the idea, or soul, of the individual. And so the gladness of the one differs in nature from the gladness of the other as much as the essence of the one differs from the essence of the other" (IIIp57s).

Despite his claim in the preface to part three to treat the passions as if they were simply points along a Cartesian grid, he cannot help but make what appear to be moral evaluations between them. Like every moralist, Spinoza distinguishes between higher and lower pleasures. The language of the affects, of joy and sadness, of love and hate, is Spinoza's equivalent of the traditional moral distinction between more and less worthy ways of life. The affects contributing to joy and our sense of power are deemed good and those contributing to sadness and sense of impotence are deemed evil. For "it follows" from what he has said, "there is no small difference between the gladness by which a drunk is led and the gladness a philosopher possesses" (IIIp57s).

The differences between the various kinds of joy suggest that the *Ethics* is working with a strongly normative conception of human nature that can serve as a model for life. Spinoza may warn against philosophy's tendency to be merely edifying, but his philosophy cannot help but edify. Despite his claim that the *Ethics* differs from the works of previous moralists because of its tough-minded realism and geometric style, he continually seeks to encourage some emotional states and discourage others. His work has often been seen as a kind of therapy for the soul in which our emotional life is actively transformed, transformed by being understood. By understanding the causes of our emotions, we cease to respond passively to them but take an active role in shaping and directing them. His use of the verbs "is led" and "possesses" to describe the drunk and the philosopher respectively points to the difference between a passive and an active personality.

The *Ethics* evaluates all the affects in terms of whether they produce joy or sadness, love or hatred. In the chain of propositions from IIIp29–35 he develops the idea that our affects grow out of an imitation of the affects of others. This process, which he calls the "imitation of the affects" (*affectum imitatio*) (IIIp27), brings out the social composition of the passions as something that emerges from a procedure of comparison and adjustment. This imitation is the source of both compassion and fellow feeling but also enmity and competition. It is the source of that singular political passion that goes under the name of ambition: "This striving to bring it about that everyone should approve his love and hate is really Ambition. And so we see that each of us, by his nature, wants the others to live according to his temperament; when all alike want this, they are alike an obstacle to one another, and when all wish to be praised, or loved, by all, they hate one another" (IIIp31s).

Ambition, the desire that all should love and hate the same as we do, is connected to another passion, pride (*superbia*), which Spinoza calls "a species of madness." Pride is defined as "Joy born of the fact that a man thinks more highly of himself than is just" (IIIp26s). In his systematic "Definitions of the Affects" appended to the end of part three, he describes this passion and its opposite at greater length. The difference between pride and overestimation is that overestimation pertains to the valuation of another, while pride concerns the valuation of oneself. Not only are we disposed to value ourselves and our powers too highly, we are prone to value others too little. If pride is a joy that grows out of an excess of self-love, the opposite of this passion is despair or despondency at thinking too little of ourselves. Spinoza strains to describe these passions less as forms of self-hatred than as sublimated forms of aggression. "These affects—Humility and Despondency—are very rare," he writes. "For human nature, considered in itself, strains against them, as far as it can be. So those who are believed to be most despondent and humble are usually most ambitious and envious" (IIIdef.aff29).

Spinoza realizes that he is in somewhat of a quandary. The *conatus* is called upon to explain both the life-enhancing and the life-negating affects, both joy and sadness, active and passive qualities. How can one cause be responsible for such a vast variety of effects? How can the same cause make some people hopeful and others fearful (IIIp50), some brave and others timid (IIIp51s), some reverent and others disdainful (IIIp52)? His answer is that the affects all derive from human nature, but are shaped by the struggle for power and preeminence. It is this struggle for prestige that makes us "troublesome to one another":

> From this it follows, again, that men are by nature envious or are glad of their equals' weakness and saddened by their equals' virtue. For whenever anyone imagines his own actions, he is affected with Joy, and with a greater Joy, the more his actions express perfection . . . So everyone will have the greatest

gladness from considering himself, when he considers something in himself which he denies concerning others.

But if he relates what he affirms of himself to the universal idea of man or animal, he will not be so greatly gladdened. And on the other hand, if he imagines that his own actions are weaker, compared to others' actions, he will be saddened, and will strive to put aside this Sadness either by wrongly interpreting his equals' actions or by magnifying his own as much as he can. It is clear, therefore, that men are naturally inclined to Hate and Envy. (IIIp55s)

The greatest obstacle to the achievement of freedom and happiness is not so much the fear of death but a condition that Spinoza calls "vacillation of mind" (IIIp17s). The idea here is that we are beings who are continually beset by conflicting emotions that alternately cause joy and sadness. In particular we are torn by hope and fear, defined as an inconstant mental state brought about by the expectation of some future state whose certainty is in doubt (IIIp18s2). Hope and fear are equally symptoms of human weakness. The aim of the *Ethics* as a whole is to liberate the mind from both hope and fear and to achieve a kind of resoluteness of mind and heart. Indeed, having a firm and constant resolution of the will is precisely the way that Descartes had defined virtue.

THE HEROIC IDEAL

A standard, even a venerable, view of modernity is that it rests upon a comprehensive "lowering of the standards" of classical political philosophy in order to guarantee or at least make more probable the realization of the right or just political order.[10] Not virtue and the virtuous republic, but peace, order, and stability will be the goal of the new politics. Whatever merit, if any, this view might hold for thinkers like Machiavelli, Bacon, and Hobbes, it is manifestly counter to Spinoza. The aim of the *Ethics* is not to disenfranchise the virtues, but to reestablish them on a new psychological foundation. This new foundation is clearly not the ancient teleological conception of nature dispatched in the appendix to part one of the *Ethics,* but the theory of the *conatus.* From this psychological vantage point, Spinoza hopes to derive a doctrine of the virtues that is at once solid and sublime. The peak of the virtues, the antithesis to the quality of weakness or vacillation of mind, is given by Spinoza the name of *Fortitudo* or strength of character.

Fortitudo has been translated a number of ways, from "strength of character" (Curley and Elwes), to "strength of mind" (Shirley), to *la Force l'âme* in the French edition, to *Charakterstarke* in German. In whatever language, *fortitudo* is intended to convey something like a form of inner strength or moral integrity that informs our actions. It is akin to the aristocratic virtue of greatness of soul (*megalopsychia)* described by Aristotle in the *Nicomachean Ethics* and carries the implications of generosity and high-mindedness.[11]

The link between Aristotle and Spinoza was forged by Descartes, who first translated Aristotelian magnanimity by the term *générosité* (AT, xi, 43).[12] *Générosité* is a Cartesian term that derives from the Latin *generosus,* meaning "noble" or "wellborn," which is in turn derived from genus meaning "class" or "family." Generosity in this older sense was an aristocratic virtue attached to those endowed with wealth, breeding, and good looks and who could afford to indulge a taste for the beautiful and the useless. It was linked to the virtue of liberality, meaning open-handedness or generosity in our common usage of the term. To be generous implied a sense of dignity and legitimate self-esteem, but also the conferring of benefactions on others. The true high-minded or great-souled man was one who made good use of his own money, but was loath to accept favors in return. His own noble pride forbade being under the obligation of another. Great-souled types are noteworthy not only for their upbringing but for their physical characteristics. Aristotle says that the great-souled man is tall (great height is necessary, apparently, to command respect), speaks with a deep voice, and walks slowly because nothing is worth his haste.[13]

Descartes endowed the concept of moral virtue with a whole new sense. In a letter to Queen Christina of Sweden of November 1647, he distinguishes his own conception of generosity and the moral virtues in general from that of the "ancient philosophers," who were unenlightened about the true source of goodness. "The supreme good of each individual," he confidently affirms, "consists only in a firm will to do well and the contentment which this produces" (AT, v, 82). Like most moral philosophers, Descartes distinguishes between things that we can and those that we cannot control, and he concludes that only our will remains "absolutely within our disposal." "I do not see," he writes to Christina, "that it is possible to dispose it [the will] better than by a firm and constant resolution to carry out to the letter all the things which one judges to be best, and to employ all the powers of one's mind in finding out what these are" (AT, v, 83). It is not any particular action but rather the firm and constant resolve to use our will that "alone really deserves praise and glory." By the end of this letter Descartes has so elevated the will as the only true good and source of praise that he avers that it makes us "in a way equal to God and seems to exempt us from being his subjects." He does not develop exactly what this exemption entails. The statement can come only as a shock. In a letter intended in part to establish its author's religious *bona fides* (he had criticized the ancients for their ignorance of "supernatural beatitude"), he ends by affirming the independence of the will even from divine supervision. "From all this," he concludes, "it follows that nothing but free will can produce our greatest happiness" (AT, v, 85).

In his study of Descartes, Corneille, and Christina, Ernst Cassirer argues that it was Descartes's conception of *l'homme généreux* that strongly appealed to the queen. The value of an action depends entirely on the character or inner disposition of the will and not on the consequences of one's actions. Virtue consists in our ability to be freely self-determining. "That which we call grandeur and historical glory," Cassirer writes, "is meaningless if it does not possess this quality [inner fortitude]." "The true heroes of universal history are not those who have accomplished the greatest deeds but who have possessed the greatest self-mastery and have given proof of it. True greatness consists not in doing anything one wants; it consists of the will's ability to propose legitimate goals and to pursue them in spite of all difficulties. The state to which one is born or the particular conditions under which one lives matters little. One can be free while in slavery or a slave while on a throne for one is a king only by virtue of heart and mind. Cyrus, Alexander, and Cesar were great men not because of the goods that fortune bestowed on them, but by their own greatness and force of soul."[14]

Two years later Descartes published his definitive treatise on the virtues, dedicated to Queen Christina. In the *Passions of the Soul* Descartes elaborates an entire moral code that culminates with the virtue of *générosité*, which he calls "the key to all the other virtues and a general remedy for every disorder of the passions" (AT, xi, 454). The first and most obvious difference is that the term is no longer restricted to the high and well-born, those possessed of "moral luck," but is given a decidedly more democratic or egalitarian flavor. It is in principle a quality anyone can aspire to possess because it consists in a disposition to use one's freedom. The *généreux* are those who, above all, are able to make a firm and resolute use of the will: "They will not consider themselves much inferior to those who have greater wealth or honor, or even to those who have more intelligence, knowledge, or beauty, or generally to those who surpass them in some other perfections; but equally they will not have much more esteem for themselves than for those they surpass. For all these things seem to them to be very unimportant by contrast to the virtuous will for which they alone esteem themselves, and which they suppose to be present, or at least capable of being present, in every other person" (AT, xi, 446–47).

The morality of *l'homme généreux* is still concerned with the legitimate good opinion we hold of ourselves, but it has far more to do with the disposition of our inner lives. What makes us generous and thus worthy of self-esteem? Generosity, Descartes says in the *Passions,* consists of two parts. The first is knowing that "nothing truly belongs to him, but this freedom to dispose of his volitions" and the other is an inner feeling "never to lack the will to undertake and carry out what he judges to be best" (AT, xi, 446). Because the Cartesian *généreux* are "naturally led to do great deeds" and "esteem nothing more highly than doing good to others," they always act with unfailing courtesy, graciousness, and tact (AT, xi, 447–48). But the morality of generosity remains very much a program for the rational control of the passions. The *généreux* have "complete command over their passions. In particular, they have mastery over their desires, and over their jealousy and envy, because everything they think sufficiently valuable to be worth pursuing is such that its acquisition depends *solely on themselves*" (AT, xi, 448; emphasis added). Generosity is not about outward achievements, but an inner disposition of the will to virtue. An ethic of rational self-control that values strength, firmness, and resoluteness of soul is Descartes's correlate to the scientific program for achieving mastery and control of nature.[15]

How is such virtue acquired? Descartes mentions that a good upbringing and good education may correct the faults of birth, but it remains very much an act of will. However, "if we occupy ourselves frequently in considering the nature of the free will and the many advantages which proceed from a firm resolution to make good use of it . . . we may arouse the passion of generosity in ourselves and then acquire the virtue" (AT, xi, 453–54). The claim that generosity depends on ourselves alone and can be acquired through a consideration of the free will is a strong statement of the privatization or depoliticization of virtue. The natural home of the *généreux* is not in the public space, but in the inner theater of the mind. There is little room in Cartesian ethics for friendship or dialogic engagement; in fact his entire method is designed to prevent or avert connection with others. To be generous is, ultimately, to be autarchic, to be the source of one's own authority, to be the principle of one's own life and action.[16]

Charles Taylor captures nicely the transformation of the term *generosity* from its role in ancient "honor ethics" to the modern individualist or "bourgeois" morality developed by Descartes: "This was the frequently used term for the central motive of the honor ethic. Although the word was already beginning to take on its modern meaning of open-handedness, it mainly referred to that strong sense of one's own worth and honor which pushed men to conquer their fears and base desires and do great things. We might say that a generous man was a 'great soul' . . . except that the terms for this—'magnanimous'—has gone through an analogous slide since the seventeenth century towards its modern meaning: something like a being ready to forgive, to make allowances for others."[17]

Spinoza's *fortitudo*, like Cartesian *générosité*, represents an ideal state of character. Partly owing to Spinoza's influence, the shape of this character has become familiar to us. Such a person can be called the free agent or the liberated individual. Knowing himself to be subject to the passions, such a person neither weakly submits to them nor stubbornly represses them. He seeks to understand their causes and hence to redirect the emotions toward positive ends. Above all, such a person presents an active or what Spinoza refers to as a "manly" character. In the *Short Treatise* he associates this virtue with the capacity to make firm decisions. Strength of character is the capacity to act in a "manly way," and this is referred to as "tenacity" or "bravery" when the course of action is difficult (*KV*, ix, 5; I/71). The virtue of manly strength has connections not only to ancient writers like Cicero but to Renaissance and early modern figures like Machiavelli, who refers to two "humors," one the desire to command characteristic of the *grandi* and the other the desire to be left alone, neither to rule nor be ruled, characteristic of the people.[18]

This neoclassical understanding of virtue holds true not only for the political theory of the early modern period but for the literature and dramaturgy. "One can say with justice," Cassirer writes, "that the term 'virtue' as used in classical French tragedy has a different and more expressive meaning than we today typically associate with it. It is closer to the Latin *virtus* or the Italian *virtù* that according to their etymological sense indicates a certain ideal of manliness. The style of manliness with all the duties that attach to it dominates and penetrates the dramas of Corneille."[19]

The themes of honor, nobility, and generosity figure prominently in the works of Corneille. In his Roman tragedies the true heroes are those who sacrifice everything, including their love and happiness, for honor. By honor Corneille understands not simply firmness of will, but the subordination of the will to the great interests of politics and the state. Tragedy consists in the sacrifice of personal interests and the desire for happiness for the good of the state. Thus in *Horace* old Horatio consoles his daughter Camilla, who has just lost her fiancé, by reminding her of the greater glory of Rome:

> Ma fille, il n'est plus temps de répandre des pleurs;
> Il sied mal d'en verser où l'on voit tant d'honneurs;
> On pleure injustement des pertes domestiques,
> Quand on en voit sortir des victoires publiques.
> Rome triomphe d'Albe, et c'est assez pour nous;
> Tous nos maux à ce prix doivent nous être doux.
> En la mort d'un amant vous ne perdez qu'un homme
> Dont la perte est aisée à réparer dans Rome.
>
> [My daughter, this is now no time for tears.
> 'Tis ill to shed them when we have such honor.
> One should not weep for personal misfortunes
> When victory for the State is their result.
> Rome triumphs over Alba. That should be
> Enough for us; and we should gladly purchase
> With all of our bereavements such an outcome.
> Thou losest but one man by thy lover's death,
> Whose loss can easily be repaired in Rome.]
> (*Horace*, IV, 3)[20]

Corneille was obviously not insensitive to the harshness, even inhumanity, of this moral code. In the famous soliloquy in which she is determined to avenge her fiancé's death, Camilla denounces the barbarism of Roman virtue:

> Leur brutale vertu veut qu'on s'estime heureux,
> Et si l'on n'est barbare, on n'est point généreux.
> Dégénérons, mon coeur, d'un si vertueux père;
> Soyons indigne soeur d'un si généreux frère:

C'est gloire de passer pour un coeur abattu,
Quand la brutalité fait la haute vertu.

[Their barbarous virtue would have everyone
Consider oneself happy; and if one
Is not devoid of feeling, one is base!
Well, let me, then, be the degenerate daughter
Of such a high-souled father. Let me be
The ignoble sister of my noble brother.
'Tis glorious to be deemed contemptible
When inhumanity is accounted virtue.]
(*Horace*, IV, 4)²¹

By the end of the play, however, it is not Camilla but her brother
Horace, her executioner, who emerges as the model of the Roman hero.

Spinoza retains much of this language of courage and nobility,
but transposes it to mean an inner fortitude and strength of soul.
He returns to and develops this virtue in the *Ethics*. But this
time strength of character has acquired two main tributaries,
one inner-directed and the other outer-directed. Just before his
enumeration of the definition of the affects at the end of part
three, he describes this virtue as follows: "All actions that follow from affects related to the Mind insofar as it understands
I relate to Strength of character which I divide into Tenacity
and Nobility. For by Tenacity I understand the Desire by which
each one strives, solely from the dictate of reason, to preserve his
being. By Nobility I understand the Desire by which each one
strives, solely from the dictate of reason to aid other men and
join them to him in friendship. Those actions, therefore, which
aim only at the agent's advantage, I relate to Tenacity, and those
which aim at another's advantage, I relate to Nobility. So Moderation, Sobriety, presence of mind in danger, etc., are species of

Tenacity whereas Courtesy, Mercy, etc., are species of Nobility" (IIIp59s).

The idea that the individual of strong character is characterized by tenacity (*animositas*) or the desire to preserve one's own being demonstrates once again the power of moral egoism and self-interest in the *Ethics*. In contrast to the Cartesian emphasis on "the firm and constant resolution of the will," the entire basis of Spinoza's ethic is the idea of the *conatus*. It is based on the imperative of self-preservation. But the self to be preserved is tied to a world of other selves, with whom we must enter into collaborative relations. The *conatus* that each of us possesses to preserve our own being is necessarily connected to the preservation and well-being of others.

The ethical world is a social world, a world lived *inter homines*, and for this reason the second part of moral strength dictates *nobilitas* or the joining with others in friendship and society. There are those who doubt that Spinoza can successfully bridge the gap between the egoism and subjectivism characteristic of part three and the collaborative, social morality developed in part four.[22] We will turn to this problem in the next chapter. But far from a council of sheer egoism, the *Ethics* is much interested in the virtues required for social and political life, chief among these being friendship. It is at this point that Spinoza's discussion of the passions turns from the individual to the broader needs of society.

5

Thinking about Politics

The subject matter of part four of the *Ethics* marks a change
from moral psychology to political theory. The *conatus* that impels each person to seek to preserve him or herself has a social
character that leads us to seek out the company and friendship of
others as a means not only of survival but of enhancing our power
and freedom. The theme of this part of the book is the transition
from the state of nature to civil society, from individual psychology to membership in a polity. It takes up the great question
posed earlier by Hobbes, namely, How is political order possible
given the egoistic and selfish nature of the passions? Are society
and social cooperation natural or artificial? Do the passions pre-
dispose us to a condition of peace or a state of war? These are
themes that Spinoza had developed at length in the *TTP* and
returns to in an abbreviated form in the *Ethics*. Part four is a
political anthropology that lays the foundation of a democratic
state.

SPINOZA'S "ECCENTRIC" HOBBESIANISM

Spinoza's political theory has often been thought of as derivative
of Hobbes. His treatment of such concepts as the state of nature, natural right, and the social contract are clearly borrowed
from his great English predecessor. They both refer their political theory back to a completely amoral state of nature in which
persons have the natural right to do whatever is in their power to
achieve. For each, the problem of politics consists of convincing
or persuading persons who are by nature egoistic and insecure to

cooperate for the sake of their common utility. Despite the presence of a common political vocabulary, Spinoza often uses his terms in a distinctive and original manner, leading one reader to observe that if Spinoza is indebted to Hobbes he is nonetheless an "eccentric Hobbesian."[1] Others have wondered whether it is correct to call him a Hobbesian at all.[2]

Like Hobbes's, Spinoza's political philosophy is premised on the concept of natural right. In his formulation, natural right is coextensive with our natural power (*TTP*, xvi, 3; III/189). Right and might are identical. Spinoza offers two different arguments for this thesis. The first derives from his metaphysical premises about the nature of God. God or nature exercises power over all things; the power of God and the right of God are inseparable. It follows, or at least Spinoza argues, that what is true for nature as a whole is true for every individual component of nature, that is, it has the right to do whatever it can do (*TTP*, xvi, 4; III/189).

The second argument grows out of a set of psychological postulates about the nature of the passions. The natural right of every individual is determined by his or her desires. These desires are not determined by reason but by the power and strength of each individual to persevere in his being: "Thus the natural right of every man is determined not by sound reason, but by his desire and his power. . . . All men are born in a state of complete ignorance, and before they can learn the true way of life and acquire a virtuous disposition, even if they have been well brought up, a great part of their life has gone by. Yet in the meantime they have to live and preserve themselves as far as in them lies, namely, by the urging of appetite alone, for Nature has given them nothing else and has denied them the actualized power to live according to sound reason" (*TTP*, xvi, 7; III/190).

So far Spinoza's account of natural right is in perfect keeping with that of Hobbes. The task of politics, as both conceive it, is to find a way that the natural right of each individual can coexist with the natural right of all. The social contract is the mechanism whereby each can unite with others for the sake of ensuring mutual peace and well-being. But here is where Hobbes and Spinoza begin to part company. The Hobbesian contract is meant to create a third party, the sovereign, who is authorized to represent and command the wills of each of the members. The Spinozist contract, by contrast, authorizes the transfer of right from the individual to the people in their collective capacity. In order to remedy the defects of the state of nature, "the unrestricted right naturally possessed by each individual should be put in common ownership and this right should no longer be determined by the strength and appetite of the individual, but by the power and will of all together" (*TTP,* xvi, 13; III/191). The idea that the sovereign represents the common property of those represented marks a decisive difference from Hobbes. Such a community Spinoza calls a democracy, which he defines as "a united body of men which corporately possesses sovereign right over everything within its power" (*TTP,* xvi, 26; III/193).

Spinoza's most important departure from Hobbes concerns his understanding of the very purpose of the state created by the contract. Hobbes famously regarded the state as a defensive mechanism created to ensure peace and security from all manners of "intestine" disorder (*Lev,* xxix, 1). Its purpose is to protect the liberty of the subject, where liberty is understood to mean the freedom to do or forbear from doing whatever it is in one's power to do. "By liberty," Hobbes writes, "is understood . . . the absence of external impediments which impediments may oft take away a part of a man's power to do what he would" (*Lev,* xiv, 2). Liberty is thus being able to do what we have a will to do without being obstructed by any external obstacles. By external obstacles, Hobbes means not only physical objects or processes but also such conventional obstacles as laws and civil institutions. Thus in civil society, liberty consists in acting whereof the law is silent. Where the law is silent, the individual has perfect liberty to act according to his own discretion (*Lev*, xxi, 18).

Spinoza, by contrast, regards liberty more expansively to incorporate not just the freedom of the individual but the freedom of the state. By freedom Spinoza means at least two things. First, it means freedom in the sense of "negative liberty," freedom from external interference. Freedom is understood here as the opposite of coercion, where this implies "the deliberate interference of other human beings within the area in which I wish to act."[3] He offers powerful arguments against the coercion of belief and opinion and wants to allow ample room for freedom of thought and discussion. Not only is coercion self-defeating—it breeds rebellion and discontent—but it violates the natural right of the individual. The purpose of the state, he says near the end of the *TTP*, is not "to transform men from rational beings into beasts or puppets, but rather to enable them to develop their mental and physical capacities in safety" (*TTP*, xx, 12; III/241).

However, he also endorses a sense of "positive liberty," according to which one can only be free in a self-governing community where every citizen participates in the creation of law. It is not enough to enjoy the protection of the law; one must be a creator of the law that one in turn obeys. Only thus can obligation be assured. This is an allusion to the classical ideal of the *civitas libertas* or what Quentin Skinner has referred to as "the neo-Roman theory of the free state."[4] According to this theory, a people is free not if its members possess rights against the intrusion of other individuals or even political agencies, but if the state as a whole is able to protect itself from foreign intrusion, using its power to protect itself at will. Freedom is enjoyed by individuals only insofar as the state that they inhabit is free from interference from others. Freedom in this sense has less to do with individual liberty than with the right of a community to determine its collective affairs. Freedom is thus most likely to be achieved in a democratic polity where the people in their collective capacity exercise sovereign power.

Hobbes had used his theory of individual liberty as a polemical weapon to discredit the republican theory of the state. In his own time Hobbes had seen this republican theory flourish among those who would seek to delegitimize monarchy and establish a republic as the only legitimate form of state. Unlike Machiavelli and other "neo-Romans" who attempted to revive the model of ancient republicanism, Hobbes set out to show just why this model of politics was more likely to produce war and slavery than peace and freedom. "The liberty whereof there is so frequent and honorable mention in the histories and philosophy of the ancient Greeks and Romans, and in the writings and discourse of those that from them have received all their learning in the politics, is not the liberty of particular men, but the liberty of the commonwealth" (*Lev*, xxi, 8). Such is the liberty of the *res publica*, the freedom to take part in public affairs.

Hobbes here formulates an argument that to speak of liberty as a property of a collective body like a commonwealth is to commit a kind of category mistake by endowing it with the individual qualities of will and agency. The sinister implication of this theory is that freedom consists in obeying whatever the laws of the state say it is. In what is still one of the most powerful formulations of the standpoint of individual liberty, Hobbes writes: "The Athenians and Romans were free, that is, free commonwealths, not that any particular men had the liberty to resist their own representative, but that their representative had the liberty to resist or invade other people. There is written on the turrets of the city of Lucca in great characters at this day the word LIBERTAS; yet no man can thence infer that a particular man has more liberty, or immunity from the service of the commonwealth, there than in Constantinople. Whether a commonwealth be monarchical or popular, the freedom is still the same" (*Lev*, xxi, 8). Hobbes's conclusion is that individuals may be freer in monarchical regimes that essentially leave them alone than in republics where they are obligated to engage in public life, where they are "forced to be free," so to speak.

This is not all. Not only are republics more restrictive of individual liberty, Hobbes believed, but they remain a permanent invitation to civil war, in part because they were based on an erroneous view of liberty. Among the most important causes of civil disorder were the examples of ancient Greek and Roman republics and those who teach about them either through their histories or "books of policy." Hobbes was not blind to the attractions of the ancient republics and the "strong and delightful impression of the great exploits" of their leaders and armies. The great danger of the republican model and their theoreticians was their view that citizens are only free when they are active participants in the affairs of state. The result of this view of freedom is to undercut all lawful and legitimate states that are not republics. From the ancients, young men developed an excessive hatred of monarchy, which Hobbes calls by the name "tyrannophobia": "From the reading . . . of such books, men have undertaken to kill their kings, because the Greek and Latin writers, in their books and discourses of policy, make it lawful and laudable for any man so to do, provided, before he do so, he call him a tyrant" (*Lev*, xxix, 14).

Hobbes repudiates the popular form of government on the old ground that too many cooks spoil the broth. In *De Cive* he considers the claims for public deliberation only to reject them as wildly utopian. The deliberative model of democracy requires a close knowledge of both domestic and foreign policy, which large assemblies by their nature do not possess. But more importantly, Hobbes is deeply alive to the dangers of demagoguery inherent in popular assemblies. Government by assembly turns out to be rule of the cleverest speaker: "Another reason why a great assembly is not so fit for consultation is, because every one who delivers his opinion holds it necessary to make a long-continued speech; and to gain the more esteem from his auditors, he polishes and adorns it with the best and smoothest language. Now the nature of eloquence is to make good and evil, profitable and unprofitable, honest and dishonest appear to be more or less than indeed they are; and to make that seem just which is unjust, according as it shall best suit with his end that speaketh."[5] Hobbes denies that the above opinion holds only for unscrupulous politicians, but maintains it is a truth about public deliberations in general, which "as all the masters of rhetoric teach us, is not [about] truth (except by chance), but victory; and whose property is not to inform, but to allure."[6]

The differences between Hobbes and Spinoza derive not only from theoretical first principles, but from historical experience and their readings of history. For Hobbes, the decisive political experience was the execution of Charles I and what he saw as the ill-fated experiment with republicanism under Cromwell and the Protectorate. A life-long student and translator of Thucydides, Hobbes saw the regicide and the ensuing civil war as the direct outgrowth of a popular infatuation with ancient conceptions of democracy and self-government. Drawing on Thucydides' account of the break-down of post-Periclean Athens, it was easy for Hobbes to regard the distemper of his times as the result of the absence of strong leadership and the increasingly anarchic tendencies of the mob. Although Hobbes's account of the origins of the civil war in his *Behemoth* is strongly overdetermined, he pays special attention to the rise of "democratical men," who are more inclined to liberty than order.[7]

Hobbes's analysis differs diametrically from Spinoza's. If Hobbes was a member of the party of order in England, Spinoza was, in Etienne Balibar's phrase, a member of the "freedom party" in Dutch politics.[8] For Spinoza, it was above all the Orangist monarchy in collusion with the Calvinist pastorate that conspired to keep the people in a state of ignorance and superstition. Accordingly, it was not the Athenian Thucydides but the Roman historian Tacitus whom Spinoza found the most useful guide for understanding the politics of his age.[9] While for many Renaissance readers the name of Tacitus was only a thinly concealed code for Machiavellianism, Spinoza read him as a moral psychologist with a strong libertarian bent.

Renaissance Tacitism took many forms. A notoriously cautious and guarded writer who rarely vented his own opinions directly, Tacitus remained, at least until Montesquieu, the unrivaled analyst of the perils of despotic power.[10] Like Machiavelli, he took his readers into the courts of princes and displayed their machinations for all to see. To be sure, Tacitus wrote with sufficient ambiguity to satisfy both princes and their subjects. Guicciardinni said that "Tacitus teaches the tyrants how to be tyrants and their subjects how to behave under tyrants."[11] Most importantly, he taught his readers how to navigate the perils of their times without sacrificing either their consciences or their lives. While Spinoza's Amsterdam was scarcely Nero's Rome, this did not stop Spinoza from appealing to Tacitus as an apostle of individual liberty. The final chapter of the *TTP* bears the title "In a Free State everyone is permitted to think what he likes and say what he thinks" (*TTP*, xx; III/239). This is a passage taken directly from Tacitus and indicates the Roman historian's praise of the republic.[12]

Spinoza's Machiavellian Moment

The influence of Machiavelli upon Spinoza is frequently framed in terms of his professed realism.[13] While there are no references to the great Florentine political theorist in the *Ethics,* Spinoza makes explicit and approving references to Machiavelli several times elsewhere, especially in the *Political Treatise.* He endorses Machiavelli's realistic attitude toward the passions and seeks to construct a polity for human beings who are far from perfect. Accordingly, the *Political Treatise* begins with a stern rebuke to the "philosophers" who have treated the passions as vices to be deplored rather than the natural state of embodied beings. Like Machiavelli, he criticizes those who have created principalities in the air rather than addressing "men as they are": "The result is that they have generally written satire instead of ethics, and have never conceived a political system which can be applied in practice; but have produced either obvious fantasies, or schemes that could only have been put into effect in Utopia, or the poets' golden age, where, of course, there was no need for them at all. Thus while theory is supposed to be at variance with practice in all the sciences which admit of application, this is held to be particularly true in the case of politics, and no men are regarded as less fit to govern a state than theorists or philosophers" (PT, i, 1; III/273).

Long before modern scholars opened up the debate over whether Machiavelli was an advisor to tyrants or a Florentine patriot, Spinoza claimed to have discerned "some uncertainty" about his real intention.[14] In the *Prince* Machiavelli had warned against the aristocracy's *libido dominandi,* the love of domination. Instead of a politics of glory and ambition, he praised the virtues of the people who desire neither to rule nor be ruled but to be left alone. Similarly the *Discourses* praise the people as more "decent" than the great because they desire to be left alone in freedom.[15] The alleged teacher of evil may well have been more truly in love with popular liberty than is often believed. Machiavelli, he believed, warned citizens to be wary of princes and alerted them to the cause of popular government (PT, v, 7; III/296).[16]

Spinoza's preference for the democratic free state is based on a combination of reasons that derive from both Hobbes and Machiavelli. In the first instance, his democratic theory follows from his Hobbesian doctrine of natural right. Democracy is the form of government most compatible with natural right. If our natural right is coextensive with our powers, as Spinoza believes, then it follows that the right of the majority in any community will have the greatest share of power behind it. Spinoza is not a sentimental democrat. He does not necessarily believe in the superior wisdom of popular assemblies or the inherent virtues of deliberation. His preference is dictated by considerations of pure *Realpolitik*. Under the terms of the social contract, citizens actually increase their power by joining together to achieve their common purposes.

But Spinoza also has other distinctively "Machiavellian" reasons for preferring democracy to princely rule. Like Machiavelli, he is deeply suspicious of elites and their desire to dominate.[17] He is alive to the danger of tyranny, especially ecclesiastical tyranny, which masks itself as a form of piety and solicitousness for the souls of others. The *TTP* had warned eloquently against the dangers of priestcraft and its tendency to align itself with monarchy: "Granted, then, that the supreme mystery of despotism, its prop and stay, is to keep men in a state of deception, and with the specious title of religion to cloak the fear by which they must be held in check, so that they will fight for their servitude as if for salvation, and count it no shame, but the highest honor, to spend their blood and their lives for the glorification of one man" (*TTP*, pref., 10; III/7). Such a system, Spinoza writes, has been brought to perfection in Turkey, i.e., Islam, where open discussion and the free exercise of reason has become a sign of impiety (*TTP*, pref., 9; III/7).

Spinoza's answer to the problem of religious persecution was to look to ancient Israel. Just as Machiavelli had held up ancient Rome as a reflecting mirror, so did Spinoza look to the example of the ancient Hebrew state as both a model and a cautionary tale for his own time.[18] He interprets the exodus from Egypt as a kind of reenactment of the original social contract story (*TTP*, xvii, 26–28; III/205). Spinoza describes the original transfer of power to Moses in the desert as an act of the democratic will. Moses was interpreted as a statesman, something like a Machiavellian "armed prophet," who establishes good laws and institutions through the force of his own charismatic authority. The key to his success was a careful attention to the strict separation of powers. Moses was a federalist *avant la lettre*. The political authorities were charged with the administration and enforcement of laws, while the priestly class was charged with interpreting them. Taking a page from the *Prince*, Spinoza praises Moses for establishing citizen armies that ensured the people of Israel remained fellow citizens (*TTP*, xvii, 48; III/209).

Moses did not adequately provide for a succession, and after his death the Levites grew restless and slowly began the usurpation of power. As there was no one to fill the role of supreme commander, the priests claimed the right not only to interpret the laws but to enforce them (*TTP*, xvii, 100; III/218). The special privileges claimed by this class became an irritant to the people, and that gradually gave rise to civil conflict and instability. The ongoing strife between the kings and priests, not divine disfavor, was the real cause for the collapse of the Hebrew state. The moral of Spinoza's story is that the institutionalization of the priesthood is the cause that leads to the state's demise (*TTP*, xvii, 112; III/220). The thinly veiled allusion to the Dutch Calvinist clergy could not have been more evident.[19]

Spinoza's answer to the problem of ecclesiastical tyranny is his theory of the free republic. He has greater faith in popular assemblies than Hobbes, not because the individuals who compose them are individually trustworthy but because he believes a people will not unite to oppress themselves (*TTP*, xvi, 28; III/194). Spinoza endorses democracy because he regards it as a more realistic alternative to Hobbes's *Leviathan*. Hobbes had correctly diagnosed the problem of anarchy and civil war, but had only gone half way toward a solution. Spinoza is by no means convinced that Hobbes ever solved the problem of what prevents a sovereign from behaving to his subjects as those subjects behave to one another in the state of nature. Why would a rational person agree to be governed by someone who has absolute power and who is unconstrained by law? What limits a monarch's avarice and ambition once he is equipped with armies and taxes? Despite his professed realism, Hobbes turns out to have been utopian in his expectations about monarchical power. Spinoza's turn to Machiavelli was necessitated ironically not because Hobbes was too Hobbesian but because he was not Hobbesian enough.

"An Idea of Man"

Part four of the *Ethics* begins with a meditation on the meaning of good and evil, perfection and imperfection. Earlier in the work Spinoza had proposed that these terms were the expressions of our desires and appetites. Nothing is good or bad in itself; only our desire or aversion makes it so (IIIp9s). Some of this reduction of moral categories to our psychological states is repeated in the preface. "Perfection and imperfection," Spinoza writes, "are only modes of thinking." Here the terms are given not just a psychological but a cognitive content. They are instances of human judgment and reasoning. "As far as good and evil are concerned," he says, "they also indicate nothing positive in things, considered in themselves, nor are they anything other than modes of thinking or notions we form because we compare things to one another" (IVpref/208).

The idea being expressed here is not that moral terms are reducible to our individual dispositions, but that they are relational concepts whose meaning grows out of a comparison between individual items of the same species. The presence of perfection or imperfection may not reside in the object under consideration, but in our judgment of the object in relation to others of a similar sort. We form the idea of what is a good or bad chair by experience of different sorts of chairs and coming to a judgment of which ones are the best examples of what a chair is. It is out of this comparative ability that the mind is led to an idea of perfection that is more than simply the sum of its parts.

This transition from the psychological to the cognitive foundation of our moral and evaluative terms testifies to a "Platonic" turn in the *Ethics,* expressed in Spinoza's reference to an "idea" or "model" (*exemplar*) of human nature: "For because we desire to form an idea of man, as a model of human nature which we may look to, it will be useful to retain these same words . . . In what follows, therefore, I shall understand by good what we know certainly is a means by which we may approach nearer and nearer to the model of human nature that we set before ourselves. By evil, what we certainly know prevents us from becoming like that model" (IVpref/208).

The *exemplar* clearly serves a normative function, allowing us to judge the quality of our lives and identify the obstacles that stand in the way of achieving this ideal. The idea of human nature mentioned above is clearly an allusion to the life of the free person developed in the last two parts of the *Ethics.*[20] The free person as described in the *Ethics* has a host of qualities. Such a person is active, not passive, and this activity arises from adequate ideas (IIIp3). Likewise, the free person is led by reason alone, and reason leads one to join others in friendship and in a society governed by common laws (IVp37, 70). The free person avoids giving offense, acts honestly not deceptively, and strives, as far as possible, to avoid accepting favors bestowed by the ignorant. In the final resort the free person endeavors to uphold the integrity of the state out of the belief that the rule of law is the precondition for all other goods.[21]

Above all, the free person understands and appreciates the value of life, his own and that of others. "A free man," he writes, "thinks of nothing less than of death and his wisdom is a meditation on life" (IVp67). The value of life as an end in itself forms the cornerstone of Spinoza's ethical theory. It follows that no one can ever take his life willingly or from "the necessity of his own nature": "Those who do such things are compelled by external causes, which can happen in many ways. Someone may kill himself because he is compelled by another, who twists his right hand (which happened to hold a sword) and forces him to direct the sword against his heart; or because he is forced by the command of a Tyrant (as Seneca was) to open his veins, i.e., he desires to avoid a greater evil by [submitting to] a lesser, or finally because hidden external causes so dispose his imagination, and so affect his Body, that it takes on another nature" (IVp20s).

Spinoza's brief digression on suicide is revealing of his larger purpose. The idea that no one takes his own life voluntarily is deeply counterintuitive. It goes against our ordinary experience of people who take their lives every day. But Spinoza's point is not about descriptive psychology. Life is not simply a biological category but a moral imperative. A person who takes his own life must be acting out of extreme physical coercion, as in the case of Seneca, or must have become someone other than he was. When Spinoza denies the rationality of suicide—and we could include here all forms of self-mutilation and abuse—he wants us to recognize the supreme value of life as an end in itself. He does not even want to hint at the possibility that self-destruction is ever a rational alternative to life. This view about the impossibility of rational self-destruction may seem odd to our ears, but it is not the task of a great thinker to confirm what we already believe. The *Ethics* provides us new reasons for resisting claims about the value of euthanasia, physician-assisted suicide, and all forms of the destruction of life.

RATIONAL NATURE

The model of human nature announced in the preface to part four is clearly related to the political theory developed later in the work. By nature, Spinoza reaffirms, all beings strive to preserve themselves. "Desire is the very essence of man," he writes (IVp18d). We are all creatures of desire and can no more cease to be so than a stone can cease to roll down hill. This doctrine taken by itself would be little cause for comment, except that the desires of one person must necessarily coexist with the desires of another. It is not just the fact of desire, but that our desires are multiple and inconstant that brings them into conflict with one another. The solution to the problem of the conflict of desires lies in Spinoza's theory of the unity of rational nature. Our powers of attaining the objects of our desires depend upon the help and cooperation of others. Reason dictates cooperation as a means to our self-preservation.

Spinoza asserts the rationality of social cooperation at IVp37: "The good which everyone who seeks virtue wants for himself, he also desires for other men; and this Desire is greater as his knowledge of God is greater." This conception of the unity of rational nature assumes that while the passions are the cause of conflict, reason is the source of community and consensus. Reason helps us see our common advantage. The premise on which Spinoza relies here is spelled out earlier when he argues that rational agents never seek something for themselves that they do not simultaneously wish for all others. "From this it follows," he writes, "that men who are governed by reason . . . want nothing for themselves that they do not desire for other men. Hence, they are just, honest, and honorable" (IVp18s).

The idea of mutual reciprocity lies at the foundation of Spinoza's lengthy reflection on the social contract and the state of nature as well as the related distinction between natural and civil right. The passage appearing at the literal center of part four deserves to be cited at length:

> Everyone exists by the highest right of nature, and consequently everyone, by the highest right of nature, does those things that follow from the necessity of his own nature. So everyone, by the highest right of nature, judges what is good and what is evil, considers his own advantage according to his own temperament, avenges himself, and strives to preserve what he loves and destroy what he hates.
>
> If men lived according to the guidance of reason, everyone would possess this right of his without any injury to anyone else. But because they are subject to the affects, which far surpass man's power, or virtue, they are often drawn in different directions and are contrary to one another, while they require one another's aid.
>
> In order, therefore, that men may be able to live harmoniously and be of assistance to one another, it is necessary for them to give up their natural right and to make one another confident that they will do nothing which could harm others. How it can happen that men who are necessarily subject to affects, inconstant and changeable should be able to make one another confident and have trust in one

another, is clear from P7 and IIIP39. No affect can be restrained except by an affect stronger than and contrary to the affect to be restrained, and everyone refrains from doing harm out of timidity regarding a greater harm.

By this law, therefore, Society can be maintained, provided it appropriates to itself the right everyone has of avenging himself, and of judging concerning good and evil. In this way Society has the power to prescribe a common rule of life, to make laws, and to maintain them — not by reason, which cannot restrain the affects, but by threats. This Society, maintained by laws and the power it has of preserving itself, is called a State, and those who are defended by its law, Citizens.

From this we easily understand that there is nothing in the state of nature which, by the agreement of all, is good or evil; for everyone who is in the state of nature considers only his own advantage, and decides what is good and what is evil from his own temperament, and only insofar as he takes account of his own advantage. He is not bound by any law to submit to anyone except himself. So in the state of nature no sin can be conceived.

But in the Civil state, of course, it is decided by common agreement what is good or what is evil. And everyone is bound to submit to the State. Sin, therefore, is nothing but disobedience, which for that reason can be punished only by the law of the State. On the other hand, obedience is considered a merit in a Citizen, because on that account he is judged worthy of enjoying the advantages of the State.

Again in the state of nature there is no one who by common consent is Master of anything, nor is there anything in Nature which can be said to be this man's and not that man's. Instead, all things belong to all. So in the state of nature, there cannot be conceived any will to give to each his own, or to take away from someone what is his. I.e., in the state of nature nothing is done which can be called just or unjust. (IVp37s2)

This stunning passage has been quoted in full to indicate the deeply political nature of the *Ethics*. At the core of the book is a political problem. By the right of nature all men have the power to determine what they believe to be good and bad for themselves. The state of nature is precisely one of those conditions, alluded to above, wherein there are no agreed upon standards, no shared criteria, for adjudicating conflicts of interest. It is a world of radical moral subjectivism. Nature provides no common standard by which to resolve conflicting moral claims. Rather, each person is equally judge, jury, and executioner of his or her own natural right. Consequently, Spinoza says provocatively, in the natural state nothing is either just or unjust: all things are permitted. It is only in society that our conflicting desires come to have moral force. Morality is a product of social agreement and can have no force outside of society. So far the logic of the contract is perfectly Hobbesian.

But even within the same set of propositions Spinoza indicates his differences with the Hobbesian contract. His account of the transition from the state of nature to civil society may be less detailed than that of Hobbes, but it differs in a number of important particulars. The most important is that fear plays a much less significant role in Spinoza's account. In the passage cited above Spinoza mentions the problem of a person "avenging himself" where there are no common rules of life. But there is no sense that the state of nature is one of overwhelming terror or dread. For Hobbes, "the passion to be reckoned upon is fear" (*Lev*, xiv, 31). Mutual fear makes reasoners of us all. Typically, Spinoza believes we enter into society not just to alleviate our fear at the possibility of death but in order to increase our powers of virtue and rationality. "Virtue," he says earlier, "is human power itself" (IVp2od). The Spinozistic contract is not so much an agreement to transfer our natural rights to a third party for the sake of security, but an exercise in the increase in our powers of rational nature and agency.

Spinoza differs most notably from Hobbes in his view that society exists not just to avoid the evils of nature but to facilitate the attainment of harmony among rational agents. The contract serves not just the primary end of achieving security of person and property, but the higher-order goal of attaining morality and a kind of rational freedom among citizens. The contract performs not just a legal but a moral function. Once again it is important to cite Spinoza's own words at some length:

> Insofar as men are torn by affects which are passions, they can be different in nature and contrary to one another. But insofar as men live according to the guidance of reason, they are said only to act. Hence, whatever follows from human nature, insofar as it is defined by reason, must be understood through human nature alone, as through its proximate cause. But because each one, from the laws of his own nature, wants what he judges to be good, and strives to avert what he judges to be evil, and moreover, because what we judge to be good or evil when we follow the dictate of reason must be good or evil, it follows that insofar as men live according

to the guidance of reason, they must do only those things that are good for human nature, and hence, for each man, i.e., those things that agree with the nature of each man. Hence, insofar as men live according to the guidance of reason, they must always agree among themselves.

Cor. 1: There is no singular thing in Nature that is more useful to man than a man who lives according to the guidance of reason.

For what is most useful to man is what most agrees with his nature, i.e., (as is known through itself), man. But a man acts entirely from the laws of his own nature when he lives according to the guidance of reason, and only to that extent must he always agree with the nature of the other man. . . .

Cor. 2: When each man most seeks his own advantage for himself, then men are most useful to one another.

For the more each one seeks his own advantage, and strives to preserve himself, the more he is endowed with virtue, or what is the same, the greater is his power of acting according to the laws of his own nature, i.e., of living from the guidance of reason. . . .

Schol.: What we have just shown is also confirmed by daily experience, which provides so much and such clear evidence that this saying is in almost everyone's mouth: man is a God to man.

Still, it rarely happens that men live according to the guidance of reason. Instead, their lives are so constituted that they are usually envious and burdensome to one another. They can hardly, however, live a solitary life; hence, that definition which makes man a social animal has been quite pleasing to most. And surely we do derive, from the society of our fellow men, many more advantages than disadvantages.

So let the Satirists laugh as much as they like at human affairs, let the Theologians curse them, let Melancholics praise as much as they can a life that is uncultivated and wild, let them disdain men and admire the lower animals. Men can still find from experience that by helping one another they can provide themselves much more easily with the things they require, and that only by joining forces can they avoid the dangers that threaten on all sides. (IVp35d,c,s)

Spinoza's focus in this passage is on the attainment of rational nature. The idea that rational beings "must always agree among themselves" is by no means evident. In activities governed by shared criteria, we are more likely to find agreement than in those wherein the standards of evaluation are unsettled or subject to dispute. Activities like presenting evidence in a law court, testing a scientific hypothesis, or determining a move in a game are all subject to rules for which reasons can be given. Yet it is not clear why Spinoza believes that if people are equally rational they all necessarily seek agreement, that is, they not only share the same nature but desire the same things, even think the same thoughts. Do all rational minds really think alike? Spinoza's idea of rational nature appears to deny that there will always be winners and losers in the game of life. The attainment of rational nature seems to obliterate all the individual differences between persons that make us human.

Spinoza differs most notably from Hobbes in his view that society exists not just in order that its members may avoid the evils of nature but for the purpose of advancing an idea of the human good. At its most basic level he recognizes the utility of society as a means for the satisfaction of needs. If the *Ethics* teaches us anything it is that we are embodied creatures fully articulated within the natural order and it is mutual dependence that makes society necessary. He raises the banner of utility as the foundation of society. What is just and unjust is determined by what is most useful to us. "To man," he writes, "there is nothing more useful than man" (IVp18s).

The standard of utility is brought out in a brief digression on our relationship with other species in which all of nature is presented as a means to human advantage: "The law against killing animals is based more on empty superstition and unmanly compassion than sound reason. The rational principle of seeking our own advantage teaches us the necessity of joining with men, but not with the lower animals, or with things whose nature is different from human nature. We have the same right against them that they have against us . . . Not that I deny that the lower animals have sensations. But I do deny that we are therefore not permitted to consider our own advantage, use them at our pleasure, and treat them as is most convenient for us" (IVp37s1). So much, one might say, for the "green" Spinoza.[22]

Although our relation to other species and even to the rest of nonhuman nature may be one of utility, our relation to others of our own kind contains a moral component. Society may grow out of need and the desire for security, but the aim of the social contract is fundamentally the enhancement of human freedom. Not mere utility but empowerment is the goal of a democratic community. The aim of the social contract is fundamentally the enhancement of human freedom. Freedom is possible not only in a state in which our mutual protection is ensured, but one in which our rationality and powers of action are enhanced. In a remarkable passage that has gone largely neglected, Spinoza attempts to show how human nature itself is virtually transformed through the art of association: "There are . . . many things outside us which are useful to us, and on that account to be sought. Of these, we can think of none more excellent than those that agree entirely with our nature. For if, for example, two individuals of entirely the same nature are joined to one another, they compose an individual twice as powerful as each one . . . Man, I say, can wish for nothing more helpful to the preservation of his being than that all should so agree in all things that the Minds and Bodies of all would compose, as it were, one Mind and one Body" (IVp18s).

This passage sounds almost like a proof-text for Rousseau's theory of the general will in the *Social Contract*, where the freedom of each is said to be enhanced by joining with others for the sake of pursuing some common goal (*SC*, i, 8). For both, the social contract confers on individuals a moral liberty that they did not possess in the pure state of nature. In the state of nature each person has a right to whatever his power can secure. But in civil society natural right is superseded by civil right, which not only limits the rights of each but establishes the general rules of social morality. The social contract is more than a legal device; it is a moral institution that establishes not merely peace but liberty.[23] In this respect both Spinoza and Rousseau break from an earlier Stoic and Ciceronian tradition of natural law according to which we have moral obligations to all human beings, even across societies. For Spinoza and Rousseau, moral obligations are a creation of the social contract and we have no duties to those with whom we have not specifically contracted.

For both Spinoza and Rousseau, only in a democratic republic do one's actions acquire the force of morality, for only in a republic can one freely consent to the laws. The opposite of freedom is not necessity but slavery, where slavery means arbitrary rule or dependence on the will of another. Thus the social contract creates a general will (*volonté générale*) or "one mind and one body" where previously there had been only particular minds and particular bodies. It is only with this transfer of power from the individual to the sovereign that our freedom acquires a civil and moral dimension. A person who follows his or her instincts or affects is not free, but a slave to the passions. Freedom means acting from the laws of reason (IVp35d). We are only truly active, really alive, when we allow ourselves to be led by reason. Rational action is the very opposite of lawlessness; it means acting from laws that we give to ourselves. Freedom equals self-legislation.[24]

There is, then, a strongly democratic character to Spinoza's account of the social contract. The democratic state is one in which all follow laws to which every member has contributed. This view is confirmed near the end of part four: "A man who is guided by reason is more free in a state, where he lives according to a common decision, than in solitude, where he obeys only himself" (IVp73). The idea that freedom is realized by membership in a community of rational agents is confirmed by the following proof: "A man who is guided by reason is not led to obey by fear, but insofar as he strives to preserve his being from the dictate of reason, i.e., insofar as he strives to live freely, desires to maintain the principle of common life and common advantage. Consequently, he desires to live according to the common decision of the state. Therefore, a man who is guided by reason desires, in order to live more freely, to keep the common laws of the state, q.e.d." (IVp73d).

On the basis of IVp18 Spinoza's conception of liberty can be made to seem deeply anti-liberal, not to say, collectivist. His attempt to derive "one mind and one body" from many minds and many bodies suggests a communitarianism that leaves little room for expressions of individual difference and personality. Underlying this belief is the assumption that no person, at least no rational person, ever desires for himself something that he does not simultaneously desire for all others. This is the formula for the generalization of the will that Rousseau made into the standard for justice. Spinoza's belief is that if persons are equally rational they will be motivated by the same desires and seek the same ends, that there is a kind of harmony of interests that follows spontaneously from our rational nature (IVp30–31). Whether this is psychologically persuasive has been held up to doubt.[25] Will not conflicts of interest inevitably arise even among people who are alike in rationality? Competition for scarce resources would seem to be a permanent cause of enmity and conflict. Further, his view that all rational beings "must always agree among themselves" (IVp35d) appears to sanction harmony over difference and the subordination of the individual to the unity of a rational consensus. The identity, separateness, and self-sufficiency of the individual all seem to be denied by Spinoza's emphasis on the unity of rational nature.[26]

To be sure, there is much to support the communitarian reading of the *Ethics*. Beginning with a hard core of egoism, Spinoza tries to demonstrate the rationality of social cooperation. Our freedom to persevere in our being is always part of the social context. It follows that rational persons will seek out the company of others for the sake of enhancing their power and mutual freedom. The common stock of freedom is enhanced rather than diminished by cooperation and harmony. Spinoza gives this conception of freedom a strongly democratic twist. Freedom is only achieved inside a community of rational persons. This follows from his premise that free persons are united not just by utility but by bonds of friendship: "Only free men are very useful to one another, are joined to one another by the greatest necessity of friendship, and strive to benefit one another with equal eagerness for love" (IVp71d).

There is much in the political theory of the *Ethics* that seems to anticipate the communitarianism of Rousseau or even Hegel. He seems to endow the state with a higher purpose and moral idealism not present in the more prosaic visions of Hobbes and Locke. Yet Spinoza falls far short of attributing to the state or any institutional noun a general will or mind independent of the agents who have shaped it. From his defense of the rationality of cooperation, it would be false to draw the conclusion that he advocated the subordination of the individual to the will of the community or any other collective being. Those who live according to reason are rare. More commonly, men are motivated by hatred and envy rather than friendship and good will (IVap13). It may be rational to seek out the company and friendship of others for the sake of living well; it can never be rational to alienate our powers and freedom of the mind to another being.

Running throughout the *Ethics* is a profound awareness of the limits of rationality. The imaginative and passionate aspects of human nature run deep. Communities are composed of the rational and the irrational alike, so that the problem of politics is to discover institutional means to ensure freedom and security from the mobilized forces of superstition, intolerance, and hatred. "The mob is terrifying if unafraid," Spinoza remarks (IVp54s). The task of politics is not to create an ideal community of Spinozistic reasoners but to institute laws and rules that protect the rational from the tyranny and collective irrationalities of the multitude.

The *Ethics* differs from any kind of collectivist morality in its "epicurean" endorsement of joy, especially the pleasure of laughing and joking. There is nothing of either Spartan austerity or Christian asceticism in the *Ethics*. It is a work devoted to the celebration of the self. Self-esteem is thus said to be the highest thing we can hope for. True self-esteem can be neither conferred nor withheld by the opinion of others. It is entirely self-generated or grows out of the good opinion we hold of ourselves (IVp52). Among the pleasures the *Ethics* endorses are cheerfulness (*hilaritas*), gladness (*gaudium*), and joy (*laetitia*). "The greater the joy with which we are affected," he writes, "the greater the perfection to which we pass." "Nothing forbids our pleasures except a savage and sad superstition" (IVp45s).

The *Ethics* is nothing if not a tribute to the pleasures of individuality. Many of these pleasures depend upon the body and can only be attained through the companionship of others. The passage cited above continues as follows: "It is the part of a wise man . . . to refresh and restore himself in moderation with pleasant food and drink, with scents, with the beauty of green plants, with decoration, music, sports, the theater, and other things of this kind, which anyone can use without injury to another. For the human body is composed of a great many parts of different natures, which constantly require new and varied nourishment, so that the whole Body may be equally capable of all thing which can follow from its nature, and hence, so that the Mind also may be equally capable of understanding many things" (IVp45s).

Spinoza's statement that the body itself is composd of "many parts of different natures" bespeaks his awareness of the variety of human pleasures and the different sources of satisfaction. His reference to good food and drink, the arts and beautiful objects, all testify to a cultivated aesthetic sense at odds with a cramped Calvinism. He appears here to reject a monistic view of human flourishing, the one-size-fits-all model of the good life. Instead his awareness of diversity both within and between human beings not only indicates an appreciation of the role of human freedom but makes the *Ethics* an important, although frequently unacknowledged, source of moral pluralism.

The *Ethics* is a democratic manifesto through and through. The issue is whether Spinoza's idea of democracy is favorable or hostile to the freedom of the individual. To be sure, at times Spinoza sounds deeply communitarian. The "one mind and one body" passage discussed above seems to surrender the individual to the general will of society. Similarly the view that rational beings always agree among themselves appears to favor the attainment of consensus over the expression of individual differences. The civil condition is not for Spinoza just a legal state but a moral state in which the individual is more free the more he or she lives under laws made by the entire community. Although Spinoza, as we have seen, is frequently compared to Hobbes because of his theory of the state of nature and natural right, he radically departs from Hobbes in his belief that freedom is only possible in a democratic republic where the laws are literally made by all and not merely "authorized" by the sovereign, as in the case of Hobbes. Public liberty is here clearly given priority over the interests and liberties of the individual.

Some readers of the *Ethics* have gone so far as to find a sinister, even totalitarian, component to Spinoza's democratic theory. Berlin associates Spinoza's conception of positive liberty with the tradition of political paternalism and coercion in which persons are deemed free only when they are playing out their allotted parts, acting from their true nature, as players in a "cosmic drama." Berlin regards this conception of freedom as premised on the rationalist assumption that for every question there must be one true answer and that all solutions seamlessly fit into a single whole which can be called rational nature. Freedom has nothing to do with acting spontaneously, irrationally, or impulsively, but with acting rationally, where this means not just the ability to give reasons for our actions, but acting as part of some overall plan or pattern of behavior. Spinoza's theory of freedom means, then, acting in accordance with the laws or rules presented by reason.[27]

The obliteration of the individual is said to follow necessarily from the ascription of a kind of universal cosmic necessity to the natural order. If determinism is true, then freedom can consist only in the recognition of and adaptation to the laws of causal necessity. It took as perspicacious an observer as Tocqueville to observe the affinity between Spinoza's democratic pantheism and the diminution of the individual. Today pantheism sounds like a relatively harmless doctrine often associated with the Emersonian cult of nature worship and some of the more extravagant ejaculations of the environmental movement. In a little-noted chapter from *Democracy in America* entitled "What Causes Democratic Nations to Incline toward Pantheism," Tocqueville catches something of the spirit, if not the letter, of Spinoza's doctrine: "If one finds a philosophical system which teaches that all things material and immaterial, visible and invisible, which the world contains are only to be considered as the several parts of an immense Being who alone remains eternal in the midst of all the continual flux and transformation of all that composes Him, one may be sure that such a system, although it destroys individuality, or rather just because it destroys it, will have secret charms for men living under democracies."[28]

The belief that democratic pantheism leads to the debasement of the individual may be true for some of the more enthusiastic nature worshippers. It is not, however, true for Spinoza, whose *Ethics* is a testimony to the empowerment and liberation of the individual. The individual is free to the extent that his actions are self-caused (IIIp3). The opposite of freedom is not necessity but slavery, where slavery means dependence on the will of another or ignorance of the causes of our own behavior.

A person is a slave to the extent that he is unaware of or unable to control his desires and actions. The purpose of Spinoza's doctrine of necessity is not to enslave the individual but to liberate the mind from a whole range of angry or negative passions such as bigotry, hatred, intolerance, resentment, and all those "savage and sad" superstitions that stand in the way of our happiness and pleasure.

Something of this combination of belief in necessity and devotion to the cause of liberty was central to Tocqueville's great American contemporary Abraham Lincoln. It seems that from a relatively early age Lincoln was strongly attracted to a kind of Spinozistic doctrine of cosmic determinism. There is no evidence that Lincoln ever read Spinoza, but he did know the work of many of the eighteenth-century natural theologians. His law partner and subsequent biographer, William Herndon, later recounted that Lincoln was particularly impressed with the new doctrine of evolution of which he became a "warm advocate."[29] In several conversations Lincoln defended a necessitarian view of the world:

> "There are no accidents," he said one day, "in my philosophy. Every effect must have its cause. The past is the cause of the present, and the present will be the cause of the future. All these are links in the endless chain stretching from the finite to the infinite." From what has been said it would follow logically that he did not believe, except in a very restricted sense, in the freedom of the will. We often argued the question, I taking the opposite view; he changed the expression, calling it the freedom of the mind, and insisted that man always acted from a motive. I once contended that man was free and could act without a motive. He smiled at my phi-

losophy, and answered that it was impossible, because the motive was born before the man.[30]

Lincoln's belief in a doctrine of cosmic necessity did not lead
to resignation or despair. Nor did it entail an abandonment of
a sense of justice and responsibility to relieve the suffering of
others. Spinozistic natural theology is entirely consistent with
a commitment to human activity and rationality as well, as in
Lincoln's case, a desire to redeem the world from injustice and
cruelty. This point has been nicely captured by David Bidney, the
only previous writer to acknowledge Lincoln's Spinozistic combination of determinism and devotion to the cause of human
liberty:

> The conviction that man was the necessary product
> of the universal forces of nature taught Lincoln for-
> bearance and tolerance toward others so that he felt
> "malice towards none and charity towards all," in
> spite of bitter provocation in his domestic and po-
> litical life. But this fatalistic attitude was blended in
> him as in Spinoza with a profound respect for the
> natural worth and dignity of man and the inalien-
> able right of each person to be his own master. Lin-
> coln's success in emancipating the slaves of America
> was one of the supreme, creative acts of history and
> altered what seemed to be the inevitable destiny of
> millions. In this respect he carried into practical so-
> cial life the principles on which Spinoza founded his
> *Ethics*.[31]

6

Thinking about Love

In his posthumously published *Love and Friendship* Allan Bloom remarks that while Rousseau may have been "the most erotic of modern philosophers," Socrates was "the most erotic of philosophers, period."[1] I will not quarrel with this statement except to note that it fits with a number of fairly standard views on modernity. Marxist historians and their acolytes have long contended that the older traditions of chivalry and courtly love no longer conformed to the imperatives of the new market-oriented economy of the sixteenth and seventeenth centuries. The great ethical philosophers of the early modern period devoted themselves to exonerating the loveless "bourgeois" virtues of work, instrumental rationality, and deferred gratification. "Don Quixote," Marx himself wrote, "long ago paid the penalty for wrongly imagining that knight errantry was compatible with all economic forms of society."[2]

Contemporary feminist critics maintain that reason and rational knowledge—the code words for the traditional philosophical and scientific enterprise—are associated with the typically "male" urge to transcend, transform, and conquer nature. These are believed to be distinctively masculine characteristics in which the feminine sphere of the affects and emotions are either ignored or else ruthlessly suppressed.[3] In neither case does either of these perspectives have much to say about Spinoza, precisely because he makes love a dominant theme of the *Ethics*.

Perhaps no aspect of Spinoza's work has given rise to greater perplexity than the fifth and final part of the *Ethics*, entitled "On the Power of the Intellect or on Human Freedom." His description of the eternity of the mind, the immortality of the soul, and, above all, the intellectual love of God has both baffled and infuriated readers. According to many, these sections provide evidence that Spinoza was a mystical pantheist, the "god intoxicated man" of the Romantics; for others, they demonstrate that Spinoza never managed to free himself from the hold of medieval philosophy and forms of thought; while for still others of a contemporary analytical bent, Spinoza's discussion of intellectual divine love is nothing less than an embarrassment unworthy of a philosopher of the first order. For those of a more psychological disposition they can be explained as a form of self-hatred and intellectual masochism. The one thing that can be said with certainty is that Spinoza's *amor Dei intellectualis* has provoked controversy.

According to Jonathan Bennett, the current dean of the "analytical" school of Spinoza scholarship, Spinoza's views in the fifth part of the *Ethics* are said to be "unintelligible" and "pretty certainly worthless."[4] He accuses Spinoza of betraying the highest insights of his philosophy, yet Bennett himself seems overcome by a very unspinozistic paroxysm of rage. What Spinoza has written is worthless. "Worse," he writes, "it is dangerous: it is rubbish which causes others to write rubbish."[5] Bennett can only offer a psychological explanation for Spinoza's views on divine love and immortality. Perhaps, he speculates, Spinoza was "terrified of extinction" and with "a scatter of perverse arguments" hoped to grasp at some shred of immortality. In other words part five is entirely the product of Spinoza's fear of divine punishment, exactly what he had spent his life telling his readers that they had no reason to fear. "Those of us who love and admire Spinoza's philosophical work," Bennett concludes, "should in sad silence avert our eyes from the second half of Part 5."[6] Would that the author had heeded his own advice.

An equally negative opinion was expressed by Lewis Feuer, who traced Spinoza's ideas about the love of God back to his own emotional and sexual frustrations. It is here that "the ethically-minded psychiatrist merged into the mystic lover of God."[7] What especially bothers Feuer is the proposition that "He who loves God cannot strive that God should love him in return" (Vp19). The idea of an eternally unrequited love strikes Feuer as "strange," if not an example of a colossal mistake: "Is not Spinoza's theory of the intellectual love of God a colossal example of an 'inadequate idea'? Is there not a streak of masochism that runs through this doctrine which insists that we love God though He never loves us? We are asked to love this substance without feeling, this entity of geometrical perfection and indifference. How would this 'love of God' have fared if Spinoza the psychiatrist had placed it under analytic scrutiny? Would not the first act of the free man have been to affirm his independence of this nonmoral geometrical entity, this whole which, by definition, contains all things? Why, indeed, worship a logical tautology?"[8]

Feuer believes a more logical response to Spinoza's God would be one of "Byronic defiance," a hatred for this vast impervious being whom we are expected to love but from whom we can expect nothing in return. This strikes him as nothing more than "gallows humor written into metaphysics":

> The human race is asked to admire the power of nature which may destroy it and to take delight in the beauty of the mathematical laws which threaten it with annihilation. The soldier killed by a bullet is

asked to rejoice in the laws of motion which govern the bullet's trajectory. And it is false to say that
with knowledge, we can only desire what is necessary; for we can long for a more just order of things
even when the powers of injustice and indifference
overwhelm us. Behind Spinoza's metaphysics lies an
injunction to love that which is necessary, a cosmic
acquiescence. To love that which destroys you, however, is a sign of a "disease of the mind." The mas-
ochist hates himself and Spinoza has abundantly
said that reason demands "that every person should
love himself." The intellectual love of God, as a form
of self-hatred, is a neurotic manifestation or, as Spinoza would say, an "inadequate idea."⁹

To be sure, there is a deep paradox entailed by a philosopher
like Spinoza enjoining his readers to the intellectual love of God.
The paradox is captured by considering the end of the *Ethics* in
the light of its beginning. Part one presents Spinoza's conception of God not as the divine creator of heaven and earth, but as
an extended substance that has neither beginning nor end. The
God of the *Ethics* is a God that is purely immanent in its effects,
that is, God is inseparably bound up with nature and its infinity of attributes. Part five, however, culminates with Spinoza's
exhilarating vision of intellectual divine love (Vp32). This is a
condition described as the highest human perfection and peace
of mind, something approximating eternal blessedness and joy
(Vp42). This is a kind of love freed from the imagination and
the desires of the body and based on a purely intellectual union
with God.

The question is how can such an abstract, even inhuman,
deity be considered the object of human affection? How can a
God allegedly indifferent to justice and injustice be worthy of

love? Is it not absurd to ask us to love a being that is the cause of famine, war, disease, of so much pain, suffering, and misery? How is it possible to love a being that is literally beyond good and evil? The God of Spinoza, we have seen earlier, is knowable principally through the operations of nature and events of history. This may include not only beneficial happenings like the creation of laws and the institution of society, but can also include the extermination of entire peoples.

The One True Plan of Life

The great theme of part five is nothing less than the freedom of mind or, what is the same thing, blessedness (*beatitudo*) (Vpref/277). The idea that blessedness or salvation (*salus*) is the goal of philosophy is not unique to Spinoza. His predecessors are Plato, Augustine, and Maimonides. Philosophy is for him endowed with not just rational but also redemptive power, an ability to transform one's life and turn one's soul. Having repudiated historical religions based on revelation and prophecy, he was free to endorse a new kind of philosophy endowed with much of religion's salvific power, but divested of its otherworldly orientation. The salvation to be achieved remains very much a worldly or secular redemption based on the moderation of the passions and leading the one true way of life.

The attribution of a redemptive power to philosophy was evident from Spinoza's earliest writings. In the preface to *TIE*, he polemicizes against the futility of attaching absolute value to things outside of our control, among which he counts riches, honors, and pleasures. The problem with these goods is that they remain contingent on a host of circumstances that perpetually elude human control. Since all of these goods are perishable, they cannot be enjoyed absolutely. Insofar as we love wealth or honor or pleasure, our love will be tinged with an awareness of sadness as we contemplate their transience. Consequently, these goods have only a relative, not absolute, value. Furthermore, such goods are frequently the cause of conflict and animosity. They are part of a zero-sum game in which there are winners and losers. In place of these false goods, Spinoza declares a resolution to seek a good that is both sought for its own sake and that is not at the same time an object of competition, that can be shared without being diminished. The true good must be indestructible, impervious to the shifts of fortune. To find such a good, he realizes, will take a change in one's "plan of life" (*TIE*, vii; II/6-7).

Spinoza writes here like a philosophically minded physician seeking a remedy for these false goods. In this case he is both physician and patient. He describes himself as being "like a man suffering from a fatal illness" who is forced to seek a cure or accept certain death (*TIE*, vii; II/7). The cure he prescribes for himself is a new philosophy that holds out both the right way of knowing and the right kind of life. It is philosophy understood as the art of living. Moreover, this new philosophy is described in explicitly erotic terms. This new love is alluded to only dimly as "the eternal and infinite thing" that "feeds the mind with a joy entirely exempt from sadness" and that is "greatly to be desired and sought with all our strength" (*TIE*, x; II/7).

This new philosophy requires a "turning" away from the older goods and life plan toward a new way of life and set of objectives. It must begin with a sense of dissatisfaction with the way of life one has been leading and a search for a more worthy one. He continually stresses the difficulties standing in the way of adopting this new plan of life. In his most programmatic statement of the redemptive mission of philosophy he writes:

> Here I shall only say briefly what I understand by the
> true good, and at the same time, what the highest

good is . . . The highest good is to arrive—together with other individuals if possible—at the enjoyment of such a nature. What that nature is we shall show in its proper place: that it is the knowledge of the union that the mind has with the whole of Nature.

This, then, is the end at which I aim at: to acquire such a nature, and to strive that many acquire it with me. That is, it is part of my happiness to take pains that many others may understand as I understand, so that their intellect and desire agree entirely with my intellect and desire. To do this it is necessary, *first* to understand as much of Nature as suffices for acquiring such a nature; *next* to form a society of the kind that is desirable, so that as many as possible may attain it as easily and surely as possible.

Third, attention must be paid to Moral Philosophy and to instruction concerning the education of children. Because health is no small means to achieving this end, *fourthly,* the whole of Medicine must be worked out. And because many difficult things are rendered easy by ingenuity, and we can gain much time and convenience in this life, *fifthly,* Mechanics is in no way to be despised.

But before anything else we must devise a way of healing the intellect, and purifying it, as much as we can in the beginning, so that it understands things successfully, without error and as well as possible. Everyone will now be able to see that I wish to direct all the sciences toward one end and goal, viz., that we should achieve, as we have said, the highest human perfection. (*TIE,* xii–xvi; II/8–9)

Spinoza's language of "healing" and "purifying" the mind reveals his therapeutic intentions. The mind must be purged of errors and superstitions before we will be able to ascend to the one true plan of life. This plan entails an entire regimen of not only moral education but social and political transformation. Spinoza speaks here of a new plan for the instruction of children and future generations. His plan requires a new kind of society that is open to and fosters this new kind of life. Like Descartes in the preface to the *Principles of Philosophy*, Spinoza envisages a redirection of the sciences, chiefly medicine and physics, toward this new goal. Here he speaks both as a prophet and a physician of the soul.

THE LADDER OF LOVE

The *TIE*'s mention of the highest human perfection as the mind's union with nature as a whole is an authoritative anticipation of what is called the intellectual love of God in the final part of the *Ethics*. Both works indicate that human perfection is attainable only after a purification of the mind of previously held false beliefs and values; both stress that philosophy is more than a method of knowing but a way of life; and both believe that the decisive link unifying nature and mind is love. Running through the *Ethics* is nothing less than a phenomenology of love, from the lowest form of desire to the most exalted spiritual love. This ladder of love, to recall an image from Plato's *Symposium*, mirrors the different stages of knowledge we have seen from *imaginatio* to *ratio* to *scientia*. Each form of knowledge has its corresponding type of love culminating in the mind's union with God or nature.

Spinoza defines love in the most general sense as pleasure accompanied by the idea of an external object (IIIp13s). This definition is, of course, so broad as to encompass virtually anything. There are potentially as many objects of love as there are causes of pleasure. The problem with love of the imaginative or passionate sort is that it is caused by things or persons largely outside of our control. Such love renders us passive and helpless before the objects of our desires. Passionate love is presented throughout the *Ethics* as the cause of emotional uncertainty and anguish, what we have seen Spinoza call vacillation of mind (IIIp17s).

The first kind of love is identified with physical attraction and is defined as "a desire for and love of joining one body to another." Spinoza adds in an explanatory note that "whether this desire for sexual union is moderate or not, it is called lust [*libido*]" (IIIdef.aff48). Love of this sort is connected to bodily pleasures such as gluttony, avarice, and sexual obsession. Passionate love is shown to be the cause of jealousy, conflict, and hatred. Not only is this kind of love the cause of erotic competition between rival lovers, but it also causes feelings of anger, jealousy, and hatred. There is, in other words, a dialectical relationship between erotic love and hatred. I am prepared to do anything for the beloved but only on the condition that she love me for it in return; if she ceases to love me or prefers another, love turns to hatred. Jealousy and possessiveness are thus a part of passionate love.

Sometimes one suspects that Spinoza's own biographical experiences are coming to the surface in his description of intense feelings of hatred caused by erotic love: "For he who imagines that a woman he loves prostitutes herself to another not only will be saddened, because his own appetite is restrained, but also will be repelled by her, because he is forced to join the image of the thing he loves to the shameful parts and excretions of the other. To this, finally, is added the fact that she no longer received the jealous man with the same countenance as she used to offer him. For this cause, too, the lover is saddened" (IIIp35s).

There is a Platonic dimension to Spinoza's analysis of sexual love. He associates it with temporal, impermanent objects such as physical beauty. The idea seems to be that because physical beauty is inconstant so are the passions associated with it. Only the permanent, imperishable One can be truly considered an object of love. Passionate love is an unstable emotion because when the object to which it is attached changes, so too does the emotion. Love, then, turns into its opposite: "A purely sensual love, moreover, i.e., a lust to procreate that arises from external appearance, and absolutely, all love that has a cause other than freedom of mind, easily passes into hate—unless (which is worse) it is a species of madness. And then it is encouraged more by discord than by harmony" (IVap19).

The text quoted above cross-references an earlier passage in which Spinoza develops the tyrannical character of passionate love. It is connected to the *libido dominandi*, the desire to dominate and control. The passions are such that we want all people to love, desire, and hate exactly as we do. The fact that each of us wants everyone else to love and hate the things we do is a principal cause of social conflict. In one of the few passages from the *Ethics* in which Spinoza calls on the help of a poet to make his case, he shows how social disapproval is an important goad to erotic conquest. The passions lead us to want what is forbidden and this adds to the sweetness of the quest:

> From this . . . it follows that each of us strives, so far as he can, that everyone should love what he loves, and hate what he hates. Hence the passage of the poet:

Speremus pariter, pariter metuamus amantes;
Ferreus est, si quis, quod sinit alter, amat.
[Lovers need a coexistence of hope and fear;
Love by another's leave is too cold-blooded.
—Ovid, *Amores*, 2.19.4–5]

This striving to bring it about that everyone should
approve his love and hate is really ambition.
(IIIp31c,s)

Passionate love is, then, connected to our sense of pride and
ambition. Although human desires are various, the effect of love
is to fixate the mind on one object to the exclusion of everything
else. Passionate love is a source of obsessive behavior that not
only agitates the mind but makes us into an object of ridicule
and contempt: "Generally, then, the affects are excessive, and
occupy the mind in the consideration of only one object so much
that it cannot think of others . . . When this happens to a man
who is not asleep, we say that he is mad or insane. Nor are they
thought to be less mad who burn with love, and dream, both
night and day, only of a lover or a courtesan. For they usually
provoke laughter" (IVp44s).

Spinoza's own views on the subject of passionate love have
been attributed to a variety of causes. He has been seen by some
as a misogynist; he frequently associates women in the above
passages with images of courtesans and prostitutes. These views
have also been explained by his own disappointments in love,
especially those references to spurned lovers and the obsessive-
compulsive character of erotic love. They have also been attributed to a sort of moral prudery and a "repressed" personality;
he frequently describes erotic love as a species of insanity.[10] Spinoza's own experiences with the opposite sex seem to have been
extremely limited. One may wonder whether he is the most re-
liable judge of such matters.

Dr. Fischelson's Spinoza

The most sensitive and illuminating treatment of the issue of passionate love has been developed not by a philosopher but by a novelist, Isaac Bashevis Singer in his wonderful short story "The Spinoza of Market Street."[11] Here Singer depicts an aging Spinoza scholar, Dr. Nachum Fischelson, who has tried to live his life in accordance with the strict teaching of the *Ethics*. Fischelson knows every proposition, demonstration, and scholium by heart. His barren attic room is filled with slips and notes for the grand commentary on Spinoza he has yet to complete. But Dr. Fischelson is consumed with worries about his body. At the beginning of the story he is ill; he has stomach cramps and believes he may have a cancerous tumor. He is barely able to eat without feeling nauseous. He is obsessed with death despite Spinoza's admonition that the free man thinks only of life (IVp67).

One day after returning from the market, Fischelson is taken ill and is helped back to his apartment by a spinster neighbor known as Black Dobbe. Dobbe is initially reluctant to help Fischelson. She has heard stories that he is a convert and takes his copy of the *Ethics* to be a gentile prayer book. But the two talk, and after a life of asceticism and solitude, Fischelson suddenly falls in love with this illiterate bagel seller from his Warsaw neighborhood. Singer describes the wedding night as nothing short of a "miracle." The old Spinozist promises his bride nothing, but inexplicably discovers himself revived. The unlikely couple consummate their marriage, after which Dr. Fischelson gets out of bed, goes to the window, and reflects:

> Dr. Fischelson looked up at the sky. The black arch was thickly sown with stars — there were green, red, yellow, blue stars; there were large ones and small ones, winking and steady ones. There were those that were clustered and those that were alone . . .

In the chaos of nebulae primeval matter was being formed . . . Yes, the divine substance was extended and had neither beginning nor end; it was absolute, indivisible, eternal, without duration, infinite in its attributes. Its waves and bubbles danced in the universal cauldron, seething with change, following the unbroken chain of causes and effects, and he, Dr. Fischelson, with his unavoidable fate, was part of this. The doctor closed his eyelids and allowed the breeze to cool the sweat on his forehead and stir the hair on his beard. He breathed deeply of the midnight air, supported his shaky hands on the window sill and murmured, "Divine Spinoza, forgive me. I have become a fool."[12]

At the story's end Fischelson clearly believes that he has betrayed everything his life has stood for. His ideal of the philosopher, the quintessential man of reason, has succumbed to his own passions. The life of the mind has come to grief before the needs of the body. One can, of course, read the story as a satire on the philosophic life. What kind of philosophy is it, Singer seems to ask, that leads to such as joyless and impoverished existence? Is such a philosophy, cut off from all human warmth and affection, worth having? Singer seems to be playing Aristophanes to Spinoza's Socrates.

In this story Singer has reopened Plato's "old quarrel between philosophy and poetry." But this begs another possible reading of the story. The question is: How well did Dr. Fischelson understand Spinoza? Is Singer mocking Spinoza or merely Fischelson's understanding of him? Fischelson believes that erotic love is at odds with the life of reason, but Spinoza constantly reminds us that mind and body are not two substances at war with one another, but two aspects of the same individual.

The passions are not the antithesis of reason, but "inadequate ideas" waiting to be developed. Erotic love contains shards of reason that at least point to the love of God. There is a continuum between the earthiest form of sexual desire and the most exalted state of spiritualized love.

The issue is whether passionate love of the kind felt between Fischelson and Dobbe is always irrational and contrary to the teachings of the *Ethics*, as Fischelson clearly believes, or whether it may serve a higher interest. When Singer says that on their wedding night "powers long dormant" were awakened in Fischelson, he includes not just sexual powers but the recollection of love poetry ("Long forgotten quotations for Klopfstock, Lessing, Goethe rose to his lips"). It appears from this that even passionate love is connected to the powers of the mind. If Spinoza is correct that only "a savage and sad superstition" prevents our pleasure, why should Fischelson deny himself the pleasures of the body? These surely constitute a legitimate source of human happiness.

Despite Fischelson's belief that he has become a fool, Singer raises the possibility that passionate love may also be empowering. Fishelson's infirmities, which occupy so much of his thinking before he meets Dobbe, are at least temporarily overcome on their wedding night, when he appears physically revived and imagines himself as a young man skiing down an alpine mountain. This would seem to confirm, not negate, Spinoza's belief about the importance of the body. The stronger are the powers of the body, the stronger the powers of the mind (IIp13). If it is a principle of the *Ethics* that anything that empowers the body must also empower the mind, then the love between the two characters must play a positive role whatever its source. The wedding of Fischelson and Dobbe could even be a confirmation of Spinoza's belief that "if two individuals of entirely the same nature are joined to one another, they compose an individual twice as strong as each one" (IVp18s).[13]

Rational Love

The second kind of love is connected to our powers of reason and critical reflection. Rational love, so called, has its basis in *ratio*, or the general concepts and categories that are used to organize experience. To speak of rational love might seem like a contradiction in terms. Isn't love blind? But for Spinoza, all the affects contain a cognitive content and can be ranked accordingly. By rational love Spinoza refers not just to intimate relations outside the family, but to the full range of family relations (husband and wives, parents and children) as well as to the broader bonds of society and citizenship. It describes a relationship closer to what the Greeks called *philia* than to *eros*.

A key feature of this kind of love is its connection not to the attractions of the body but to the "freedom of the mind." Spinoza uses the phrase *animi libertatem* to indicate the active, self-affirming character of this kind of love. The implication here is clear. In contrast to the love that is just a desire to possess the body of the beloved, this love is also a desire for a genuine union of minds. Love is ultimately a meeting of the minds, thus confirming the adage that the mind is the most erogenous zone. The desire of one mind for another has the features of stability and permanence lacking in purely passionate relationships. Not only is such love more enduring, it forms the only solid basis for marriage and the family: "As for marriage, it certainly agrees with reason, if the desire for physical union is not generated only by external appearance but also by a love of begetting children and educating them wisely, and moreover, if the love of each, of both the man and the woman, is caused not by external appearance only, but mainly by freedom of mind" (IVap20).

This brief description of marriage and the family is notable for the absence of romantic love. Spinoza's treatment of marriage as an institution in agreement with reason makes it appear more like a long-term friendship of character than a passionate relationship. The statement that marriage is "caused" by freedom of mind shows that he believes the love between man and woman has an intellectual, not just an emotional, content. The love that one mind has for another leads to a growth in self-knowledge and reflectivity. Men and women help each other to exercise their rationality and pass it on to the next generation. This type of love—sober, rational, self-reflective—is most closely connected with the life of society. Friendships of mind make possible social cooperation and all the other social virtues. Such long-term character relations may lack the quality of erotic intensity typical of passionate love, but they encourage virtues and dispositions of mind such as justice, fidelity, and honor, which all fall under the term *morality* (IVp37s1; IVap15).

Intellectual Love

The second kind of love that one mind feels for another is but a step to the third and highest love, described in the *Ethics* as the intellectual love of God. Describing these three kinds of love as steps or rungs on a ladder is to emphasize their continuity and interconnectedness. There is the suggestion that the three kinds of love, like the three kinds of knowledge discussed in part two, mutually presuppose one another. They are not so much discrete experiences as way stations on the path to redemption. The *amor Dei intellectualis* is not merely an afterthought appended to Spinoza's metaphysics but the basis for a new philosophical theology, a theology without dogmas and sacraments but one that performs a powerful transformative function nonetheless. Spinoza explicitly states that this kind of love is based on an intuitive apprehension of God. According to his final word on the subject, this kind of love is based on a knowledge of individual things in their singularity. All genuine knowledge is for Spinoza ultimately knowledge of particulars. "The more we understand singular things, the more we understand God," Spinoza writes at Vp24. Apparently, to know God is to know the details.

Spinoza's use of the expression *amor Dei intellectualis* draws on a wide range of Platonic as well as medieval sources. "It is useless to speculate from whom Spinoza took it; it was as common a property of philosophy as the term 'substance,'" Wolfson writes. "He could have taken it from various sources, and had he had no sources to guide him he could have coined it himself to describe what was generally meant by the love of God."[14] Nevertheless, a usual suspect is Leone Ebreo, whose *Dialoghi d'Amore* Spinoza possessed in Spanish translation and from which he derived his views on the superiority of intellectual to passionate love. Another source is often attributed to Maimonides, whose treatment of the love of God combines elements of both the knowledge of the divine attributes and the imitation of God's acts of kindness and charity.[15] But if Spinoza could have taken the idea from a number of sources, he uses it in a distinctive way to depict not just a form of love but a way of life. Intellectual love is the dominant characteristic of what could be called the exemplary life or what is essential for the attainment of complete human perfection.

The rules circumscribing the exemplary life are set out in the fourth chapter of the *TTP*, called "Of the Divine Law." Spinoza is aware that he is using this term in an idiosyncratic sense and takes some pains to define what he means by it. The divine law is not something given through a suprarational revelation. It has nothing to do with a revealed law. Rather the *lex divina* is simply Spinoza's term for the power of nature as a whole. Insofar as human beings are themselves a part of nature, the laws governing and regulating our conduct can be called part of the divine law. The divine law does not indicate some supernatural order of things, but is entirely consonant with the steady and constant operations of nature. Knowledge of God is essentially identical to "the universal laws of nature according to which all things happen and are determined" (*TTP*, iii, 8; III/46).

Spinoza sketches four features of the divine law understood as a system of natural necessity. First, he says, it is "universal or common to all men" because it derives from premises embedded in a common human nature. Second, it is independent of faith in any particular historical narrative or text. Third, it does not require ceremonies or rituals; and fourth, the reward for knowledge of the law is the law itself: "So the sum-total of the divine law, and its highest precept, is to love God as the highest good . . . not from fear of some punishment or penalty, nor from love of some other thing in which we desire to take pleasure. For the idea of God dictates this: that God is our greatest good or that the knowledge and love of God is the ultimate end toward which all our actions are to be directed" (*TTP*, iv, 15: III/61).

The sentiment that knowledge and love of God are the ends toward which all our actions should be directed is reiterated at the end of the *Ethics*. At Vp41 Spinoza distinguishes between "the usual conviction of the multitude" who obey the law out of hope for benefits or fear of punishments and those who obey it as the fulfillment of their rational nature, as an end in itself. This distinction corresponds to two very different states of character. Those determined by hope and fear are essentially passive personalities, reacting to the promise or threat of external incentives. Those who regard the law as an end in itself are rewarded by an increase in their powers of activity and capacity for self-determination. Spinoza associates this heightened state of activity with a condition of blessedness in the final proposition of the work: "Blessedness consists in Love of God, a Love which arises from the third kind of knowledge. So this Love must be related to the Mind *insofar as it acts*. Therefore it is virtue itself" (Vp42d; emphasis added).

The highest injunction of the divine law is, then, to love God before all things. Spinoza denies that this injunction is a burden or a yoke, but when understood correctly is a precept of our own reason. When we love God not from mercenary reasons but as the fulfillment of our rational nature, we are actually participating in the very love by which God loves himself (Vp36). Spinoza identifies intellectual divine love exclusively with the third kind of knowledge or *scientia intuitiva*. Such a love is intellectual because it is based on knowledge of natural causes. It is not a form of mystical intuition incommunicable through ordinary language. Neither is it accessible through prayer or supplication, but derives entirely from our ability to form adequate ideas about the nature of things. "The more we know natural things," Spinoza writes, "the more perfectly do we know God's essence, which is the cause of all things" (*TTP*, iv, 11; III/60). Intellectual divine love describes not just knowledge of facts but of natures. It describes a passionate relationship between the knower and the world.

Spinoza's arguments regarding divine love are further supported by his theory of the eternity of the mind sketched out in the final propositions of the *Ethics*. His "proof" of the eternity of the mind is often taken as evidence that at the end of the book he fell back on traditional dualist and theological beliefs about the immortality of the soul. To be sure, he sometimes writes as if the mind existed before the body and will continue to persist even after the body perishes. "The human mind," he says, "cannot be absolutely destroyed with the body, but something of it remains which is eternal" (Vp23). In the scholium to this proposition, Spinoza makes a remarkable appeal to the reader's "experience" in support of his argument: "There is . . . this idea, which expresses the essence of the body under a species of eternity, a certain mode of thinking, which pertains to the essence of the Mind, and which is necessarily eternal. And though it is impossible that we should recollect that we existed before the Body . . . still, we feel and know by experience that we are eternal. For the Mind feels these things that it conceives in understanding no less than those it has in the memory" (Vp23s).

This proof of the eternity of the mind is supplemented a few propositions later by another, more naturalistic, argument. Earlier in the *Ethics* Spinoza had defended the dependence of the mind on the body. Bodies vary enormously in regard to their internal complexity. The greater and more complex the power of the body, the greater and more complex will be the mind that inhabits it. Spinoza returns to this point again later on: "He who has a body capable of a great many things has a mind whose greatest part is eternal" (Vp39). He adds to this proposition the following clarification: "Because human bodies are capable of a great many things, there is no doubt but what they can be of such a nature that they are related to Minds which have a great knowledge of themselves and of God, and of which the greatest, or chief, part is eternal. So they hardly fear death" (Vp39s).

For an even "clearer understanding" of this passage, Spinoza adds that human life is continual change from one bodily state to another, from childhood to adulthood, from happiness to sadness, and so on. For those organisms with simple bodies that are largely dependent upon "external causes," the mind will have a correspondingly limited capacity, while bodies capable of activity and self-direction will have minds "very much conscious of itself, and of God, and of things" (Vp39s). Still it is not altogether clear why a body capable of a "great many things" necessarily has a mind whose "greatest part" is eternal.

Spinoza's theory of the eternity of the mind has caused fits for those who conceive him as a strict materialist for whom mind and body are one and the same.[16] How can the mind persist after the extinction of the body? Spinoza denies that he is committed to Christian beliefs about personal immortality or an afterlife. Rather, the eternity of the mind is based on the recognition that the contents of our minds cease to be ours alone and become the common property of mind in general. At some level our ideas are not simply our ideas but belong to the common stock of knowledge. Euclid's theorems, for example, are not simply the property of a man named Euclid who lived at a particular time and place, but take on a life of their own that confers a certain eternity on them. In this sense our bodies may cease to exist, but the contents of our minds may live on forever as a part of the knowledge of God or nature.

Despite Spinoza's "proof" of the eternity of the mind, the *Ethics* provides no clear or compelling account of how we can bootstrap ourselves into eternity. Much of the psychology of the work is devoted to showing that the mind cannot exist apart from the body. The mind, Spinoza continually reminds us, is not a separate soul substance but is itself embedded within a network of causal processes; as finite and limited, the mind will always share the limitations of the vessel within which it is contained. The mind is immanently connected to the body, not as a cause that makes the body function or gives it life, but as a part of a complex individuated substance that we call a person or a self. Given the embodied character of the mind, it is hard to see how we can ever rise above our own transitoriness as a finite mode of being to adopt the standpoint of eternity.

Even if we accept that Spinoza's doctrine of the eternity of the mind is not the same as theological doctrines of the immortality of the soul, he still leaves the reader with a host of unanswered questions. Do all minds have a share in eternity or only some? If only some minds do, which ones? Further, if it is not the whole mind but only the "greatest part" that is eternal, what part of the mind is that? Finally, how can the mind be said to partici-pate in eternity if it is fully articulated within nature, within the system of which it is a part? Presumably if nature is eternal, then mind, which is a part of nature, must share in that eternity. But if this is so, then the eternity of the mind pertains not to indi-vidual minds but to mind insofar as it is, along with extension, one of the two primary attributes of being. The *Ethics* seems to embody this ongoing tension between a desire to liberate the mind from the confines of time and the merely human perspec-tive and a keen awareness of the limitations and embeddedness of the mind in a vast network of causal processes.

The Satisfactions of Mind

Intellectual divine love is distinguished from the two previous loves inasmuch as its object, *Deus sive Nature,* is eternal. Un-like the other transient objects of desire, the love of God is freed from the powers of the imagination and the needs of the body. It is based on a union of the mind with its object. Most importantly, this kind of love represents a gain in human self-knowledge. The love of God is ultimately a form of self-love. If all things are in God, then to love God is to love those things that participate in God. "He who understands himself and his affects clearly and distinctly loves God," we read at Vp15, "and does so the more, the more he understands himself and his af-fects." In other words, the more we understand nature, the better we understand ourselves, and the more we understand ourselves, the better we understand nature. The *Ethics* likens this kind of self-knowledge to a form of salvation or blessedness because it liberates the knower from dependence on unrefined passions and emotions and puts the mind in touch with something eternal.

Spinoza describes this type of love as affecting a kind of Pla-tonic turning of the soul away from the transient toward the absolute: "From what we have said, we easily conceive what clear and distinct knowledge—and especially that third kind of knowledge whose foundation is the knowledge of God itself—can accomplish against the affects. Insofar as the affects are passions, if clear and distinct knowledge does not absolutely remove them, at least it brings it about that they constitute the smallest part of the Mind. And then it begets a love toward a thing immutable and eternal, which we really fully possess, and which therefore cannot be tainted by any of the vices which are in ordinary love, but can always be greater and greater, and occupy the greatest part of the Mind, and affect it extensively" (Vp20s).

Spinoza sometimes writes as if there is a Stoic dimension to intellectual divine love. Love of God requires an acceptance of how things are, a recognition of and submission to necessity. He is often taken to task for believing that freedom is only the recognition of necessity. From the third kind of knowledge is said to arise "the greatest satisfaction of mind" (*mentis acquiescentia*) (Vp27). Yet far from extolling a Stoic acquiescence (*ataraxia*), the *Ethics* everywhere celebrates the intensely held feelings of joy that come with the love of God. Throughout this part of the work, Spinoza continually refers to feelings of pleasure (*titillatio*) and joy (*laetitia*) that come from the contemplation of God: "From this kind of knowledge, there necessarily arises intellectual Love of God. For from this kind of knowledge, there arises Joy, accompanied by the idea of God as its cause, i.e., Love of God, not insofar as we imagine him at present, but insofar as we understand God to be eternal. And this is what I call intellectual love of God" (Vp32c).

Spinoza explicates his understanding of the intellectual love of God by means of the biblical term for glory: "Our salvation, or blessedness, or freedom, consists viz. in a constant and eternal love of God or in God's love for men. And this love or blessedness is called Glory in the Sacred Scriptures—not without reason" (Vp36s). Now the biblical term for glory, *kabod,* appears in almost two hundred places in the Hebrew Bible, although it is not clear to which of the many uses of the term Spinoza may be referring. It has been argued that this is a reference to the passage "the whole earth is full of His glory" (Isaiah 6:3). Wolfson maintains that we must look for a passage in which glory is associated with love and joy and this he thinks he has discovered in Psalms 16:9: "Therefore, my heart is glad, and my glory rejoiceth; My flesh also dwelleth in safety." According to Ibn Ezra's commentary on this passage, in the phrase "my glory rejoiceth" glory refers to the rational soul. This use of glory is further confirmed by Psalms 73:24, which reads: "Thou dost guide me with thy counsel, and afterward thou wilt receive me to glory."[17]

Recently, Zev Harvey has argued that the reference to glory at Vp36 is more likely a reference to Isaiah 58:8: "Your righteousness shall go before you, the glory of the Lord shall be your rear guard."[18] Maimonides cites this passage in the *Guide of the Perplexed* to indicate the intense feeling of passionate joy that accompanies the love of God. Commenting on this passage, Maimonides writes: "After having reached this condition of enduring permanence, that intellect remains in one and the same state, the impediment that sometimes screened him off having been removed. And he will remain permanently in that state of intense pleasure, which does not belong to the genus of bodily pleasures, as we have explained in our compilations and as others have explained before us" (III/51). Further evidence for this reading is provided by Spinoza himself, who cites Isaiah 58:8 in the *TTP* to confirm his own views on the divine law: "In return for the freeing of the oppressed and for charity, the prophet promises a healthy mind in a healthy body and the glory of the Lord after death" (*TTP,* v, 10; III/71).

Spinoza's reference to the "Sacred Scriptures" is rare in the *Ethics* (cf. IVp68s). Part five is certainly that part of the book that lends itself to more orthodox readings. However, an overly theological interpretation of his treatment of the themes of immortality and eternal beatitude can just as easily obscure the worldly and humanistic interpretation of these themes. The passage about the "Sacred Scriptures" referred to above continues as follows: "For whether this Love is related to God or to the Mind, it can rightly be called satisfaction of mind, which is really not distinguished from Glory" (Vp36s). Spinoza here references his earlier definitions of praise and esteem. "Self-esteem is a joy born of the fact that a man considers himself and his own power of acting" and "Love of esteem is a joy accompanied by the idea of some action of ours which we imagine that others praise" (IIIdef.aff 25, 30). In other words, glory, the love of self, is the greatest pleasure a person can enjoy, while the biblical virtues of repentance and humility are cast as evils (IVp53, 54).

Spinoza recognizes that self-esteem is not a vice, but is related to a kind of noble ambition for recognition and distinction. Although he defines ambition as an "*excessive* desire for esteem," he also acknowledges that it is the desire "by which all the affects are encouraged and strengthened": "For as long as a man is bound by any desire, he must at the same time be bound by this one. As Cicero says, Every man is led by love of esteem, and the more so, the better he is. Even the philosophers who write books on how esteem is to be disdained put their names to these works" (IIIdef.aff44; emphasis added).

The emphasis on the love of glory, joy, ambition, and self-esteem gives the *Ethics* both a liberatory and redemptive tone quite at odds with the spirit of Stoicism. The Stoic may aspire to a sort of contemplative autonomy brought about by the control of the passions, but this is a far cry from Spinoza's exaltation of life. Joy is related to an increase in our powers of activity (Vp42d). Stoicism is based on a ruthless suppression of the passions, while Spinoza's conception of well-being elevates the emotions of gladness (*gaudium*) and cheerfulness (*hilaritas*) to constitutive aspects of virtue. To be sure, joy is a passion, but Spinoza affirms the existence of active emotions. The *amor Dei intellectualis* describes an active passionate relationship between the knower and the world. It is not a static fund of information but an activity that engages both our intellectual and emotional powers.

There remains a puzzle regarding the relation between intellectual divine love and the love for other human beings. The issue raised in the final propositions of part five is the old question of the relation between the moral and intellectual virtues. Is the love of God an ultimately solitary activity that leaves the knower no room or time for relations with, to say nothing of love for, other finite embodied creatures? Or does the love of God encourage us to seek out other beings in relations of love and friendship? Does intellectual love of God make us lovers of the world or does it entail a retreat from human attachments into a life of solitary contemplation? In short, does complete rationality require the companionship of others or is it best achieved when we have essentially freed ourselves from dependence upon society? How one answers these questions will determine what kind of life Spinoza believes one should live.

There is considerable evidence to suggest that the love of God is intended to strengthen our connectedness to others. "This love toward God," he writes, "is the highest good which we can want from the dictate of reason, and is common to all men; we desire that all should enjoy it" (Vp2od). Spinoza here suggests that we all aspire to the love of God even if we do not realize it, and that this aspiration includes a desire that everyone should participate in it. The love of God is only truly good if it is shared with others. The view is substantiated by the passage cited earlier from the *TIE*, where Spinoza writes that not only is the mind's union with nature to be sought, but so is the goal that "many acquire it with me" (*TIE*, xiv; II/8). A part of my happiness is that others agree with me in intellect and desire. There is on this view an ultimately unitary conception of the human good as something in which all rational persons can share. On this reading, the highest end, the intellectual love of God, is best realized as part of a community of reasoners or learners, each of whom contributes to the enhancement of the common store of adequate ideas. People working in harmony with one another are in a sense freer and more powerful than any one person operating alone.

At the same time, this is not Spinoza's last word on the subject. The *Ethics* as a whole can be seen as an ascent from lesser to more adequate ideas of God and freedom. It is a work that begins with the most general properties of the cosmos and ends with an intensely private intellectual experience. The collaboration with other learners is only a step to the highest kind of love. At the pinnacle of the work can be found a vision of intellectual divine love that consists of emancipation not only from the passions and affects but from the needs and society of others. This is the point in the *Ethics* at which Spinoza seems closest to Maimonides's appreciation of the virtues of the solitary. At the end of the *Guide* Maimonides considers the philosopher as a passionate lover of God. The passionate lover is one who devotes himself entirely to reflection on God's nature and attributes and does so as far as possible apart from the company of others: "Thus it is clear that after apprehension, total devotion to Him and the employment of intellectual thought in constantly loving Him should be aimed at. Mostly this is achieved in solitude and isolation. Hence every excellent man stays frequently in solitude and does not meet anyone unless it is necessary" (III/51).

This all-consuming passion excludes every other desire and is exhibited, according to Maimonides, especially at night: "When, however, you are alone with yourself and no one else is there and while you lie awake upon your bed you should take great care during these precious times not to set your thought to work on anything other than that intellectual worship consisting in nearness to God and being in His presence in that true reality that I have made known to you and not by way of affections of the imagination" (III/51).

Like Maimonides, Spinoza is struck by an ideal of divine love that is intensely personal. Such a love is achieved in solitude without the necessity of another. To use another Platonic metaphor, Spinoza provides a conception of liberation from the cave of the imagination and the needs of the body, but no compelling justification for why we should feel obligated to others except out of motives of sheer utility. It is hardly surprising that this idea of the self liberated from obligations to the community has found more favor among novelists and artists than among moral philosophers, who have often been shocked by Spinoza's apparent immoralism.[19]

It is not at all unreasonable to identify Spinoza's *amor Dei intellectualis* with the life of the solitary. We cannot entirely disassociate this conception of liberation from Spinoza's own life, which he devoted almost single-mindedly to the cultivation of his independence from his community and its traditions. The love of God seems to require a life so completely and passionately absorbed in the object of one's study as to leave virtually no time to cultivate relations with others. To be sure, he urges us to seek out the company of others and to live with them peaceably and sociably, but largely as a means to increase one's own sense of power. Love and friendship, marriage and sexuality, are encouraged, but as means to our rational self-sufficiency. As is the case with all truly great thinkers, Spinoza's conception of freedom of mind comes with a price tag. His idea of human perfection, the rational love of God, is extremely private, not to say utterly solitary. The concluding sentence of the *Ethics* confirms this point: "All things excellent are as difficult as they are rare" (Vp42s).

7

The Authority of Reason

The *Ethics* is a singular book written by someone who valued his singularity. Even the title of the book remains something of a mystery, for it is a work that contains very few of what we would call ethical propositions. As a result, although Spinoza's influence has been widespread, there are very few people today who would call themselves Spinozists, or, if they do, they are happy to recognize or appropriate one aspect of Spinoza's thought and declare allegiance to it while ignoring or disavowing the others. In a world where there are still Platonists, Aristotelians, Thomists, Kantians, and even Marxists, the legacy of Spinoza remains highly contested and Spinoza himself a lonely figure in the history of moral and political philosophy. He remains, in the phrase of Antonio Negri, a "savage anomaly."[1] What he has done is to bequeath a series of problems to think through, the most important of which concerns the authority of reason to govern life and thought.

That the *Ethics* is regarded as a classic work of philosophical rationalism goes without saying. The question concerns the scope and limits of reason. There are those, primarily the students of Hume and Kant, who believe that attempts like Spinoza's to deduce what is from the postulates or categories of pure reason is an inherently futile enterprise, that the issues with which the *Ethics* deals are better left to empirical or experimental science, that we can learn nothing valuable about the world from the deductive series of propositions that constitutes the work. This view, widespread among logical empiricists and positivists of various types, typically contrasts what it believes to be Spinoza's closed, dogmatic system of metaphysics to the open, skeptical, and experimental spirit of the modern sciences. This contrast is false to the extent that it overlooks the experiential basis of the *Ethics* and the extent to which the modern sciences often take for granted and presuppose philosophical assumptions derived from Spinoza. The idea that nature is a single homogeneous system without beginning or purpose is an assumption that scientists take for granted in their work, in large part due to the success of the *Ethics* and other works of early modern philosophy. The challenge posed by the book is not to the authority of modern science, for which Spinoza is at least in some sense responsible, but to the claims of Scripture or orthodoxy, whose authority he set out to undercut.

The *Ethics* stands or falls by its claim to refute the authority of biblical orthodoxy, with its belief in such things as the creation of the world, the revealed character of truth, and the possibility of miracles. The comprehensive goal of the work is to replace the God of orthodoxy with the light of reason as the authoritative guide to life, to replace the opening chapters of the book of Genesis with the opening definitions and axioms of the *Ethics* as the definitive account of the nature and origins of the universe. The *Ethics* is poorly understood, or rather it is not understood at all, unless it is seen as casting the initial broadside in the Enlightenment's war against orthodoxy. It carries on and perpetuates the "theologico-political" struggle that Spinoza had inaugurated in the *TTP*. The *Ethics* is an appendage to the *TTP* and builds on, even as it deepens, its arguments against the tradition of scriptural hermeneutics. The question is whether Spinoza's refutation of orthodoxy is successful or if it is ultimately a castle built on sand.

Jacobi's Affirmation of Faith

The first person to indicate the problematic status of Spinoza's rationalism was F. H. Jacobi. Jacobi was a minor figure of the German Counter-Enlightenment who, along with Hamann and Herder, was the principal instigator of the famous *Pantheismus-streit* or the pantheism dispute that raged throughout Germany in the 1780s and 1790s.[2] The pantheism debate was occasioned by the rehabilitation of the reputation of Spinoza in Germany in the last quarter of the eighteenth century. Although he had been anathematized for approximately a century after his death, the fortunes of Spinoza took a dramatic turn once it was revealed that Gotthold Lessing had been a secret admirer and even a closet Spinozist for much of his life. The pantheism debate, however, was much more than a dispute over the reputation of Spinoza or over the Lessing's alleged Spinozism. It was at bottom a debate about the authority of reason.

Jacobi and the Romantics were not simply opposed to reason, as they are often made out. They were opposed to the Enlightenment's conception of sufficient reason. By the principle of sufficient reason is meant that for any possible state of affairs there are reasons capable of explaining it. To accept the principle of sufficient reason is, then, tantamount to accepting Spinoza's view that everything that is happens for a reason and that to understand that reason is to see that events could not have happened otherwise. It is ultimately equivalent to accepting some form of determinism according to which for every event, A, there must be some prior event, B, that is sufficient to explain A. Whether this is an accurate depiction of Spinoza's understanding is not the issue. The point for the Romantics is that accepting the principle of sufficient reason meant denying that we are free and responsible agents who can choose to do this rather than that on the basis of our free will and understanding.

The Romantic critique of reason was, therefore, less an epistemological than a moral one. Its aim was ultimately to save the possibility of morality from all forms of determinism.

In the Romantics' crusade against the Spinozist principle of sufficient reason, they acquired an unlikely ally in David Hume.[3] In the *Treatise of Human Nature* Hume had demonstrated that reason has a far more restricted scope than the Enlightenment had alleged. Applying reason to itself, Hume contended that there are no necessary or causal relations between events. That we see the sun rise in the morning and set at night is not a necessary truth of reason. It is at most an observed regularity, but there are no sufficient reasons capable of explaining it. At most what we believe to be universal and necessary laws are no more than judgments made on the basis of habit, custom, and experience. The truths of reason may be applicable to limited areas of thought like mathematics and logic, but to the vast areas of human experience there are no necessary consequences following from the nature of things, only loosely associated sequences of events. The most we are entitled to say is that it is probable that events will occur in the future as they have in the past; there is no necessity for them to do so. In some respect these claims seem modest enough, but for the Romantics, Hume's deconstruction of the claims of reason came as a liberation. They extended his claim to mean that the way we perceive and understand the world is not the product of reason, but of faith.

Jacobi achieved notoriety after publishing his *Letters to Herr Moses Mendelssohn Concerning the Doctrine of Spinoza* (1785).[4] The *Letters* took the form of a series of conversations between the author and G. E. Lessing, in which the latter allegedly professed to being a disciple of Spinoza. According to the account of these conversations, not published until after Lessing's death, Jacobi told how he journeyed to Wolfenbuttel to discover Lessing's opinions on a range of philosophical and theological topics.

Among the topics the two men discussed was a copy of Goethe's then-unpublished poem "Prometheus." After reading the poem Jacobi reports the following exchange:

> *Jacobi:* Do you know the poem?
>
> *Lessing:* The poem I have never seen before; but I think it is good.
>
> *Jacobi:* It is good in its kind, I agree; otherwise I would not have shown it to you.
>
> *Lessing:* I mean it is good in a different way . . . The point of view from which the poem is treated is my own point of view . . . The orthodox concepts of the Divinity are no longer for me; I cannot stomach them. *Hen kai pan!* I know of nothing else. (*MPW,* 187)

Jacobi professed to express surprise at Lessing's endorsement of the philosophical principle of pantheism (*Hen kai pan*) or the belief that God is immanent in the world. When the two spoke again the next day, Lessing continued his defense of Spinozism as follows:

> *Lessing:* I have come to talk to you about my *hen kai pan*. Yesterday you were frightened.
>
> *Jacobi:* You surprised me, and I may indeed have blushed and gone pale, for I felt bewilderment in me. Fright it was not. To be sure, there is nothing that I would have suspected less, than to find a Spinozist or a pantheist in you. And you blurted it out to me so suddenly. In the main I had come to get help from you against Spinoza.
>
> *Lessing:* Oh, so you do know him?
>
> *Jacobi:* I think I know him as only very few can know him.

Lessing: Then there is no help for you. Become his
friend all the way instead. There is no other philosophy than the philosophy of Spinoza. (*MPW,*
187)

The issue of Lessing's Spinozism is hardly the point. The
point at issue is Jacobi's belief that a pantheistic system, a religion of divine immanence, leads not only to atheism but to
a radical determinism with no room for human freedom and
agency. The result is to turn human beings into passive effects
of a system of immanent causality rather than self-governing
agents capable of initiating new chains of causality. Jacobi takes
this to mean that in Spinoza's world there can be no "I" who
acts or thinks, but only a conjuncture of forces governed by the
same laws that govern everything. Jacobi expresses this opinion
in a lengthy rejoinder:

> The whole thing comes down to this: from fatalism
> I immediately conclude against fatalism and every-
> thing connected with it. If there are only efficient,
> but no final, causes, then the only function that the
> faculty of thought has in the whole of nature is that
> of observer; its proper business is to accompany the
> mechanism of the efficient causes. The conversation
> that we are now having together is only an affair
> of our bodies; and the whole content of the con-
> versation, analyzed into its elements, is extension,
> movement, degree of velocity, together with their
> concepts, and the concepts of these concepts. The
> inventor of the clock did not ultimately invent it;
> he only witnessed its coming to be out of blindly
> self-developing forces. So too Raphael, when he
> sketched the *School of Athens,* and Lessing, when he

composed his *Nathan*. The same goes for all philosophizing, arts, forms of governance, sea and land
wars—in brief, for everything possible. (*MPW,* 189)

Jacobi's point is that if Spinoza and the principle of sufficient
reason are correct, then the inevitable result is not only determinism but fatalism and atheism, in other words a complete
denial of human agency and freedom. Once again, this is not
intended to be simply an attack on Spinoza's *Ethics* but an attack on all systems of rationalistic metaphysics. While Hume
had chastised reason in order to show that our moral beliefs were
rooted in certain preexisting natural sentiments, Jacobi and the
Romantics limited reason in order to make room for faith. No
more than Spinoza did Jacobi mean by faith belief in the God
of Scripture. Faith meant for him simply the place at which
all rational demonstration came to an end. All argument rests
on certain assumption and beliefs about what counts as true or
valid. My belief that a glass of water is on the table is possible
because of certain assumptions I make about the veracity of per-
ception and the nature of physical reality. But these assumptions
cannot in turn be justified in terms of the beliefs they validate
without falling into circularity. Reason is incapable of establishing its own premises. This means for Jacobi that all of our assumptions—the assumption that everything is determined no
less than the assumption that we possess free will and choice—
rest ultimately on an act of faith. Jacobi's answer to Spinozistic
determinism is his concept of the *salto mortale,* a death-defying
leap of faith confirming a belief in freedom and individual moral
responsibility.

Jacobi's brief against Spinoza is ultimately carried out in defense of morality. Spinozistic determinism, like all systems of
philosophical rationalism, undermines faith, the sole basis for
morality, Jacobi believed. Jacobi's case was not directed at Spi-

noza ad hominem, but rather against all philosophical systems, of which the *Ethics* was simply the limiting example. The *Ethics* had taken the rationalism of all philosophy and simply pushed it to its outer limits. Rationalism can only lead to a loss of faith and hence to skepticism and indecision, a moral posture that he was the first to call *Nihilismus* (*MPW,* 519). Although Jacobi carried out his critique of rationalism in the name of Christianity, he ultimately saw it as applicable to all forms of moral belief. Moral beliefs and commitments require faith, not reason. Reason can analyze and criticize, but morality requires belief, at a minimum belief in human freedom and individual responsibility. Jacobi is not saying that morality can dispense with reason. He is not an irrationalist, although he sometimes looks like one. He is arguing, rather, that reason presupposes faith or choice and that choice presupposes the primacy of ourselves as moral agents. The difference between freedom and determinism is not a theoretical matter, a question of truth; it is a moral question, a matter of choice between two competing systems. We can choose to affirm our freedom through a leap of faith or we can deny it. The one thing we cannot do is to ignore it altogether.

Strauss's "Theologico-Political Predicament"

The issue raised in Jacobi's *Letters* was developed at length by Leo Strauss, the twentieth century's most profound critic of Spinoza. Strauss had written a doctoral dissertation in 1921 on the epistemology of Jacobi in Hamburg under the direction of the Kantian philosopher Ernst Cassirer.[5] He well understood the challenge to rationalism posed by the Jacobian critique of the Enlightenment, but unlike Jacobi, Strauss was less concerned with defending the possibility of faith than with what he termed orthodoxy. The claims of orthodoxy—revelation, miracles, the immutability of the law—had all been shaken by Spinoza and the radical Enlightenment that he helped to launch. This challenge was taken up in Strauss's first book, *Spinoza's Critique of Religion* (1930).[6] The challenge to orthodoxy posed by Spinoza was turned by Strauss into nothing less than the fate of modern Judaism torn between a fundamental choice: either join the party of Spinoza and the radical Enlightenment with its belief in the death of God or return to orthodoxy and all that it entails. Nothing less was at stake.[7]

In the preface to the English translation of his Spinoza book, written over thirty years later, Strauss describes himself as "a young Jew born and raised in Germany who found himself in the grips of a theologico-political predicament" (*LAM*, 224). The most immediate and urgent manifestation of this dilemma was the tenuous situation of the Jews in Weimar. Weimar was a republic, a liberal democracy that came into being in that brief period between the Treaty of Versailles and the Reichstag fire. Weimar was a product of the French Revolution and the Enlightenment but was also connected to the home of Goethe and the tradition of German Idealism, which contributed to its "moderate, nonradical character." As such Weimar struck a balance between dedication to the principles of 1789 and dedication to the highest German tradition (*LAM*, 225).

The problem with Weimar was in the first instance its weakness and instability. The weakness of Weimar became most evident not with the economic crisis of 1929—other democracies faced similar economic problems—but with its inability to protect the Jews. This dilemma was made all the more acute because the Jews of Germany, more than Jews of any other nation, had put their faith in liberal democracy to provide a solution to the "Jewish Question." Liberal democracy was understood as the regime devoted to ending persecution not only of Jews but of all religious and ethnic minorities. Liberal democracy was the first political regime to grant full citizenship and equal rights to Jews while recognizing their right to remain Jews. If for this reason only, the assassination of Walter Rathenau, the Jewish minister of foreign affairs, in 1922 proved a moment of profound crisis.

The dilemma of modern Jewry has a long genealogy going back before Weimar to the time of Spinoza. Spinoza was to Strauss and many of his generation the first example of the modern Jew. Spinoza championed not only a break with orthodoxy and the burdens of the ceremonial law, but was the first Jewish thinker to endorse liberal democracy in something like its modern form (*LAM*, 246). Although Spinoza had been anathematized by the Jewish community of Amsterdam, he was subsequently canonized by generations of Jewish modernists, who celebrated him not only for showing the way out of the ghetto but for establishing a new kind of secular religion and culture based on the highest aspirations of the educated middle class. Spinoza is depicted by Strauss as nothing short of the prophet of a new kind of ethical culture: "He thus showed the way toward a new religion or religiousness which was to inspire a wholly new kind of society, a new kind of Church. He became the sole father of that new Church which was to be universal in fact, and not merely in claim as other churches, because its foundation was no longer any positive revelation—a Church whose rulers were not priests or pastors, but philosophers and artists and whose flock were the circles of culture and property" (*LAM*, 241).

In particular Spinoza opened the door to liberal democracy, a society that was neither Christian nor Jewish but above or impervious to each. Central to the liberal solution to the theologico-political predicament was the distinction between public and private and the belief that religion belonged exclusively to the private sphere of life. Henceforth religion would be deprived of the tools of force and coercion and turned into a matter of conscience and private belief, something quite different from the authoritative character of the law. This effort to divest religion of its public character was to have far-ranging consequences: "The millennial antagonism between Judaism and Christianity was about to disappear. The new Church would transform Jews and Christians into human beings — into human beings of a certain kind: cultured human beings, human beings who, because they possessed science and art, did not need religion in addition. The new society, constituted by an aspiration common to all its members toward the True, the Good, and the Beautiful, emancipated the Jews in Germany. Spinoza became the symbol of that emancipation which was to be not only emancipation but secular redemption. In Spinoza, a thinker and a saint who was both a Jew and a Christian and hence neither, all cultured families of the earth, it was hoped, would be blessed" (*LAM*, 242).

Strauss's critique of Spinoza is twofold: Jewish and philosophical. As a Jewish thinker, Strauss regards Spinoza as "the greatest man of Jewish origin who had openly denied the truth of Judaism and had ceased to belong to the Jewish people without becoming a Christian" (*LAM*, 239). The God of Spinoza was certainly not the God of orthodoxy, but neither was it the God of the German Romantics. Spinoza's God is that of "the hardheaded, not to say hardhearted, pupil of Machiavelli": "The biblical God forms light and creates darkness, makes peace and creates evil; Spinoza's God is simply beyond good and evil. God's might is His right, and therefore the power of every being is as such its right; Spinoza lifts Machiavellianism to theological heights. Good and evil differ only from a merely human point of view; theologically the distinction is meaningless. The evil passions are evil only with a view to human utility; in themselves they show forth the might and right of God no less than other things which we admire and by the contemplation of which we are delighted" (*LAM*, 242–43).

In the same paragraph this "Machiavellian" deity is in turn

given a Nietzschean twist: "All human acts are modes of the one God who possesses infinitely many attributes each of which is infinite and only two of which are known to us, who is therefore a mysterious God whose mysterious love reveals itself in eternally and necessarily bringing forth love and hatred, nobility and baseness, saintliness and depravity, and who is infinitely lovable not in spite but because of His infinite power beyond good and evil" (*LAM*, 243).

Strauss does not reject out of hand the Spinozist conception of God. If Spinoza offered the possibility of emancipation in a secular liberal society, so too did he hold out the possibility of reconstituting a Jewish state. The Torah, he taught, just like all ostensibly revealed works, is in fact a human book. The Torah is not "from heaven" but is a product of the Jewish mind or the Jewish nation. Judaism, like all religions, is a human invention designed to secure worldly happiness and well-being. Moses was not a prophet to whom God spoke, but a statesman and political leader who used prophetic language to found and maintain a nation.

The Jewish religion was thus from the beginning a political religion founded by Moses to instill obedience to law. Spinoza holds out the possibility that what Moses did in the past can under new circumstances be done again. Strauss quotes from the third chapter of the *TTP* to indicate Spinoza's call for an independent Jewish state: "Indeed, if the foundations of the religion did not effeminate their hearts, I would absolutely believe that some day, given the opportunity, they will set up their state again and that God will choose them anew, so changeable are human affairs" (*LAM*, 229; translation modified). On the basis of this sentence, Strauss assigns to Spinoza an honored role among the founders of political Zionism.

In a number of places Strauss alludes to the fact that he was a political Zionist in his youth and until the end of his life regarded it as a highly "honorable" solution to the Jewish Question. However, the appropriation of Spinoza for the cause of political Zionism could not but prove doubtful from the standpoint of orthodoxy. As the passage just quoted indicates, Zionism ascribes responsibility for establishing a state not to prayer or patient waiting for the messiah, but to the force of one's own arms, fighting. It turns responsibility for the security and even the redemption of the Jewish people into a purely human, political problem. Works like Herzel's *Judenstaat* or Pinsker's *Auto-emanzipation* understood the fate of the Jews as having nothing to do with divine promises but with power politics pure and simple. The use of human, even crudely political, means to attain an end previously reserved for God is a further example of Strauss's complaint that Spinoza raised Machiavellianism to "theological heights."

The Zionist solution to the Jewish Question appears to preserve Jews even at the expense of Judaism, something Strauss calls "a most dangerous game": "Spinoza may have hated Judaism; he did not hate the Jewish people. However bad a Jew he may have been in all other respects, he thought of the liberation of the Jews in the only way in which he could think of it, given his philosophy. But precisely if this is so, we must stress all the more the fact that the manner in which he sets forth his proposal—to say nothing of the proposal itself—is Machiavellian: the humanitarian end seems to justify every means; he plays a most dangerous game; his procedure is as much beyond good and evil as his God" (*LAM*, 246).

The Jewish critique of Spinoza points to a second critique, which cuts to the core of the ancient problem of faith and reason. The *Ethics* is based on the assumption that human reason alone can give a theoretically and practically satisfying explanation of nature, of everything that is. This is the principle of sufficient reason, that there is nothing in the world (or outside of it) that escapes the powers of human rationality. The question is whether the *Ethics* proves this claim or merely begs the question. Strauss appears to doubt whether the premises of orthodoxy have been or ever can be refuted by reason alone. "The *Ethics*," he writes, "thus begs the decisive question—the question as to whether the clear and distinct account is as such true and not merely a *plausible hypothesis*" (*LAM*, 254: emphasis added). The merely "hypothetical" character of the *Ethics* would seem to cast doubt on its claims to provide the one true or necessary account of the whole.

The apparent failure of Spinoza to refute orthodoxy stems in large part from the incommensurability of their premises. "The genuine refutation of orthodoxy," Strauss writes, "would require the proof that the world and human life are perfectly intelligible without the assumption of a mysterious God" (*LAM*, 254). But the assumption of an unfathomable mysterious God, whose ways are not our ways, is "irrefutable" at least by reason. The Enlightenment's recourse to such devices as mockery and ridicule in their critique of religion provides an "indirect proof" of the failure to penetrate the bridgehead of orthodoxy. The difference, then, between Spinoza and even the most fundamentalistic orthodoxy is not based on truth, but on an act of will or faith.

The conflict between faith and reason, Jerusalem and Athens, is in the final instance a moral, not a theoretical, choice: "Spinoza's *Ethics* attempts to be the system, but it does not succeed; the clear and distinct account of everything which it presents remains fundamentally hypothetical. As a consequence, its cognitive status is not different from that of the orthodox account. Certain it is that Spinoza cannot legitimately deny the possibility of revelation. But to grant that revelation is possible means to grant that the philosophic account and the philosophic way of life are not necessarily, not evidently, the true account and the right way of life: philosophy, the quest for evident and necessary knowledge, rests itself on an unevident decision, on an act of will, *just as faith*" (*LAM*, 255; emphasis added).

The critique of philosophy contained in the above passage is far-reaching. There is no proposition more central to the *Ethics* as a whole than that the mind can aspire to knowledge of nature (= God) and therefore that there is nothing in nature that is not susceptible to a rational explanation. This is the principle of rational sufficiency. However, philosophy that aspires to provide a rational account of nature, of everything that is, itself rests on an act of will, on an "unevident decision." Philosophy that attempts to explain everything cannot account for itself. The idea that philosophy or reason rests on a prior act of faith is obviously not damaging to the standpoint of orthodoxy, which assumes that the choice between good and evil rests on a decision whose origin is in the will. It is the standpoint of philosophy, or at least that of the *Ethics*, that is compromised, perhaps fatally, by this awareness.

There is finally a "Pascalian" or Jacobian flavor to Strauss's claim that rational philosophy rests on a mysterious leap of faith. The implication is that philosophy is inferior to faith because philosophy is unwilling to recognize that it rests on faith, on an act of will. In this respect philosophy flunks the test of "intellectual probity," which Strauss, following Nietzsche, defines as "the willingness to look man's forsakenness in its face, being the courage to welcome the most terrible truth" (*LAM*, 256). Apparently philosophy is unwilling to look itself in the face and consider the most terrible truth. Spinoza's claim to overcome orthodoxy radically cannot overcome the fact that the basis of his critique rests on an act of will, of arbitrary subjectivity. There appears to be no critical necessity for philosophy, only critical necessity within philosophy. At the root of all philosophy stands a stark epistemic abyss where reason simply comes to an end. Strauss here endorses the view of Wittgenstein, another of the great "fideists" of modernity—not, to be sure, the Wittgenstein of the *Philosophical Investigation* but of the Spinoza-inspired *Tractatus Logico-Philosophicus*, which concludes with the words: "Whereof we cannot speak, thereof we must keep silent."[8]

Like Jacobi, Strauss argued that our situation is one of radical existential choice, either for orthodoxy, revealed faith, or resolute atheism. There is no third way. In the conflict between faith and reason, Jacobi clearly took the side of faith. Only a radical leap of faith could affirm life and our status as moral agents. But the subordination of philosophy to theology or, what comes to the same thing, reason to revelation, was not for Strauss, as it was for Jacobi, a cause for celebration. He regarded the conflict between these two alternatives as the source of a genuine paradox. "The victory of orthodoxy through the self-destruction of rational philosophy was not an unmitigated blessing," he wrote (*LAM*, 256).

Although Strauss often presents himself as a defender of morality against philosophy, he is even more alive to the threats to philosophy and rational truth posed by the claims of morality. Uncriticized or unchastened by reason, the return of orthodoxy could only lead to fanaticism and obscurantism. The victory of orthodoxy would likely mean the victory not of Jewish orthodoxy but of orthodoxy in general. This opens up the possibility of a world of competing orthodoxies, of a plurality of revealed faiths, each engaged in a life and death struggle for recognition and power. A bad situation is made even worse when some superstitions claim for themselves the mantle of science, either in the Marxian doctrine of class struggle or the Nietzschean form of the will to power. In such a world the first victim of orthodoxy will be the truth. "Other observations and experiences," Strauss averred, "confirmed the suspicion that it would be unwise to say farewell to reason" (*LAM*, 257).

The conflict between faith and reason does not result in nihilism or a paralysis of the will, as Jacobi believed; still less did it authorize some grand synthesis that would provide the common basis for faith and reason and yet be superior to both. Strauss was highly skeptical of all such efforts at harmonization because they detracted from the original power of each. The task is to keep alive the tension or conflict between faith and reason. This conflict between the Bible and philosophical notions of the good life are said by Strauss to provide the "core" or "nerve" of Western intellectual history. The philosophy of Spinoza, perhaps more than that of any other individual, allows us to think through this conflict by taking seriously one side of the tension and thus bringing us to the brink of the other. The answer to the *Ethics* is neither an uncritical endorsement of rationalism nor an equally uncritical endorsement of faith, but rather an attentiveness to both while remaining open to each, as Strauss stresses: "No one can be both a philosopher and a theologian, nor, for that matter, some possibility which transcends the conflict between philosophy and theology, or pretends to be a synthesis of both. But every one of us can be and ought to be either one or the other, the philosopher open to the challenge of theology or the theologian open to the challenge of philosophy."[9]

Philosophy as a Way of Life

The *Ethics* gives to modernity one of its boldest and most articulate expressions. According to Spinoza's formulation, there is no pattern for human life set either by God (revelation), nature, custom, or tradition. We may be natural beings insofar as we are fully articulated into the overall structure of nature, but nature itself sets no ends of purposes for human life. If there is no preexisting pattern, then it is up to us to create one. The geometrical method of the *Ethics* represented for Spinoza precisely such a model of human self-making, a construction of the mind that could serve as an expression of human power and freedom. Mathematics was for him not so much the ultimate form of knowledge as an expression of human creativity and the moral imagination.

The *Ethics* is of special interest today because it remains a founding document of modern democratic individualism. It is the first systematic attempt to work out the psychology and ethics of the modern democratic soul. The first and most fundamental aspect of the *Ethics* is the desire for freedom, as an aspect of both individual psychology and political institutions. The free individual is someone capable of acting on and for reasons, whose actions are an intelligible response to an understood situation. Freedom means the ability to act rationally, where this means that our activities are self-determined and not simply the outcome of unconscious or mechanical patterns or processes. The free person is not one, however, who stands alone and apart from the needs of others. Freedom is ultimately achieved only in a society of individuals who have joined with one another, first for the sake of securing peace and security but ultimately for the purpose of enhancing their powers of agency and self-direction. The free society will be a democracy in which each person has some say in the creation of the laws under which they choose to live, one in which men and women live under conditions for which they must take responsibility. The free society will be the responsible society.

Spinoza's is in many respects a bleak and loveless view of the universe in which the individual is forced to confront his solitude before an unimaginably large empty space. The willingness to view the human situation without recourse either to metaphysical comfort or to despair constitutes a new kind of bravery, which Spinoza calls *fortitudo* or strength of character—what Nietzsche later described as intellectual probity. Whether this probity founders on the shoals of its own rationalism, as Jacobi

and Strauss later maintained, does not settle the moral and political problem. Above all, *fortitudo* is the virtue of the free individual, someone who certainly understands the causal context of
his or her situation but who uses this knowledge to act resolutely
and responsibly. Spinoza underscores especially the inner quality
of this virtue. It is not dependent on the recognition or good
opinion of others, but derives from the good opinion we have
of ourselves. It could be called self-esteem properly understood.
This is the first virtue of the new democratic individual.

The *Ethics* is, above all, a great work of moral pedagogy. It
is addressed to anyone who suffers—and who doesn't?—from
mental confusion, frustration, and emotional conflict. It is a virtual guide for the perplexed. Its claim is to emancipate the reader
from *fluctuatio animi,* vacillation of mind, the external symptoms of which are war, hatred, conflict, and aggression. But the
Ethics is not only about relieving various forms of mental and
emotional distress; it encourages the qualities of joy, friendship,
sociability, and love. The free individual described in the last two
parts of the book, the *exemplar* of human nature to which we
can look, is fearless before death, resolute in action, and fiercely
independent in mind and judgment. Despite his statement that
his philosophy would simply describe human nature as it is, not
as it ought to be, Spinoza could not help but transform everything that he touched. The point of his philosophy is not just to
interpret the world, but to redeem it.

NOTES

PREFACE

1. Richard Popkin, "The Excommunicant," *London Review of Books*, October 15, 1998, p. 38.

2. Among the most prominent are Jonathan Bennett, *A Study of Spinoza's Ethics* (Indianapolis: Hackett, 1984); Michael Della Rocca, *Representation and the Mind-Body Problem in Spinoza* (New York: Oxford University Press, 1996); Susan James, *Passions and Actions: The Emotions in Seventeenth-Century Philosophy* (Oxford: Clarendon, 1997).

INTRODUCTION

1. The best recent biography is Steven Nadler, *Spinoza: A Life* (Cambridge: Cambridge University Press, 1999); there is still much valuable information contained in K. O. Meinsma, *Spinoza et son cercle* (Paris: Vrin, 1983) and Madelaine Francès, *Spinoza dans les pays néerlandais de la seconde moitié du XVIIe siècle* (Paris: Alcan, 1937).

2. For the details of Spinoza's excommunication, see Nadler, *Spinoza*, pp. 116–54; Yirmiyahu Yovel, *Spinoza and Other Heretics*, vol. 1: *The Marrano of Reason* (Princeton: Princeton University Press, 1989), pp. 3–14, 76–80; Genviève Bryckman, *La Judéité de Spinoza* (Paris: Vrin, 1972), pp. 16–31.

3. Pierre Bayle, "Spinoza," *Historical and Critical Dictionary*, trans. Richard Popkin (Indianapolis: Hackett, 1991), p. 292.

4. I. S. Revah, *Spinoza et le Dr. Juan de Prado* (Paris: Mouton, 1959); Joseph Kaplan, *From Christianity to Judaism: The Story of Isaac Orobio de Castro*, trans. Raphael Loewe (Oxford: Oxford University Press, 1989).

5. Lewis Feuer, *Spinoza and the Rise of Liberalism* (New Brunswick, N.J.: Transaction, 1987), pp. 25–26.

6. Nadler, *Spinoza*, pp. 125–27, 147–53.

7. Jean Lucas, *La vie et l'espirt de Mr. Benoit de Spinoza [1719]: The Oldest Biography of Spinoza*, trans. A. Wolf (London: Dial Press, 1928).

8. Pierre Bayle, *Various Thoughts on the Occasion of a Comet*, trans. Robert C. Bartlett (Albany: SUNY Press, 2000), pp. 214–16; see Isabelle Delpla,

"Bayle: Pensées diverses sur l'atheisme ou le paradoxe de l'athée citoyen," *Figures du theologico-politique,* ed. E. Cattin, L. Jaffro, A. Petit (Paris: J. Vrin, 1999), p. 117–47.

9. Leszek Kolakowski, *Chrétiens sans église: La conscience religieuse et le lien confessional au XVIIe siècle* (Paris: Gallimard, 1969).

10. See Steven B. Smith, *Spinoza, Liberalism, and the Question of Jewish Identity* (New Haven: Yale University Press, 1997); Etienne Balibar, *Spinoza and Politics,* trans. Peter Snowdon (London: Verso, 1998), pp. 1–24.

11. This story is told at length in Jonathan Israel, *The Dutch Republic: Its Rise, Greatness, and Fall, 1477–1806* (Oxford: Oxford University Press, 1995).

12. Bryckman, *La Judéité de Spinoza,* pp. 117–30, regards this as evidence for Spinoza's interest in returning to the Jewish community.

13. Cited in Bennett, *A Study of Spinoza's Ethics,* p. 34; see also Georges Friedmann, *Leibniz et Spinoza* (Paris: Gallimard, 1946), pp. 107–8.

14. Among other works in this genre, see Isaac Bashevis Singer, "The Spinoza of Market Street"; Bernard Malamud, *The Fixer;* Paul Auster, *Mister Vertigo.*

15. Friedrich Nietzsche, *The Portable Nietzsche,* ed. Walter Kaufmann (New York: Viking, 1965), p. 92.

Chapter 1. Thinking about the *Ethics*

1. Every reader of Spinoza is indebted to, among others, Frederick Pollock, *Spinoza, His Life and Philosophy* (London: Duckworth, 1899); H. H. Joachim, *A Study of the Ethics of Spinoza* (Oxford: Clarendon, 1901); Richard McKeon, *The Philosophy of Spinoza* (New York: Longmans, 1928); David Bidney, *The Psychology and Ethics of Spinoza* (New Haven: Yale University Press, 1940); Sylvan Zac, *L'idée de la vie dans la philosophie de Spinoza* (Paris: PUF, 1963); Martial Gueroult, *Spinoza,* vol. 1: *Dieu;* vol. 2: *L'Ame* (Paris: Aubier, 1968, 1974); Pierre Machery, *Introduction à l'Ethique de Spinoza,* 5 vols. (Paris: PUF, 1994–98).

2. Leon Roth, *Spinoza* (London: Ernest Benn, 1929), p. 234.

3. Harry A. Wolfson, *The Philosophy of Spinoza: Unfolding the Latent Processes of His Reasoning* (Cambridge: Harvard University Press, 1934), 1:vii.

4. G. W. F. Hegel, *Lectures on the History of Philosophy,* trans. E. S. Haldane and F. H. Simson (London: Routledge and Kegan Paul, 1955), 3:283: "Of modern philosophy it may truly be said: You are either a Spinozist or not a philosopher at all." Louis Althusser, in *Lire le Capital* (Paris: Maspero, 1965), describes Spinoza as "le seul ancêtre diret de Marx" (p. 128).

5. Edwin Curley, *Behind the Geometrical Method: A Reading of Spinoza's "Ethics"* (Princeton: Princeton University Press, 1988).

6. Yovel, *Spinoza and Other Heretics*, vol. 1.

7. P. O. Kristeller, "Stoic and Neoplatonic Sources of Spinoza's 'Ethics,'" *History of European Ideas* 5 (1984): 1–15; Susan James, "Spinoza the Stoic," in *The Rise of Modern Philosophy: The New and Traditional Philosophies from Machiavelli to Leibniz*, ed. Tom Sorell (New York: Oxford University Press, 1993), pp. 289–316; Martha C. Nussbaum, *Upheavals of Thought: The Intelligence of the Emotions* (Cambridge: Cambridge University Press, 2001), pp. 500–510.

8. For some recent efforts to characterize modernity as a whole, see Hans Blumenberg, *The Legitimacy of the Modern Age*, trans. Robert Wallace (Cambridge, Mass.: MIT Press, 1983; Stephen Toulmin, *Cosmopolis: The Hidden Agenda of Modernity* (New York: Free Press, 1990); Robert B. Pippin, *Modernism as a Philosophical Problem: On the Dissatisfactions of European High Culture* (Oxford: Blackwell, 1991).

9. Leo Strauss, *Persecution and the Art of Writing* (Chicago: University of Chicago Press, 1980), p. 24.

10. For some of the views on Spinoza's use of the geometrical method, see Joachim, *A Study of the Ethics of Spinoza*, pp. 9–13, 115–19; Wolfson, *The Philosophy of Spinoza*, 1:40–60; Roth, *Spinoza*, pp. 36–39; Gueroult, *Spinoza*, vol. 2: *L'Ame*, pp. 473–87; for a useful survey of the debate, see Thomas Carson Mark, "Ordine Geometrica Demonstrata: Spinoza's Use of the Axiomatic Method," *Review of Metaphysics* 29 (1975): 263–86.

11. Stuart Hampshire, *Spinoza* (New York: Penguin, 1951), pp. 24–25.

12. Hampshire, *Spinoza*, p. 25.

13. For a contemporary expression of this view, see Richard Rorty, *Philosophy and the Mirror of Nature* (Princeton: Princeton University Press, 1979).

14. Yitzhak Melamed, "On the Exact Science of Nonbeings: Spinoza's View of Mathematics," *Iyyun* 49 (2000): 3–22.

15. Charles Adam and Paul Tannery, eds., *Oeuvres de Descartes* (Paris: J. Vrin, 1974–86); henceforth cited as AT with reference to volume and page number.

16. Pippin, *Modernism as a Philosophical Problem*, pp. 23–25.

17. Galilei Galileo, "The Assayer," in *Discoveries and Opinions*, trans. Stillman Drake (New York: Doubleday, 1957), pp. 237–38.

18. John Aubrey, *Brief Lives*, ed. Andrew Clarke (Oxford: Clarendon, 1898), p. 357.

19. Thomas Hobbes, *Leviathan*, ed. Edwin Curley (Indianapolis: Hackett,

1994); henceforth cited as *Lev* with reference to chapter and section numbers.

20. Harry A. Wolfson, "Behind the Geometrical Method," *Spinoza: A Collection of Critical Essays*, ed. Marjorie Grene (Garden City: Anchor, 1973), pp. 3–24.

21. Wolfson, "Behind the Geometrical Method," p. 17.

22. Wolfson, "Behind the Geometrical Method," p. 18.

23. Wolfson, "Behind the Geometrical Method," p. 18.

24. Wolfson, "Behind the Geometrical Method," p. 19.

25. Efraim Shmueli, "The Geometrical Method, Personal Caution, and the Idea of Tolerance," in *Spinoza: New Perspectives*, ed. Robert W. Shahan and J. I. Biro (Norman: University of Oklahoma Press, 1978), pp. 197–215.

26. Shmueli, "The Geometrical Method," pp. 208–09.

27. Shmueli, "The Geometrical Method," p. 209.

28. Gilles Deleuze, "Spinoza and the Three 'Ethics,'" in *The New Spinoza*, ed. Warren Montag and Ted Stolze (Minneapolis: University of Minnesota Press, 1997), pp. 20–33.

29. Deleuze, "Spinoza and the Three 'Ethics,'" p. 27.

30. Deleuze, "Spinoza and the Three 'Ethics,'" p. 28.

31. Stuart Hampshire, "Two Theories of Morality," *Morality and Conflict* (Cambridge: Harvard University Press, 1983), p. 66; the connection between Spinoza and Kant needs to be more fully explored.

32. For the relation between geometry and constructivist metaphors of knowledge, see Amos Funkenstein, *Theology and the Scientific Imagination: From the Middle Ages to the Seventeenth Century* (Princeton: Princeton University Press, 1986), pp. 290–345; for the relation between the ancient and modern conceptions of mathematical concepts, see Jacob Klein, *Greek Mathematical Thought and the Origin of Algebra*, trans. Eva Brann (Cambridge, Mass.: MIT Press, 1968), pp. 117–25.

33. Funkenstein, *Theology and the Scientific Imagination*, p. 316.

34. On the constructivist character of Hobbesian political science, see Leo Strauss, *Natural Right and History* (Chicago: University of Chicago Press, 1953), pp. 171–77.

35. David Lachterman, *The Ethics of Geometry: A Genealogy of Modernity* (London: Routledge, 1989).

36. Lachterman, *The Ethics of Geometry*, pp. 2–3.

37. For the source of *verum = factum*, see Vico, *On the Most Ancient Wisdom of the Italians*, trans. L. M. Palmer (Ithaca, N.Y.: Cornell University Press, 1988), pp. 45–47; for the uses to which this principle has been put,

see Jürgen Habermas, *Theory and Practice*, trans. John Viertel (Boston: Beacon Press, 1974), pp.45–46; Hannah Arendt, *The Human Condition* (Chicago: University of Chicago Press, 1958), pp. 294–304; Karl Löwith, "Vico's Grundsatz: Verum et factum convertuntur," *Aufsätze und Vorträge* (Stuttgart: Kohlhammer, 1971), pp. 157–88.

38. Lachterman, *The Ethics of Geometry*, p. 5.

39. Alexis de Tocqueville, *Democracy in America*, trans. George Lawrence (New York: Doubleday, 1969), p. 429.

40. Tocqueville, *Democracy in America*, p. 429.

41. Hampshire, "Two Theories of Morality," p. 43.

42. For the Promethean theme in early modern thought, see Francis Bacon, "Prometheus or the State of Man," in *Of the Wisdom of the Ancients* in *Works*, ed. James Spedding, Robert Ellis, and Douglas Heath (New York: Garrett Press, 1870), 6:745–53.

43. See Avishai Margalit, "The Crooked Timber of Nationalism," *The Legacy of Isaiah Berlin*, ed. Mark Lilla, Ronald Dworkin, and Robert Silvers (New York: NYRB, 2001), p. 151.

44. For the idea of philosophy as a way of living, see Alexander Nehamas, *The Art of Living: Socratic Reflections from Plato to Foucault* (Princeton: Princeton University Press, 1998).

45. See Steven Nadler, *Spinoza's Heresy: Immortality and the Jewish Mind* (New York: Oxford University Press, 2001).

46. Roth, *Spinoza*, pp. 233–34.

CHAPTER 2. THINKING ABOUT GOD

1. Aristotle, *Physics*, II, 1 (192b–93b).

2. See Umberto Cassuto, *A Commentary on the Book of Genesis Part One: From Adam to Noah*, trans. Israel Abrahams (Jerusalem: Magnes, 1989), pp. 7–70.

3. For a useful discussion of the idea of creation, see Kenneth Seeskin, "Maimonides, Spinoza, and the Problem of Creation," *Jewish Themes in Spinoza's Philosophy*, ed. Heidi Ravven and Lenn E. Goodman (Albany: SUNY Press, 2002), pp.115–30.

4. The locus classicus of this debate is Judah Halevi, *The Kuzari*, trans. Hartwig Hirschfeld (New York: Schocken, 1964), 4:25–27; see also Maimonides, *The Guide of the Perplexed*, trans. Shlomo Pines (Chicago: University of Chicago Press, 1963), II:25; for Spinoza's response to the debate, see *TTP*, vii, 75–78; III/113–14.

5. For the source of this story, see Steven S. Schwarzschild, "Franz Rosen-zweig's Anecdotes about Hermann Cohen," *Gegenwart im Rückblick: Festgabae für die Judische Gemeinde zu Berlin, 25 Jahre nach dem Neubeginn,* ed. Herbert Strauss and Kurt Grossmann (Heidelberg: Stiehm, 1970), p. 211.

6. Bayle, "Spinoza," *Historical and Critical Dictionary,* pp. 311–12.

7. Roger Scruton, *Spinoza* (Oxford: Oxford University Press, 1986), p. 53.

8. Richard Mason, *The God of Spinoza: A Philosophical Study* (Cambridge: Cambridge University Press, 1997), pp. 23–25.

9. Bennett, *A Study of Spinoza's Ethics,* p. 35.

10. Bennett, *A Study of Spinoza's Ethics,* p. 35.

11. Descartes's ethical theory has until recently been largely overlooked, espe-cially by Anglo-American writers; for an exception see John Marshall, *Descartes's Moral Theory* (Ithaca: Cornell University Press, 1998); the classic studies are Pierre Mesnard, *Essai sur la morale de Descartes* (Paris: Boivin, 1936); Geneviève Rodis-Lewis, *La morale de Descartes* (Paris: PUF, 1970).

12. Scruton, *Spinoza,* p. 18: "In choosing the universal language of our cul-ture, Spinoza wrote the last indisputable Latin masterpiece . . . He chose a single word from that language for his device: *caute*—'be cautious'—in-scribed beneath a rose, the symbol of secrecy. For having chosen to write in a language that was so widely intelligible, he was compelled to hide what he had written."

13. Leo Strauss, *Spinoza's Critique of Religion,* trans. E. M. Sinclair (New York: Schocken, 1965), p. 215.

14. The denial of all teleology in Spinoza is claimed by Bennett, *A Study of Spinoza's Ethics,* pp. 215–16; Bennett's position has been recently endorsed by Mason, *The God of Spinoza,* pp. 122–27.

15. See Edwin Curley, "On Bennett's Spinoza: The Issue of Teleology," in *Spinoza: Issues and Directions,* ed. Edwin Curley and Pierre-Francois Moreau (Leiden: E. J. Brill, 1990), pp. 39–52.

16. Mason, *The God of Spinoza,* pp. 123–24.

17. Bennett, *A Study of Spinoza's Ethics,* p. 215.

18. Karl Marx, *Capital* (London: Lawrence and Wishart, 1970), 1:178.

Chapter 3. Thinking about Thinking

1. For some of Spinoza's possible sources, see Wolfson, *The Philosophy of Spinoza,* 2:226; see also Zev Harvey, "A Portrait of Spinoza as a Maimo-nidean," *Journal of the History of Philosophy* 20 (1981): 151–71.

2. Gilles Deleuze, *Expressionism in Philosophy: Spinoza*, trans. Martin Joughin (New York: Zone, 1990), pp. 107–11; how the term came to be applied to Spinoza is a subject worthy of consideration.

3. Gilbert Ryle, *The Concept of Mind* (New York: Barnes and Noble, 1949), pp. 11–18.

4. R. G. Collingwood, *The New Leviathan*, ed. David Boucher (Oxford: Clarendon, 1992), pp. 8–9.

5. Deleuze, *Expressionism in Philosophy*, p. 109.

6. Stephen Jay Gould, "The Brain of Brawn," *New York Times*, May 25, 2000.

7. Boris Berman, *Notes from the Pianist's Bench* (New Haven: Yale University Press, 2000), p. 170.

8. For a useful survey of the issues involved, see Timothy O'Connor, ed., *Agents, Causes, and Events: Essays on Indeterminism and Free Will* (New York: Oxford University Press, 1995).

9. Isaiah Berlin, "From Hope and Fear Set Free," in *The Proper Study of Mankind*, ed. Henry Hardy and Roger Hausheer (London: Chatto and Windus, 1997), pp. 103–4.

10. Berlin, "From Hope and Fear Set Free," pp. 106–7.

11. I owe this example to Joseph Cropsey.

12. This point has been developed persuasively by Donald Davidson, "Actions, Reasons, and Causes," *Essays on Actions and Events* (Oxford: Oxford University Press, 1980), pp. 3–19; see also Alasdair MacIntyre, "The Antecedents of Action," *Against the Self-Images of the Age* (New York: Schocken, 1971), pp. 191–210.

13. Scruton, *Spinoza*, p. 58.

14. Stuart Hampshire, "Two Theories of Morality," p. 63.

15. Curley, *Behind the Geometrical Method*, p. 77.

16. Feuerbach describes Spinoza in his history of materialism as the Moses of "modern free spirits"; cited in Emil Fackenheim, *To Mend the World: Foundations of Future Jewish Thought* (New York: Schocken, 1982), p. 51. The identical position is taken by Marx in *The Holy Family*, in *Writings of the Young Marx on Philosophy and Society*, ed. Loyd Easton and Kurt Guddat (New York: Doubleday, 1967), pp. 393–95; for Nietzsche's appropriation of Spinoza, see the letter to Overbeck in *The Portable Nietzsche*, p. 92.

17. Louis Althusser, "The Only Materialist Tradition," *The New Spinoza*, pp. 6–7.

18. Tocqueville, *Democracy in America*, p. 437.

19. Tocqueville, *Democracy in America*, p. 437.

Chapter 4. Thinking about Desire

1. For the use of this countervailing strategy, see Albert Hirshman, *The Passions and the Interests* (Princeton: Princeton University Press, 1977), pp. 20–31.

2. James Madison, *The Federalist Papers*, ed. Jacob E. Cooke (Middletown, Conn.: Wesleyan University Press, 1961), no. 51, p. 349.

3. For a helpful discussion see David Lachterman, "The Physics of Spinoza's 'Ethics,'" *Spinoza: New Perspectives*, pp. 71–111.

4. Stanley Rosen, "Benedict Spinoza," in *History of Political Philosophy*, ed. Joseph Cropsey and Leo Strauss (Chicago: Rand McNally, 1972), pp. 432–33: "Spinoza is a student of Machiavelli, who taught that Fortuna could be mastered by strong men . . . Spinoza also retains Hobbes's (and Descartes') admiration for mathematics as the model for the new reason whereby false utopias will be replaced by a scientifically regulated will to power."

5. Roth, *Spinoza*, p. 114.

6. Bennett, *A Study of Spinoza's Ethics*, p. 223.

7. Bennett, *A Study of Spinoza's Ethics*, pp. 222–23.

8. William Shakespeare, *Twelfth Night*, III, 4, 358–59.

9. Yirmiyahu Yovel, "Transcending Mere Survival: From *Conatus* to *Conatus Intelligendi*," in *Desire and Affect: Spinoza as Psychologist*, ed. Yirmiyahu Yovel (New York: Little Room Press, 1999), p. 50.

10. See Leo Strass, *What Is Political Philosophy and Other Studies* (New York: Free Press, 1959), p. 46.

11. Hampshire, *Spinoza*, pp. 167–68.

12. For some interesting remarks on the role of Cartesian generosity, see Charles Taylor, *Sources of the Self: The Making of Modern Identity* (Cambridge, Mass.: Harvard University Press, 1989), pp. 152–56; John Cottingham, *Philosophy and the Good Life: Reason and the Passions in Greek, Cartesian, and Psychoanalytic Ethics* (Cambridge: Cambridge University Press, 1998), pp. 99–103; see also Marshall, *Descartes's Moral Theory*, pp. 148–66.

13. Aristotle, *Nicomachean Ethics*, IV, 1125a.

14. Ernst Cassirer, *Descartes, Corneille, Christine de Suède*, trans. Madeleine Francès and Paul Schrecker (Paris: J. Vrin, 1942), pp. 73–74.

15. See Richard Kennington, "Descartes and the Mastery of Nature," in *Organism, Medicine, and Metaphysics*, ed. Stuart Spicker (Dodrecht: D. Reidel, 1978), pp. 201–23.

16. For the aspiration to self-creation in Descartes, see Lachterman, *The Ethics of Geometry*, pp. 126–40.
17. Taylor, *Sources of the Self*, p. 153.
18. Machiavelli, *The Prince*, trans. Harvey Mansfield (Chicago: University of Chicago Press, 1985), ix, 39–40.
19. Cassirer, *Descartes, Corneille, Christine de Suède*, p. 115.
20. Pierre Corneille, *Horace, Theatre Completes*, ed. Roger Caillois (Paris: Gallimard, Bibliothèque de la Pleiade, 1950), 1:825; *The Chief Plays of Corneille*, trans. Lacy Lockert (Princeton: Princeton University Press, 1957), pp. 143–44.
21. Corneille, *Horace*, p. 827; *The Chief Plays of Corneille*, p. 145.
22. See Bennett, *A Study of Spinoza's Ethics*, pp. 299–308.

CHAPTER 5. THINKING ABOUT POLITICS

1. Edwin Curley, "Kissinger, Spinoza, and Genghis Khan," in *The Cambridge Companion to Spinoza*, ed. Don Garrett (Cambridge: Cambridge University Press, 1996), p. 315.
2. Strauss, *Spinoza's Critique of Religion*, p. 229, remarks that "Spinoza's political theory, in particular his theory of natural right . . . is *toto coelo* different from the theory of Hobbes, with whom his name is often coupled."
3. Isaiah Berlin, "Two Concepts of Liberty," cited in Quentin Skinner, *Liberty before Liberalism* (Cambridge: Cambridge University Press, 1998), p. 114.
4. Skinner, *Liberty before Liberalism*, pp. 1–57.
5. Thomas Hobbes, *De Cive*, ed. Noel Malcolm (Cambridge: Cambridge University Press, 1998), x, 11; references are to chapter and section numbers.
6. Hobbes, *De Cive*, x, 11.
7. Thomas Hobbes, *Behemoth or the Long Parliament*, ed. Ferdinand Tonnies (Chicago: University of Chicago Press, 1990), p. 20.
8. Balibar, *Spinoza and Politics*, p. 24.
9. See Chaim Wirszubski, "Spinoza's Debt to Tacitus," *Scripita Hierosolymitana* 2 (1955): 176–86; see also Strauss, *Spinoza's Critique of Religion*, pp. 312–14, for a catalog of Spinoza's usages of Tacitus. For a review of the revival of Tacitism, see Arnaldo Momigliano, "Tacitus and the Tacitist Tradition," *The Classical Foundations of Modern Historiography* (Berkeley: University of California Press, 1990), pp. 109–31; see also Lionel Trilling,

"Tacitus Now," *The Liberal Imagination: Essays on Literature and Society* (New York: Harcourt Brace, 1950), pp. 198–204.

10. Montesquieu, *The Spirit of the Laws*, trans. Anne M. Cohler, Basia Miller, Harold Stone (Cambridge: Cambridge University Press, 1989), bk. 30, chap. 2: "Tacitus . . . summarized everything because he saw everything."

11. Guicciardini, cited in Momigliano, "Tacitus and the Tacitist Tradition," p. 122.

12. The phrase is "Ubi sentire quae velis et quae sentias dicere licet" and comes from Tacitus, *Histories*, I, i, 4; see Wirszubski, "Spinoza's Debt to Tacitus," p. 184; the phrase is also used as the epigraph to Hume's *A Treatise of Human Nature*.

13. For the influence of Machiavelli on Spinoza, see Strauss, *Spinoza's Critique of Religion*, pp. 226–28; Curley, "Kissinger, Spinoza, and Genghis Kahn," pp. 327–33.

14. The debate goes back to Hans Baron, *The Crisis of the Early Italian Renaissance* (Princeton: Princeton University Press, 1966); it was restated by J. G. A. Pocock in *The Machiavellian Moment: Florentine Political Thought and the Atlantic Republican Tradition* (Princeton: Princeton University Press, 1975); however the premise of a continuity between ancient and modern republicanism has been challenged recently by Paul Rahe in *Republics Ancient and Modern: Classical Republicanism and the American Revolution* (Chapel Hill: University of North Carolina Press, 1992).

15. Machiavelli, *Discourses on Livy*, i, 58.

16. See Jean-Jacques Rousseau, *On the Social Contract*, trans. Roger D. and Judith R. Masters (New York: Saint Martins, 1978), iii, 6; henceforth cited as *SC* with reference to book and chapter numbers.

17. See John McCormick, "Machiavellian Democracy: Controlling Elites with Ferocious Populism," *American Political Science Review* 2 (2001): 297–313.

18. For the way in which the Hebrew commonwealth served as a model for the modern republic, see Fania Oz-Salzberger, "The Jewish Roots of Western Freedom," *Azure* 13 (2002): 88–132; Spinoza is mentioned briefly on p. 94, but otherwise his contribution to the debate is ignored here.

19. See Michael Rosenthal, "Why Spinoza Chose the Hebrews," *History of Political Thought* 18 (1997): 207–41; see also Smith, *Spinoza, Liberalism, and the Question of Jewish Identity*, pp. 145–51.

20. For the importance of the *exemplar* in the *Ethics*, see Edwin Curley, "Spinoza's Moral Philosophy," in *Spinoza*, ed. Grene, pp. 354–76; see also David Bidney, *The Psychology and Ethics of Spinoza* (New Haven: Yale University Press, 1940), pp. 272–73.

21. For an excellent discussion of Spinoza's characterization of the free man, see Bidney, *The Psychology and Ethics of Spinoza*, pp. 296–97.
22. Spinoza's attitude toward animals evoked a hostile ethnic slur from Schopenhauer. Referring to the passage at IVp37s, he writes: "Here [Spinoza] speaks in accordance with the first and ninth chapters of Genesis, just as a Jew knows how to, so that we others, who are accustomed to purer and worthier doctrines are here overcome by the *foetor judaicus* [stench of Judaism]. He appears not to have known dogs at all." See Arthur Schopenhauer, *Parerga and Paralipomena: Short Philosophyical Essays*, vol. 1, trans. E. F. J. Payne (Oxford: Oxford University Press, 1974), p. 73. Apparently he thought that anti-Semitism was acceptable, but not "speciesism."
23. PT, v, 5; III/296: "Besides, a commonwealth whose peace depends on the apathy of its subjects, who are led like sheep so that they learn nothing but servility, may more properly be called a desert than a commonwealth." The passage paraphrases Tacitus, *Agricola*, 30.
24. For the connection between Spinoza and Rousseau, see Walter Eckstein, "Rousseau and Spinoza: Their Political Theories and Their Conceptions of Freedom," *Journal of the History of Ideas* 3 (1944): 259–91; see also Paul Vernière, *Spinoza et la pensée française avant la révolution* (Paris: PUF, 1954), 2:475–94.
25. Bennett, *Spinoza*, pp. 299–307, believes that Spinoza's effort to derive a cooperative morality from an egoistic psychology necessarily fails.
26. Scruton, *Spinoza*, p. 53.
27. Berlin classifies Spinoza, along with Hegel and Marx, as a partisan of positive liberty and therefore places him among the enemies of liberalism. See "Two Concepts of Liberty," *The Proper Study of Mankind*, pp. 213, 217, 218. For an attempt to rescue Spinoza from Berlin's charge, see David West, "Spinoza on Positive Freedom," *Political Studies* 39 (1993): 284–96. In a rejoinder to West, Berlin maintains that it is not Spinoza's own views to which he objects but merely a "distortion" of them that can be "easily twisted" to prove the opposite of what Spinoza meant. As an example of the misuse of Spinoza, Berlin cites Bismarck's *Kulturkampf* against the clerics in Germany, although he doesn't mention that Spinoza was also deeply admired by Moses Hess and the intellectual founders of Zionism, of which he elsewhere approves; see Berlin, "A Reply to West," *Political Studies* 39 (1993): 297–98.
28. Tocqueville, *Democracy in America*, pp. 451–52.
29. William Herndon, *Life of Lincoln* (New York: Da Capo, 1983), p. 354.

30. Herndon, *Life of Lincoln*, p. 354.

31. Bidney, *The Psychology and Ethics of Spinoza*, p. 302.

CHAPTER 6. THINKING ABOUT LOVE

1. Allan Bloom, *Love and Friendship* (New York: Simon and Schuster, 1993), p. 431.

2. Karl Marx, *Capital*, p. 82.

3. Genevieve Lloyd, *The Man of Reason: "Male" and "Female" in Western Philosophy* (Minneapolis: University of Minnesota Press, 1993).

4. Bennett, *Spinoza*, p. 372.

5. Bennett, *Spinoza*, p. 374.

6. Bennett, *Spinoza*, p. 375.

7. Feuer, *Spinoza and the Rise of Liberalism*, p. 215.

8. Feuer, *Spinoza and the Rise of Liberalism*, p. 216.

9. Feuer, *Spinoza and the Rise of Liberalism*, pp. 217–18.

10. According to Feuer's psychoanalytic reading, "the erotic component in [Spinoza's] life seems somehow to have been twisted" by personal circumstances, by which he refers to the early death of Spinoza's mother and her succession by various stepmothers and half-siblings. It was these conditions, he opines, that "made it virtually impossible for Spinoza to have a normal emotional life." Feuer, *Spinoza and the Rise of Liberalism*, pp. 218–21. How Feur claims to know these things is not said.

11. This section draws heavily on Steven B. Smith, "A Fool for Love: Thoughts on I. B. Singer's Spinoza," *Iyyun* 51 (2002): 41–50.

12. Isaac Bashevis Singer, "The Spinoza of Market Street," *The Collected Stories* (New York: Farrar, Strauss and Giroux, 1987), p. 93.

13. See Smith, "A Fool for Love"; Genevieve Lloyd, *Spinoza and the "Ethics"* (London: Routledge, 1996), pp. 58–60.

14. Wolfson, *The Philosophy of Spinoza*, 2:306.

15. See Zev Harvey, "A Portrait of Spinoza as a Maimonidean," *Journal of the History of Philosophy* 20 (1981): 151–71.

16. See Curley, *Behind the Geometrical Method*, pp. 83–86.

17. Wolfson, *The Philosophy of Spinoza*, 2:311–16.

18. Zev Harvey, "The Biblical Term 'Glory' in Spinoza's 'Ethics,'" *Iyyun*, 48 (1999): 447–49.

19. The obvious exception is Nietzsche, who regarded Spinoza's *Ethics* as an important precursor of his own immoralism; for an appreciation of Nietzsche's debt to Spinoza, see Gilles Deleuze, *Spinoza: Practical Philosophy*, trans. Robert Hurly (San Francisco: City Lights, 1988), pp. 22–25.

Chapter 7. The Authority of Reason

1. Antonio Negri, *The Savage Anomaly: The Power of Spinoza's Metaphysics and Politics,* trans. Michael Hardt (Minneapolis: University of Minnesota Press, 1991).

2. For the context and significance of this debate, see Frederick Beiser, *The Fate of Reason: German Philosophy from Kant to Fichte* (Cambridge, Mass.: Harvard University Press, 1987), pp. 44–91; David Bell, *Spinoza in Germany from 1670 to the Age of Goethe* (London: Institute of Germanic Studies, 1984), pp. 71–96; see also Paul Franks, "All or Nothing: Systematicity and Nihilism in Jacobi, Reinhold, and Maimon," in *The Cambridge Companion to German Idealism,* ed. Karl Ameriks (Cambridge: Cambridge University Press, 2000), pp. 95–116.

3. For Hume's influence on the German debate, see Beiser, *The Fate of Reason,* pp. 3–4, 11, 54; see also Isaiah Berlin, "Hume and the Sources of German Anti-Rationalism," *Against the Current* (New York: Penguin, 1977), pp. 181–87.

4. Friedrich Heinrich Jacobi, *The Main Philosophical Writings and the Novel "Allwill,"* trans. George di Giovanni (Montreal: McGill–Queen's University Press, 1994); henceforth cited in the text as *MPW.*

5. Leo Strauss, *Das Erkenntnisproblem in der philosophischen Lehre Fr. H. Jacobis,* reprinted in *Gesammelte Schriften,* vol. 2, *Philosophie und Gesetz—Frühe Schriften,* ed. Heinrich Meier (Stuttgart: J. B. Metlzer, 1997), pp. 237–92.

6. Leo Strauss, *Spinoza's Critique of Religion,* trans. E. M. Sinclair (New York: Schocken, 1965); the extensive "Preface" is reprinted in *Liberalism: Ancient and Modern* (New York: Basic Books, 1968); henceforth cited in the text as *LAM.*

7. Some of these themes are anticipated in Steven B. Smith, "The Situation of Modern Judaism in Leo Strauss's 'Natural Right and History'" (forthcoming).

8. Ludwig Wittgenstein, *Tractatus Logico-Philosophicus,* trans. D. F. Pears and B. F. McGuinness (New York: Humanities, 1961), 6.54.

9. Leo Strauss, "Progress or Return?" *The Rebirth of Classical Political Rationalism,* ed. Thomas Pangle (Chicago: University of Chicago Press, 1989), p. 270.

INDEX OF PASSAGES CITED FROM SPINOZA'S *ETHICS*

General Index

action, 59, 68–69, 76–78, 95, 116
affects, 94–95, 109–13, 154; definition of, 98, 106, 111–13, 168; power of, 83, 97–98; understanding of, 102–4. *See also* passions
affectum imitatio, 111
agency, xv, 26, 38, 60–61, 69–70, 80–86, 146; *conatus* as, 8, 81, 102–4, 108. *See also* free will
agent-centered actions, 76–77, 78, 85
ambition, 97, 111, 164, 178
American democracy, 23–24
amor Dei intellectualis, 59, 92, 155–58, 161, 169–82
ancients and moderns, quarrel of, 21
animals, Spinoza's view of, 144
animi libertatem. See freedom of mind
animositas, 7–8, 121, 122
anthropomorphic fallacy, 34, 40–41, 48–61
appetites, 56, 83, 95, 101, 102, 162–63
aristocratic virtues, 114–15
Aristotle, xxii, 8, 26, 27, 53, 56; on greatness of soul, 114, 115; on substance plurality, 32, 33
atheism, xxi–xxii, xxiii, xxiv–xxv, 1, 44, 198; pantheism and, 39–43, 188, 189

Athenian democracy, 127, 129
athletic skill, 70–72
attribute, 1
Aubrey, John, 12, 14
Auerbach, Berthold, xxvi
Augustine, 8, 158
authenticity, 22–23
autonomy, 26, 85–86, 109

Bacon, Francis, 25, 114
Balibar, Etienne, 130
Balling, Pieter, xxiii
baseball, 70–72
Bayle, Pierre, xxiii, 1, 37–38, 42
beatitudo. See blessedness
behavioral psychology, 77, 78, 95
Bennett, Jonathan, 43, 56–57, 101–2, 155–56
Bentham, Jeremy, 27
Berlin, Isaiah, 73–75, 78, 81
Berman, Boris, 72
Bible: *Ethics* as reply to, xv, 18, 28, 29, 34, 184; on God, 18, 31, 34–35, 36, 193; historical approach to, xiv; philosophical notions of good life vs., 199; political interpretation of, 133; terms for glory, 176–77, 178; "two great books" metaphor, 12
Bidney, David, 153
blessedness, 158, 171–72, 175–76, 178
Bloom, Allan, 154

demagoguery, 128–29
Democracy in America (Tocqueville), 23–24, 151
democratic republicanism: Descartes and, 23–24; German Jews and, 191–92; Hobbes's arguments against, 127–29, 150; pantheism and, 151; Spinoza and, xiii, xxii–xxiii, 123, 125, 126–27, 132–34, 145–53, 192, 200
Descartes, René, xiii, 2, 25, 53, 94, 161; democracy and, 23–24; double teaching of, 44–45; on *générosité*, 114, 115–18; geometry and, 11–12, 19, 20, 21–23; on knowledge, 20, 21–23; on mind-body dualism, 13, 22–23, 32, 62, 66–67, 68, 97–98; new science and, xxi–xxii, 11, 44; on provisional morality, 45–48; on self, 23, 44–48, 92; Spinoza commentary on, xxiv, 10, 11; on will, 96–97, 98, 113, 115–17, 118, 122
desire, 54, 94–122; ambition and, 178; causal context of, 81; definition of, 102–3; natural right and, 124; unity of rational nature and, 137–43. *See also* appetites; *conatus*
determinism, xxv, 1, 44, 95; freedom vs., 72–86, 151, 185–86, 188, 189; Lincoln and, 152–53; pantheism and, 37, 151, 185, 188, 189; self-destructive behavior and, 83–84; as undermining faith, 189–90
Deus sive natura (God or nature), 19, 32–34, 38, 175; meaning to Spinoza of, 42–43

Dialoghi d'Amore (Ebreo), 170
Discourse on Method (Descartes), 11, 23, 25, 45–46
dissenters, xxii
diversity, human, 109–10, 149
divine law, 170–72, 177
divine love. *See* intellectual love of God
divine punishment, 155–56
divine purpose, 53, 57
divine will, 36, 41, 51–52
dualism. *See* mind-body problem
Dutch politics, xxiii, 130, 133

Ebreo, Leone, 170
efficient causes, 28, 54–56, 95, 102
ego. *See* self
egoism, 98–99, 100, 103–9, 122
Elements (Euclid), 1, 9, 12
eliminative materialism, 83
Emerson, Ralph Waldo, 1, 151
emotions. *See* affects
empowerment, 96, 104, 109, 144, 151, 167
Enlightenment, xv, xvi, 184, 185, 186, 190–91, 196
envy, 112
eternity, 1, 9, 155
eternity of God, 33
eternity of mind, 172–75, 176
Ethics of Geometry, The (Lachterman), 21
Euclid, xiv, 1, 9, 12, 20, 91, 174
event-centered actions, 76, 77–78, 85, 186
evil. *See* good and evil
evolution theory, 152
experientia vaga, 87
explanation, 32–33; agent- vs. event-centered, 75–77, 85

faith, reason vs., xv, 189–90, 195–99
false belief, 49, 91, 158–59, 161
fatalism, 188–89
fear, 52, 105–6, 113, 140–41, 155–56, 171
feminist theory, 154
Feuer, Lewis, 156–57
Feuerbach, Ludwig, 85
first cause, 33, 95
Fischelson, Dr. Nachum (fictional person), 165–68
fluctuatio animi, 8, 201
fortitudo, 8, 114–16, 118, 121–22, 200–201
freedom, xv, 3, 4; causality and, 55–56, 60, 72–86, 188; definition of, 55, 200; Descartes's concept of, 23, 63; determinism vs., 72–86; as highest human end, xiii, 23, 24, 25, 28–29, 149; Hobbes's concept of, 127–28; as illusion, 63; as intellectual love of God, 25; knowledge and, 73–75, 84, 86–93; necessity and, 55, 151, 152–53, 176; responsibility and, 26, 44; social contract and, 145–46; Spinoza's concept of, 126–27, 135–36, 145–48, 150–53, 200. *See also* liberty
freedom of mind, xxvii, 1–2, 86–93, 158–61, 180–82; from *fluctuatio animi*, 8, 201; *fortitudo* and, 8, 116, 200–201; passions and, 96–98; rational love and, 168, 169. *See also* eternity of mind
freedom of speech and thought, 126, 130
free person, attributes of, 135–36
free will, 36, 38, 57, 60, 68, 95; causal knowledge and, 84;

Descartes on, 96–97, 98, 113, 115–17, 118, 122; determinism vs., 188–89; event-centered actions vs., 76–78; faith and, 189–90; incompatibilists on, 74–76; rationality and, 78–86, 190; Romantics and, 185–86, 188–90; Spinoza's view of, 63–64, 72–73, 78–86; sufficient reason vs., 185–86
French classical tragedy, 119–21
Freudianism, 78
friendship, 4, 100, 118, 122, 123, 148, 149, 169, 181, 201
Funkenstein, Amos, 20–21

Galileo, 11, 12
gaudium, 149, 179
gender, 119, 154, 164
general ideas, 89–92
general will, 145, 146, 147
generositas (nobility), 7–8, 119–21, 121–22
générosité (Descartes concept), 114, 115–19
generosity, 47, 114–21
Genesis, xv, 18–19, 34, 184
geometrical method, xiv, 1, 8–23; moral purpose of, 19, 44; as reasoning model, 94–95, 183–84; as Spinoza's rhetorical device, 15–17, 19, 20, 31, 184, 199–200
German Counter-Enlightenment, 185–90
German Idealism, xxv, 2, 191
German Romanticism, 185–90, 193
German Weimar republic, 191–92
gladness, 149, 179
glory, 105, 176–77, 178

goals, 26, 28, 56, 58, 59, 96, 145, 157, 158

God: actions of, 40; attributes of, 33–34, 48–49, 50, 64, 151–52, 194; corporealization of, 39; *creatio ex nihilo* by, 21; deanthropomorphization of, 40–41, 48–52; existence of, 33, 34, 43, 44; false understanding of, 50–52; as greatest good, 171; love of, 25, 59, 92, 155–58, 161, 169–82; nature of, xi, 18–19, 28, 31–45, 48–52, 54–61, 63, 124, 157–58, 187, 188, 193–94

God of Spinoza, The (Mason), 41

God or nature. See *Deus sive nature*

Goethe, Johann Wolfgang von, xxv, 1, 187, 191

good: Descartes's conception of, 115–16; false, 158–59; highest, 59, 93, 108, 159–60, 171; new plan of life and, 159–60; psychological egoism and, 103–5, 107–8

good and evil, 52, 195; as comparison, 134–35, 149, 193; impersonal God and, 31, 43, 157–58; moral judgments of, 43, 103–4, 105, 107–8; in state of nature, 140

good life, 27, 199–200; plan for, 159–60; rules for, 47–48, 170–71

Gould, Stephen Jay, 70–71

Grotius, xx

Guicciardinni, Francesco, 130

guilt, 73, 74, 78, 81, 84

Halevi, Judah, 207n4

Hamann, Johann, 185

Hampshire, Stuart, 9, 19, 25

happiness, 7–8, 27, 59

Harvey, Zev, 177

hate, 110, 111, 162, 201

Hegel, G. W. F., 27, 148

Herder, Johann, 185

Herndon, William, 152

heroic ideal, 114–22

Herzel, Theodor, 195

hilaritas, 96, 104, 149, 179

Hobbes, Thomas, xiii, xx, 2, 11, 52, 53, 96; geometry and, 12–13, 14, 19; moral psychology of, 86, 94, 100, 104–9; political theory of, 21, 28, 114, 123–30, 132, 134, 140, 141, 148, 150

honor, 118, 119–21

hope, 52, 113

Horace (Corneille), 120–21

human nature: agency and, 38, 60–61, 69–70; attributed to God (*see* anthropomorphic fallacy); causal chain and, 59; common notions of reason and, 89–91; diversity and, 109–10, 149; exemplar of, 135–36, 201; joy and, 109–11, 178–79; love of God effects on, 179–80; nonhuman animals and, 144; nonhuman nature and, 95; purposiveness and, 54–61, 76–77, 101; reflexive choice and, 57, 58; self-interest and, 107; social cooperation and, 137–43, 145. *See also* passions

Hume, David, xxv, 1, 86, 183, 186, 189

Huygens, Christiaan, xxiii

Ibn Ezra, 177

ideas, 85, 87, 89–92, 135–36, 168

ideologies, 78, 87

ignorance, 52–53, 74

imagination (*imaginatio*), 48–56,

imagination (*continued*)
92; knowledge vs., 86, 87–
88; love freed from, 157, 175;
Spinoza's meaning of, 49, 86–87
immanent cause, xi, 31, 36, 37, 40,
157, 187, 188
immortality of soul, 155, 172–76,
177
impersonal God, 31, 43, 157–58
incompatibility thesis, 73, 74–77,
78, 80–81, 85
individuality, xv, xxvi, 19, 90–
93, 118, 200; authenticity and,
23–24; pleasures of, 149
individual liberty, 4, 127–28, 130,
131, 145, 150–53, 200
indivisibility of God, 33
infinity, 18, 31, 32–33, 37, 39, 41, 59,
157, 194
in more geometrico. See geometrical
method
inner strength. See *fortitudo*
intellect, 41
intellectual love of God, 25, 59, 92,
155–58, 161, 169–82
intellectual probity, 197, 200
intelligence (*intelligibilia*), 80,
90–91
interactionist theory, 67, 68
Isaiah *58:8*, 177
Israel, ancient, 133

Jacobi, F. H., xxv, 185, 186–90, 198,
200
jealousy, 162
Jellesz, Jarig, xxiii
Jewish belief. *See* Judaism
Jewish Question, 194–95
joy, xiv, 4, 10, 105, 108–13, 148, 149,
201; goal of, 26, 96, 157; from

intellectual love of God, 176,
177–79
Judaism, xiii, 18, 29, 39, 191–95,
213n.22; secular Jews and, xxvi,
192–93; Spinoza and, xx–xxii,
42, 190, 192–99
judgments. *See* moral judgments

Kant, Immanuel, xxv, 19, 27, 183
Kaplan, Yosef, xxi
Kissinger, Henry, xxv
knowledge: Cartesian model of,
20, 21–23; constructed nature of,
21–23; freedom and, 73, 74, 75,
84, 86–93; immortality as common stock of, 174; as power, 84;
singular vs. particular, 170, 171;
three kinds of, 86–93, 161, 169,
172, 176. *See also* self-knowledge
Kolakowski, Leszek, xxii

Lachterman, David, 21, 22
ladder of love, 161–75, 180
laetitia. See joy
latitudinarianism, xxii
leap of faith, 189, 197, 198
Leibniz, Gottfried Wilhelm, xxiii,
xxv, 42, 65
Lessing, Gotthold, 185, 186–89
Leviathan (Hobbes), 12–13, 21, 94,
104, 106, 134
lex divina, 170–72, 177
liberality (open-handedness),
114–15
liberty, 4, 125–28, 131, 150–53, 200;
Hobbes vs. Spinoza on, 125–27,
130, 146, 150; Rousseau on, 145
libido dominandi, 163
life: affects and, 111–13; as goal-
directed, 28; happiness and, 27;

new plan of, 159–60; preservation of, 105–7, 113; rules for exemplary, 170–71; rules for living, 47–48; valuation of, 4, 136–37. *See also* good life

Lincoln, Abraham, 152–53

Locke, John, 42, 148

logical empiricists, 183

loneliness, 3–4

love, 100, 110, 111, 148, 154–82, 201; intellectual, 59, 92, 155–58, 161, 169–82; passionate, 162–68, 181; rational, 168–69, 181

Lucas, Jean, xxii

lust, 162

Machiavelli, Niccolò, xiii, xx, 28, 114, 119, 127; as Spinoza influence, 100, 130–34, 193, 195

Madison, James, 97

Maimonides, Moses, 158, 170, 177, 180–81

manliness, 119, 154

Mann, Thomas, 27

Marranos, xix, xxi, 2

marriage, 168–69, 181

Marx, Karl, 58, 85, 87, 154

Marxist theory, 2, 78, 87, 154, 198

Mason, Richard, 41, 56

materialism, 1, 13, 63, 65–66, 83, 85, 173–74

mathematics. *See* geometrical method

mathesis universalis, 20

Meditations (Descartes), 94

Menasseh ben Israel, xix

mind. *See* eternity of mind; freedom of mind; vacillation of mind

mind-body problem: Descartes

and, 13, 22–23, 32, 62, 66–67, 68, 197–98; interactionism and, 67; mental effects on physical activity and, 70–72; Spinoza and, 30, 64–75, 84–86, 166–67, 172–75; Spinoza's view of the body and, 82–85, 149, 167, 168, 173

miracles, xv, 184, 190

misogyny, 164

mob mentality, xxiii, 148

modernity, 21, 22–23, 113–14, 119; Spinoza and, xxv–xxvi, 3, 30, 154, 192, 199–201

monarchy, xxiii, 125, 127–30, 132, 134, 150

monism, 38, 85, 149

Montaigne, Michel de, 8, 23

Montesquieu, Charles Secondat, Baron de, xxv, 130

morale par provision, 45–48

moraliste, Spinoza as, 27

morality: common standards of, 89–90; faith and, 189–90; natural law and, 145; provisional, 45–48; rational love and, 169; rational truth and, 198; self esteem and, 117; self-interest and, 107; as social agreement, 140, 141–43

moral judgments, 52, 81, 103–13, 161; common standards of, 89–90; laws of nature and, 94–95; natural state and, 140; pluralism and, 134–35, 149

moral pedagogy, 8, 27–28, 48, 201

moral psychology: Hobbes and, 86, 94, 104–6; Spinoza and, 94–122

moral responsibility, xv, 4, 24–30, 44, 60, 68–69, 73; determinism and, 74–75, 78, 81, 84, 190; faith

moral responsibility (*continued*)
and, 189–90; pantheism and, 37,
38. *See also* free will
moral terms, 73, 74, 81, 84; as
relational, 135
Moses, 133, 194
Morteira, Saul Levi, xix
motivations, 57, 76–77, 107–9
mutual reciprocity. *See* social
cooperation

Nadler, Steven, xxi
naturalism, xxvi, 60, 77, 95, 100,
101
naturalistic fallacy, 101
natural law, 145
natural right, 123, 124–25, 126, 132,
150; civil right vs., 138–41
natural state, 123, 138–40, 145, 150
nature: common order of, 87;
gendered views of, 154; God as
coterminous with, 18–19, 33–
34, 38, 39, 157; God as ordering
principle of, 40, 63; homogeneous conception of, 56, 184;
human embeddedness in, 25–26,
95; human projections of, 49–
50; mathematization of, 11–12;
moral judgments and, 94–95;
passions and, 93–95; power of,
170–72; rational understanding
of, xv, 14, 35–36, 140–43; sublimity of, 19; "two great books"
metaphor, 12; unity of, 36, 59–
60, 62. See also *Deus sive natura;*
pantheism
necessity, 1, 26, 171–72; as attribute
of God, 33; freedom and, 55, 151,
152–53, 176

Negri, Antonio, 183
new science, xxi–xxii, 11–12, 20,
44–48, 160
Nietzsche, Friedrich, xv, xxvi,
xxvii, 85, 108, 194, 197, 198, 200,
214n19
Nihilismus, 190, 198
nobility. See *generositas*
notions communes. See general ideas
Novalis, xxv, 1

obsession, 163
Oldenburg, Henry, xxiii, xxiv–xxv,
5–6
oneness, 18–19, 30, 33, 58–59, 62,
64, 95
optics, xxiii
Orobio de Castro, Isaac, xxi
orthodoxy, xv–xvi, 25, 184, 190–
944, 196; dangers posed by,
198
"ought"/"is" distinction, 100–101

pantheism, 1, 37–48, 155; atheism
linked with, 39–43, 188, 189;
democratic theory and, 151;
German debate on, 185–89
Pantheismusstreit, xxv, 185–86
parallelism, 30, 64–75; compatibilism vs., 84–85
paranoia, xxv, 11
Parmenides, 18
particularity, 93
Pascal, Blaise, 41
passionate love, 162–68, 181
passions, xiii, 7, 29, 52, 86, 94–
122; as check on other passions,
97, 105–6; *Ethics* vs. Stoics on,
178–79; imagination and, 87;

intellectual love of God and, 180–81; moral evaluations between, 110–13; natural right and, 124; political order and, 123, 141, 146; power of, 96–97; reason and, 97, 98, 117–18, 167; secular redemption and, 158; sexual love and, 162–68; value-free judgment of, 94–95

passivity, 83, 171

paternalism, 150, 154

peace of mind, 157

perfection, 35, 37–38, 39, 54, 59, 107, 108, 109, 157, 161

Perrault, Charles, 21

personal God, 48–49, 52, 155–56

personal identity, 38, 62, 72

piano playing, 72

Pinsker, Leo, 195

Plato, 8, 27, 34, 86, 158, 161, 166

Platonism, 135, 163, 170, 175–76, 181

pleasures, 149, 176

political theory, xiii, xx, xxii–xxiii, 12–13, 21, 28, 29, 114, 123–53, 192, 200; Hobbes-Spinoza comparison, 124–30, 133–34, 140–41, 144; Jews and, 194–95; modernity and, 113–14, 119

Political Treatise (Spinoza), xxiv, 131

positivism, 183–84

poststructuralism, 9

power, xv, 28, 29, 52, 54, 84, 112–13, 124, 134, 145; *conatus* as, 97, 100, 104, 105, 108, 109; of nature, 170–72

praise, 73, 74, 178

prejudice. *See* superstition

prestige, 112–13

pride, 105–6, 111–12, 164

priesthood, 132, 133

Principles of Philosophy (Descartes), xxiv, 10, 44–45, 46, 161

private sphere. *See* public vs. private spheres

prometheanism, 25

"Prometheus" (Goethe), 187

provisional morality, 45–48

Psalms *16:9*, 177

psychological egoism. *See* egoism

public vs. private spheres, 66, 192–93

purposiveness, 41, 49–61, 76–77, 101

Quakers, xxii

Rathenau, Walter, 192

ratio, 86, 89–91, 92; rational love and, 168–69

rational agency. *See* agency

rationalism, reason, xv–xvi, 8–10, 41–42, 60, 154, 171; authority of, 183–201; common notions of, 89–91; faith vs., xv, 189–90, 195–99; feminist critique of, 154; freedom as achievement of, 29, 80–81, 146; free will and, 78–86, 190; individual responsibility and, 68–69, 75; lawlessness vs., 146; morality and, 198; passions and, 97, 98, 117–18, 137–43, 167; Romanticism vs., 185–86, 188–89; scope and limits of, 183–84; self-evident truth of, 92; of social cooperation, 137–48, 150, 180; understanding of nature

of, xxiii, xxiv–xxv, xxv, 1, 39–43, 44, 188; background of, xix–xxiii, 156, 181; caution of, xxiv–xxv, 15–16, 44, 48; critics of, xxv, 185–99; as cultural icon, xxv–xxvii; as democrat, xiii, 123, 125, 126–27, 132–34, 145–53, 192, 200; excommunication of, xx–xxii, 42, 192; geometrical method of, xiv, 13–17, 19–20, 31, 44, 94–95, 183–84, 199–200; influence of, xxv–xxvii, 214n19; as Jewish thinker, xiii, xxvi, 29, 193–94; major influences on, 2–3; major tenets of, 13–14; materialism of, 63, 65–66, 83, 85, 173–74; standard view of, 8–10; on true way of life, 170–71; two-Spinoza on, 16–18; as Zionist, 194–95
"Spinoza of Market Street, The" (Singer), 165–68
Stoicism, 2, 26, 74, 96, 97, 103, 145, 176, 178–79
Strauss, Leo, 6, 49, 190–99, 200
strength of character, 8, 114–16, 119, 121–22, 171, 200–201
striving. See *conatus*
subjectivism, 23, 104–6, 107–8, 122, 140
sublime, 19
sub specie aeternitatis, 9
substance, 1, 18, 31–33, 37, 38, 41, 58–59, 64, 95, 157, 170; Spinoza's definition of, 32–33, 175
sufficient reason, 28, 35–36, 37, 195–97; definition of, 185–86, 195; Jacobi's brief against, 185–90
suicide, 136
superstition, 49, 50, 56, 86, 87, 198
Symposium (Plato), 161

Tacitus, 130
Taylor, Charles, 118
teleology, xiii, 28, 49–61, 96, 101, 102, 108
tenacity, 7–8, 121, 122
thought and extension, 64–65, 68–72
Thucydides, 129, 130
Timaeus (Plato), 34
titillatio. See pleasures
Tocqueville, Alexis de, 23–24, 90–91, 151
Torah, 2, 18, 194
totalitarianism, 150
Tractatus Theologico-Politicus (Spinoza), xxiii, xxiv, 5–6, 28, 29, 104, 123, 130, 132; on divine law, 170–72, 177; *Ethics* relationship with, xii–xiv, 5–6, 29, 184
tragedy, 119–21
transcendence, 19, 36, 48
Treatise on the Emendation of the Intellect (Spinoza), xxiv, 13, 47, 59, 161, 180
"tree of knowledge" metaphor, 44–45
tristia. See sadness
true man (*un vrai homme*), 23
truth, 1, 91, 92, 184, 198
"two great books" metaphor, 12
tyrannophobia, 128, 130, 132

universal ideas, 89–91, 168
utility principle, 27, 144

vacillation of mind, 8, 201
value judgments, 52, 161
Van den Ende, Frances, xx
verum et factum convertuntur, 21–22
Vidal, Gore, 105